Self-Governance and Sami Communities

Jesper Larsson · Eva-Lotta Päiviö Sjaunja

Self-Governance and Sami Communities

Transitions in Early Modern Natural Resource Management

palgrave
macmillan

Jesper Larsson
Department of Urban and Rural Development
Swedish University of Agricultural Sciences
Uppsala, Sweden

Eva-Lotta Päiviö Sjaunja
Department of Urban and Rural Development
Swedish University of Agricultural Sciences
Uppsala, Sweden

ISBN 978-3-030-87497-1 ISBN 978-3-030-87498-8 (eBook)
https://doi.org/10.1007/978-3-030-87498-8

This Palgrave Macmillan imprint is published by the registered company Springer Nature Switzerland AG
The registered company address is: Gewerbestrasse 11, 6330 Cham, Switzerland

Preface

This book is about early modern indigenous peoples' management of natural resources and uses a self-governance perspective. We discuss how institutions were used in early modern Lule Sami communities over two centuries, focusing on changes in property rights. It will, hopefully, contribute to a better understanding of how property rights can be negotiated in a self-governing context and indigenous peoples' rights to land. The book will go into detail about freshwater fishing, hunting, and reindeer herding: how they were practiced, and how changes in these practices came to impact rules for land use. Before we go into these topics, we first would like to thank people and institutions that were important for us in the process of making this book.

The Royal Swedish Academy of Letters, History and Antiquities has been instrumental by providing major funding for research about common-pool resources and early modern settlement development in northern Sweden. Their support was especially important in the first phase, when our thoughts took shape. We are grateful to the Academy for the generous support and even though we know it was a collective decision to support the research, we would like to particularly acknowledge Birgitta Svensson and Maria Nyström Peck, our entry points to the Academy.

The Swedish University of Agricultural Sciences also provided funding to the overarching project this book is a part of. We would like to thank former Vice-Chancellor Lisa Sennerby Forsse and gratefully acknowledge former dean, the late Barbara Ekbom, for their support.

After establishing the road map for future research and proving that our guiding idea for the project was on solid ground, the Swedish Research Council gave us a research grant (2018-01571) that made it possible for us to complete the project.

We are thankful to all financial support that made this book possible.

During the research project, we, individually and jointly, published four articles and one book chapter ("Early Modern Reindeer Husbandry, Sami Economy, and Grazing Rights" in *International Journal of the Commons* 14(1): 91–107, 2020; "Freshwater Fishing Strategies in Early Modern Sami Households" in *Arctic Anthropology* 57(2): 197–211, 2020; "Hunting by Early Modern Lule Sami Households", *Arctic* 74(3): 323–338; "Conflict-Resolution Mechanisms Maintaining an Agricultural System: Early Modern Local Courts as an Arena for Solving Collective-Action Problems within Scandinavian Civil Law" in *International Journal of the Commons* 10(2): 1100–1118, 2016; and "Livelihood Diversification in Early Modern Sami Households in Northern Sweden" in *Integrated Peasant Economy in a Comparative Perspective: Alps, Scandinavia and Beyond*, University of Primorska Press, Koper, Slovenia, 2017) that are integrated into this book, with permissions. We have expanded their content with more recent findings and within a broader context. This expansion has made it possible to compare different forms of subsistent livelihoods. We also expanded the discussion of several topics, including our theories and methods. We are grateful to the journal article editors and reviewers who helped us make the articles more coherent and to the Palgrave Macmillan editor and reviewers who helped shape this book.

Part of the research was carried out at the Ostrom Workshop at Indiana University in Bloomington. The opportunity to stay at the Workshop and discuss and present part of the research was very important. We would like to thank faculty, staff, visiting scholars, Ostrom Fellows, and other participants, including Daniel Cole, Michael McGinnis, Federica Carugati, Dean Lueck, Lee Alston, Ivo Baur, and Christopher Upton.

Our home base is the Swedish University of Agricultural Sciences (SLU), and we would like to thank our own Division of Agrarian History for being a wonderful environment for our research. At SLU, we would like to particularly thank Patrick Svensson, Janken Myrdal, Anna Westin, Tommy Lennartsson, and Anders Wästfelt (now at Stockholm University) for valuable feedback on early versions of the manuscript. Thanks to Anna Rosling and Peter Eklöv at Uppsala University.

The help and service from museums, libraries, and archives have been vital for the project. We would like to thank Ájtte, principal museum for Sami culture, in Jokkmokk and its former head Kjell-Åke Aronsson for sharing his knowledge and time, and to librarian Birgitta Edeborg for generous access to the museum's incredibly rich library. Thanks also to the Digital Library of the Commons in Bloomington, Indiana, and in particular Emily Castle. The National Archives of Sweden (Stockholm and Härnösand) gave us access to the original early modern court rulings that have been invaluable for our research. We also would like to thank Gaaltije, Center for South Sami Culture, and its head Jerker Bexelius for letting us use the center for inspiring meetings. At last, freelance editor Joanna Broderick, with her great skill, knowledge, and thoughtful insights, has followed us along the road and made it possible for us to finish the book. We are grateful that she spent so much of her time working with us.

Uppsala, Sweden

Jesper Larsson
Eva-Lotta Päiviö Sjaunja

Contents

About the Authors

Jesper Larsson is an associate professor and senior lecturer in Agrarian History at the Swedish University of Agricultural Sciences in Uppsala. His research explores historical use of common-pool resources, including transhumance in Sweden and Sami land-use governance. He is Affiliated Faculty to the Ostrom Workshop at Indiana University Bloomington, where he has been a recurrent visiting scholar. This book is part of his appointment as Research Fellow at The Royal Swedish Academy of Letters, History and Antiquities.

Eva-Lotta Päiviö Sjaunja is a researcher in Agrarian History at the Swedish University of Agricultural Sciences in Uppsala. She is a Doctor of Philosophy in Agricultural Sciences and did her postdoctoral work at the Department of Economic History at Stockholm University, where she studied transfer between generations in Sami reindeer husbandry. She also works as senior analyst at the Swedish Environmental Protection Agency. She is of Sami descent.

List of Figures

Part I

Starting Points and Background

1
Introduction

How did early modern indigenous Sami inhabitants in interior northwest Fennoscandia[1] build institutions for governance of natural resources? We answer this question by exploring how they made decisions regarding natural resource management, mainly with regard to wild game, fish, and grazing land. Furthermore, we illuminate how Sami users, in a changing economy, altered the long-term rules for use of land and water in a self-governance context. Our focus is set on the "rules on the ground," that is, how they went about to establish and change property rights on a local level, and how they solved social dilemmas associated with natural resource use.[2]

We focus on Sami users and analyze their practices with regard to natural resource use. Throughout history, human livelihoods and use of natural resources have been tightly interlinked with their natural surroundings, especially for indigenous peoples. In the circumpolar north, these settings were often unpredictable and climatically extreme.

[1] Fennoscandia comprises Norway, Sweden, Finland, and a western part of Russia, including the Kola Peninsula.

[2] Social dilemmas "occur whenever the private returns to each participant are greater than their share of a joint return no matter what other participants do" (Ostrom 2005, p. 37).

J. Larsson and E.-L. Päiviö Sjaunja, *Self-Governance and Sami Communities*,
https://doi.org/10.1007/978-3-030-87498-8_1

People also lived on land that partially consisted of low-yielding alpine tundra, so to understand the development of governance rules and changes in property rights one has to consider factors to do with both ecology and society. Pulling together the wide range of perspectives requires an interdisciplinary approach that not only focuses on social organization but also analyzes how societies and ecological settings were interwoven. Our analyses, therefore, include how ecological factors in mountains and boreal forest impacted decision-making and organization of land use for Sami users in their respective environments. Natural conditions resulted in different subsistence strategies that came to impact the inhabitants' livelihoods and set them on different economic trajectories, depending on their access to mountains and/or boreal forest.

Governance of common-pool resources (CPRs) is a major and recurring theme in the book. CPRs are resources from which it is hard to exclude users, and where the harvest is subtractable. This means that when a person harvests a resource, someone else cannot, which leads to the risk of overuse. To avoid depletion of CPRs, and to secure people's livelihoods in the long term, users need to communicate, negotiate, and create detailed rules around their common use of natural resources. In this book, we show just how skilled early modern Sami users in interior northwest Fennoscandia were in these kinds of negotiations. We suggest that the most important contribution of the book is that it gives a partially new portrayal of how proficiently and systematically indigenous inhabitants organized and governed natural assets, and how capable they were in building highly functioning institutions for governance. In the seventeenth and eighteenth centuries, Sami users still had a major influence over the governance of fishing waters, hunting grounds, and grazing lands in this part of Fennoscandia. Later, as the colonial project increased in strength and the state gained more or less complete control over lands and natural resources, almost all of this self-determination vanished. By enhancing the knowledge about early modern Sami land use, and by demonstrating how Sami users organized their livelihoods prior to colonialism or at least in its early phase, the book can also contribute to the discussion about decolonization of present-day practices and policies.

One particularly intriguing question when it comes to property rights is why interior northwest Fennoscandia developed in an opposite direction compared to most other parts of western Europe with regard to use of common lands. In the rest of Europe, more exclusive user rights were established in the early modern period and common property dissolved.[3] But in interior northwest Fennoscandia, some Sami inhabitants obtained lawful user rights at the end of the nineteenth century for large common-use areas for reindeer grazing, fishing, and hunting. By then, an old system with privately assigned lands had definitively been abolished.[4] The land was officially owned by the state. One way to decipher this development is to emphasize the early modern period as a transformative phase for property rights as a response to fundamental changes in the local Sami economy. Around this time, livelihoods changed for many Sami households, as they went from an economy based on fishing and hunting to an economy in which large-scale reindeer herding or reindeer pastoralism became the main income source. We show both how the use of different natural assets required different property rights and how complex the rules surrounding this use were.

At the same time, it is important to separate the progress of indigenous institutions and property rights from procedures where the Swedish government undeniably recognized most lands in northern Sweden as state property. The first of these processes was a bottom-up development where Sami users were involved in building institutions that gave them both rights and duties. The latter was a top-down process, where the state used its supremacy to unilaterally claim all lands and all resources in the interior of north Fennoscandia as state property without involving the indigenous population. However, for a long time, the state's claims did not keep Sami from continuing to create institutions for hunting, fishing, and reindeer grazing. Nevertheless, beginning around 1780, the government started to enforce their measures more vehemently and thereafter Sami users' influence and self-governance eroded rapidly. Two particularly prodigious events led to an almost complete dismissal of Sami self-governance. First, the local court, where well-trusted Sami

[3] de Moor (2009).

[4] Lantto (2012) and Lundmark (2006).

men had been in the majority as lay-judges with a conclusive influence over rulings, was abolished as an arena for conflict resolution in land-use matters. From then on, these conflicts were to be solved by state servants in a government agency, *Länsstyrelsen* (the County Administrative Board), where Sami had no representation at all.[5] Second, the number of settlers from other parts of Fennoscandia started to increase from rather low numbers in the first half of the eighteenth century to a steadier inflow at the end of the century. It resulted in markedly increased competition over resources, and thus a profoundly negative impact on Sami self-governance.

These events made it logical for us to stop our investigation around 1780. An additional argument would be that large-scale reindeer herding or reindeer pastoralism peaked in our focal study area, Lule lappmark, around that time. In the years to come, hardships in the form of tough grazing conditions and recurring famines would strike the Sami population there. So, parallel with the changes in conflict resolution and influx of settlers, the Sami population started to decrease.[6] Our aim was to explore how Sami economy developed and expanded prior to this declination phase. Therefore, we have concentrated our analyses to a period between 1550 and 1780, when significant changes took place in many households' economies that had great implications for land use, and when most local users still crafted their own institutions for governance. In the source materials, many different concepts have been used to describe Sami. For consistency, we have chosen to call them *users* in most cases, in the sense that they were users of resources and rights, wanting to avoid connotations that terms like *owner* and *tenant* might have for present-day readers.

Even if many of the rules were made in a self-governance context, all decisions were of course also impacted by surrounding actors and societies. Overall, in northern Fennoscandia, the early modern period inferred increased interest from governments of nearby nation-states. We consider self-governance and colonialism as two parallel processes that are not mutually exclusive. By focusing on self-governance, early modern

---

[5] Lundmark (2006, pp. 108–118).

[6] Kvist (1987, pp. 164–172).

Sami were engaged, deliberate, and diligent agents in their creation of viable lives within certain given frames, such as natural conditions and institutional boundaries. Their lives were shaped through, among other things, ongoing relations and negotiations with, for example, other Sami users, non-Sami neighbors, external tradesmen, priests, judges, bailiffs, and other government officials. Recognizing Sami self-determination does not mean they were accountable for the negative consequences they suffered due to different state measures.

In light of the colonial ambitions of most nation-states at this time, a self-governance perspective could strike the reader as naive, or as us being neglectful of prevailing power hierarchies. We acknowledge that already in the seventeenth and eighteenth centuries, there were power asymmetries between groups, especially between indigenous inhabitants and servants of the church and the state. Inhabitants, for example, had little choice but to officially subjugate to Christian Lutheran religion, and to submit to the state's judiciary and fiscal systems. They were also obliged to do involuntary chores, such as transports for church and state. Further, they had to share their lands with a growing number of settlers. Still, we argue that in the early stage of colonialism, state interventions were rather limited with regard to natural resource use, such as fishing, hunting, and reindeer grazing. The state simply lacked adequate information to be able to formulate directives that could control and tax indigenous land use in any detail. Thus, at that time, the state could not gain full control over the land and its Sami inhabitants, although it had started to lay the groundwork. In the early modern period, the state had merely started to use the northern realms for different purposes, and they had begun to design ambitious plans on how to control the land, but in many regards the implementation was still in its infancy.

Up to the 1980s, anthropology dwelled on societies that were radically different, or "other," from the anthropologist's own. From the 1990s onward, the focus on the "other" was replaced by a focus on the suffering subject.[7] Sami historiography follows a similar pattern. An ethnographic perspective where a distinction was made between people with history and people without history has been replaced with a quest to write Sami

[7] Robbins (2013, p. 448).

history.[8] In this pursuit, a major thread has been to rewrite history and to show how Sami have been deprived of rights and land. Joel Robbins points to another way forward in anthropology, focusing on people that strive to create the good in their lives.[9] In line with this notion, we argue that studies of how early modern indigenous people created their own institutions for governance can be part of a history of the good, and be used in present-day discussions about indigenous governance. The Sami's right to use land for hunting, fishing, and reindeer grazing is a highly contentious political question in present-day Sweden. During the twentieth and twenty-first centuries, the dearth of political agreement has resulted in several lengthy court proceedings between Sami representatives and both private landowners and the state.[10] This book contributes to the discussion about the nature of indigenous peoples' rights to land and water by focusing on early modern strategies for natural resource use. A deeper understanding of historic land use and how rights to land were organized in the past hopefully can contribute to more just and robust policies in the future. Acknowledgment of indigenous users' current rights is also a prerequisite before a country can ratify the ILO Convention 169 of 1989, which is the most important operative international law guaranteeing the rights of indigenous and tribal peoples.[11] Although Sweden has yet to sign the international agreement, its articles have recently been used by the Supreme Court of Sweden to rule in favor of Sami's rights claims against the state.[12]

In this book, we focus on one particular region in interior northern Sweden that historically was called Lule lappmark. In present-day

8 Hansen and Olsen (2014, p. 3).

9 Robbins (2013, p. 457).

10 One recent example would be the Sami village Girjas' legal action against the Swedish state regarding the rights to fishing and hunting. The case started in the local court in Gällivare in 2009 and was then appealed all the way to the Supreme Court of Sweden. The final verdict came in January 2020, and the court ruled in favor of the Sami village. *Högsta domstolens dom meddelad i Stockholm den 23 januari 2020, mål nr T853-18* (The Supreme Court of Sweden's verdict announced in Stockholm January 23, 2020, case number T853-18).

11 *C169—Indigenous and Tribal Peoples Convention, 1989 (No. 169).* https://www.ilo.org/dyn/normlex/en/f?p=NORMLEXPUB:12100:0::NO:12100:P12100_INSTRUMENT_ID:312314:NO. It is the forerunner of the 2007 United Nations' Declaration on the Rights of Indigenous Peoples.

12 *Högsta domstolens dom meddelad i Stockholm den 23 januari 2020, mål nr T853-18*, p. 42.

contexts, the concept is rarely used and it has been replaced by the more modern equivalent *Lulesamiskt område* (the Lule Sami region). The latter however encompasses a larger area, including parts of northern Norway, where Sami inhabitants traditionally spoke Lule Sami language and shared cultural traits such as attires and customs. Since the historical and the modern concepts do not overlap, we have chosen to use the historical term that aligns better with our sources, albeit acknowledging that the term *lapp* is currently considered derogatory and offensive. We will go into great detail about how fishing, hunting, and reindeer herding was practiced in Lule lappmark, but also show the complexity in the users' subsistence with regard to other income sources. To understand more about Sami livelihood, one has to consider the diversity of the household economy.

An important result of the book is that it shows how early modern Sami in Lule lappmark depended on many more activities than reindeer herding. In the nineteenth and twentieth centuries, *Sami* and *reindeer herder* often have been equated, leaving out many other aspects of Sami identity. This view has moreover been enforced by the state legislature, including in the Reindeer Grazing Act of 1928, where the Swedish government finally stated that only reindeer herders were Sami.[13] Thereafter, one activity came to define a people's ethnicity in a way that does not correspond to either the historical narrative or the lived experiences of people outside reindeer herding who continued to identify as Sami. It also had consequences with regard to property rights, since only reindeer herders could obtain common user rights to grazing, fishing, and hunting. To this day, the questions of who is a Sami and who has rights to land and water cause a lot of grievances within Sami society and politics. In much research about Sami land use in the twentieth century, reindeer herding has consequently been a focus, and the equation of Sami and reindeer herder has impacted the general characterization of Sami livelihood.[14] For example, statements like Sami "social life revolves around the reindeer" have reinforced the equation.[15] It is certainly valid

[13] Morell (2021, p. 47).

[14] Manker (1963), Arell (1977), and Lundmark (1982).

[15] Pehrson (1964 [1957], p. 3).

for some Sami, but not for all, just as it was not valid for all Sami in the early modern era. We join a recent trend in Sami history writing by offering a wider analysis that includes greater emphasis on the diversity in Sami cultural history, both regionally and temporally.[16]

Large-scale reindeer herding, or reindeer pastoralism, developed earlier in interior northwest Fennoscandia, including Lule lappmark, than it did in other areas inhabited by Sami in Fennoscandia.[17] Hence, our analyses of governing processes and how users negotiated and decided property rights could contribute to the understanding of these changes in other parts of Fennoscandia where they took place later. The results in the book could also be useful for understanding the development of indigenous land use elsewhere. In the early modern period, many indigenous peoples in the world had to encounter forceful European states that wanted to take control of their lands and natural assets and often turn them into good Christians. Numerous indigenous peoples subjected to these invasions had livelihoods that in many ways resembled those of Sami: an existence based on hunting/trapping, fishing, or animal husbandry. Sweden has many unique historical sources, including materials that reveal lots of detailed insights into early modern Sami land use. This circumstance enables Sami history writing in a fashion that typically is much more difficult to accomplish for other indigenous peoples around the world, and it makes the contribution of this book even more valuable in this regard. The sources make it possible to study indigenous inhabitants' governance in detail. This is especially true for the period between 1650 and 1780. Although comparisons between indigenous land uses are hazardous due to differences in ecological settings and societal structures, we hope to contribute with useful knowledge in a global indigenous context.

Many natural resources discussed in the book are under much pressure today, where indigenous and local users are being more and more marginalized. How resources, such as freshwater for fishing and boreal forest and mountains for hunting and grazing in Sweden, are being managed today is also a very important global issue. The institutions that

[16] See for example the overview of early Sami history by Hansen and Olsen (2014).

[17] Hultblad (1968) and Arell (1977).

were used to govern these resources in the past determined the sustainability of the resources and hence survival for inhabitants. Mountains and boreal forests are cultural landscapes that have been shaped by indigenous governing institutions. The current biodiversity crisis is a result of appropriation, colonization, and intensified use of resources in the biodiverse cultural landscapes long shaped and sustained by prior societies. Empowering the environmental stewardship of indigenous peoples will be fundamental for conserving future biodiversity around the world.[18] Therefore, increased consideration of early modern Sami land use is critical in current deliberations about the management of resources that impact future biodiversity in interior northwest Fennoscandia.

The book is organized in three parts and nine chapters. Part I starts with this chapter, where we have given the background of our research and the geographic area we concentrated in. Chapter 2 examines the links between long-term changes in social-ecological systems and the development of property rights by introducing the terms *self-governance*, *common-pool resources*, and *property rights* in a Sami context. We also discuss the theoretical framework that has guided us through the writing of this book. In Chapter 3, we outline the study area and sources used. We discuss our two main sources: historical accounts and court rulings. We also introduce our interpretations of some important concepts necessary to understand the development of natural resource use and governance. In Chapter 4, some important external factors that impacted indigenous users in our study area will be introduced. These are trade, taxation, and population size, all necessary to understand the development of the inhabitants' natural resource management. Part II is mostly empirical and comprises four chapters: Chapter 5 deals with fishing, Chapter 6 deals with hunting, Chapter 7 deals with reindeer pastoralism, and Chapter 8 deals with other income sources that inhabitants could have. The approach in all chapters is interdisciplinary and includes natural conditions as well as societal factors. In Part III, Chapter 9, we conclude the results by discussing some of the main topics

---

[18] Ellis et al. (2021).

of the book, including property-rights systems, equity and social justice, and how external factors impacted the development of early modern Sami economy.

References

Arell, Nils. 1977. *Rennomadismen i Torne lappmark: markanvändning under kolonisationsepoken i fr.a.* Enontekis socken. PhD diss. Umeå, Sweden: Skytteanska samfundet. http://www.diva-portal.org/smash/record.jsf?pid=diva2%3A616377&dswid=6098.

de Moor, Tine. 2009. Avoiding tragedies: A Flemish common and its commoners under the pressure of social and economic change during the eighteenth century. *Economic History Review* 62 (1): 1–22. https://doi.org/10.1111/j.1468-0289.2008.00426.x.

Ellis, Erle C., Nicolas Gauthier, Kees Klein Goldewijk, Rebecca Bliege Bird, Nicole Boivin, Sandra Díaz, Dorian Q. Fuller, Jacquelyn L. Gill, Jed O. Kaplan, Naomi Kingston, Harvey Locke, Crystal N.H. McMichael, Darren Ranco, Torben C. Rick, M. Rebecca Shaw, Lucas Stephens, Jens-Christian Svenning, and James E.M. Watson. 2021. People have shaped most of terrestrial nature for at least 12,000 years. *Proceedings of the National Academy of Sciences of the United States of America* 118 (17): e2023483118. https://doi.org/10.1073/pnas.2023483118.

Hansen, Lars Ivar, and Bjørnar Olsen. 2014. *Hunters in transition: An outline of early Sámi history*. Leiden, the Netherlands: Brill.

Hultblad, Filip. 1968. *Övergång från nomadism till agrar bosättning i Jokkmokks socken*. PhD diss., Uppsala University.

Kvist, Roger. 1987. Rennomadismens dynamik: Rennomadismen och befolkningsutvecklingen i Tuorpon och Sirkas 1760–1860. *Historisk Tidskrift* 107 (2): 161–181.

Lantto, Patrik. 2012. *Lappväsendet: Tillämpningen av svensk samepolitik 1885–1971*. Umeå, Sweden: Center for Sami Research, Umeå University.

Lundmark, Lennart. 1982. *Uppbörd, utarmning, utveckling. Det samiska fångstsamhällets övergång till rennomadism i Lule lappmark*. PhD diss., Umeå University.

Lundmark, Lennart. 2006. *Samernas skatteland i Norr- och Västerbotten under 300 år*. Stockholm: Institutet för Rättshistorisk Forskning.

Manker, Ernst. 1963. *De åtta årstidernas folk*. Göteborg, Sweden: Tre tryckare.
Morell, Ildikó Asztalos. 2021. Indigenous gender justice with a focus on Sámi reindeer herding in Sweden. In *Indigenous peoples and gender equality with special reference to Sámi reindeer herding*, authored by Maura Hanrahan, Ritva Kylli, Ildikó Asztalos Morell, Elena Bogdanova, Konstantin Filant, Praskovia Filant, Sergei Andronov, Andrei Lobanov and Maria Akrén, 37–72. Rovaniemi, Finland: University of Lapland. http://urn.fi/URN:NBN:fi-fe2021041310266.
Ostrom, Elinor. 2005. *Understanding institutional diversity*. Princeton, NJ: Princeton University Press.
Pehrson, Robert N. 1964 [1957]. *The bilateral network of social relations in Könkömä Lapp District*. First edition by Indiana University Press 1957. Oslo: Norsk folkemuseum.
Robbins, Joel. 2013. Beyond the suffering subject: Toward an anthropology of the good. *Journal of the Royal Anthropological Institute* 19 (3): 447–462. https://doi.org/10.1111/1467-9655.12044.

2

Linking Long-Term Changes in Social-Ecological Systems with Development of Property Rights

In this chapter, we examine the links between long-term changes in social-ecological systems and the development of property rights by studying self-governance, CPRs, and property rights in a Sami context, and by introducing our theoretical framework. We start with self-governance to describe how early modern Sami in interior northwest Fennoscandia built their own institutions for governance of natural resources. The main conclusion is that Sami by and large created their own rules for how resources should be harvested and consumed, as well as for how resources should be monitored and rules should be enforced. We use CPRs and property rights to describe how well-defined property rights were a prerequisite for people to engage in, and gain profits from, land-use regimes. For Sami in interior northwest Fennoscandia, land use centered around reindeer herding, fishing, and hunting. We conclude that their access to natural resources, and rights to use them, determined the households' economic performance and development. In the last section of this chapter, features of two frameworks are introduced. They give a background to our theoretical thinking and provide a means

J. Larsson and E.-L. Päiviö Sjaunja, *Self-Governance and Sami Communities*,
https://doi.org/10.1007/978-3-030-87498-8_2

of organizing the inquiry into a set of variables to examine. We also highlight how the frameworks assist in clarifying relevant explanatory factors and how these contribute to fulfilling our aim.

Self-Governance

Research about pre- and early modern natural resource management among Sami has mainly focused on three perspectives. Up to the 1970s, the research was dominated by ethnographic accounts of pre-industrial culture, religion, tools, and traditions.[1] A distinction was made between people with history and people without history. From the 1980s, scholars in archaeology and history have worked intensely to write Sami history, and over the past four decades the understanding has increased vastly. It has, among other things, shed light on the significance of natural resource management for the relations between Sami groups and non-Sami groups along two intellectual lines. First, some scholars have emphasized the encounters between Sami societies and the nation-states Sweden, Denmark/Norway, and Russia, and interpreted most changes in Sami's natural resource use as responses to state interventions.[2] Second, other researchers have underlined that Sami groups had agency and argue that they, by interacting with actors belonging to non-indigenous institutions, i.e., national and international trade networks, could generate and maintain a number of features considered integral to Sami society. However, similar to the first group of researchers, these scholars have argued that most changes in indigenous natural resource use were a response to external driving forces with the argument that the state "considerably undermined the foundation for autonomous Sámi social systems."[3] One of the most intense research discussions when it comes to pre-modern Sami land use revolves around the question of when, why,

[1] Hansen and Olsen (2014, p. 2).

[2] Hood (2015) and Lundmark (2006).

[3] Hansen and Olsen (2014, p. 229).

and how this society transitioned from hunting and fishing to reindeer herding, and the latter has been the main focus for scholars.[4]

The last four decades of historic and archaeological research has well illustrated how Sami lost many of their rights to natural resources due to actions of expanding nation-states. However, we contribute a previously rather neglected self-governance perspective to the study of early modern Sami land use that clarifies how users in interior northwest Fennoscandia, notwithstanding an ongoing colonial project, could build their own institutions to govern use of natural resources. We also contribute readings of how these self-governing institutions co-evolved with the transforming Sami economy. The study of indigenous users' self-governance, or self-organization, is important for several reasons. As pointed to in Chapter 1, it is significant to look beyond "the suffering subject" if we want to understand how indigenous groups governed natural resources.[5]

Historical studies of how indigenous people have built institutions for natural resource management and how they have changed over time are still rare. Knowledge about how Sami created rules for governance can probably bring clarity to the organization of land use among other indigenous groups. Moreover, it is not possible to understand how the household economy changed without considering the rules that were created by the users and how the users were active players in building and changing these rules. As we will show throughout this book, we argue that early modern indigenous users in interior northwest Fennoscandia, by and large, created their own property rights connected to resource use in a self-governing context.[6] Institutions—rules and norms—were not only necessary to determine who had the right to use land and water, they were instrumental in maintaining equity and ensuring household subsistence.

In the sixteenth and early seventeenth centuries, the Swedish government's interest in interior northwest Fennoscandia increased. Initially, the interest was driven by geopolitical motives, such as the power struggle over international maritime trade in the Arctic Ocean, and by the state's

---

[4] Sommerseth (2011) and Bergman et al. (2013).

[5] Robbins (2013, p. 447).

[6] Ostrom (2005, pp. 255–258).

desire to control Sami's fur trade and taxation.[7] The latter was both a means of getting revenues and an attempt to legitimize the borders of the Swedish realm. Moreover, in the seventeenth and eighteenth centuries, the government started to promote mining enterprises and agrarian colonization in interior northern Sweden. It was not until the nineteenth century that political ambitions gained pace as the agricultural colonization grew and started to have a heavy impact on the landscape.[8] In this process, the indigenous population was steadily pushed aside and their rights to land and culture gradually diminished. Nonetheless, until the nineteenth century, Sami's decisions about land use were mostly governed through internal processes. In the early modern period, by and large, Sami created their own institutions for governance and developed their own property rights connected to resource use, such as fishing, hunting, and reindeer herding. External factors, such as changing trade patterns and new government policies, certainly played a role in the Sami economy and could be interpreted as pieces in an internal decision-making puzzle regarding natural resource use.

In a self-governance context, rules about how resources should be harvested and consumed, as well as rules about monitoring and enforcement, are usually developed by the users themselves.[9] During the eighteenth century, the decisions regarding the right to use natural resources were often negotiated in the local court, and by studying court transcripts it is possible to understand how users were involved in creating policy for land use. We return to this in Chapter 3, where we explain why the local court was an important collective-choice arena. The early modern Swedish government was more or less unfamiliar with Sami land-use practices, and even less familiar with the details of users' decision-making. It could not control the economy with any accuracy. The asymmetry of information between government and local users is why a self-governance perspective could deepen the understanding of

---

[7] Göthe (1929, pp. 41–62), Hansen and Olsen (2014, pp. 229–231, 257–262) and Wallerström (2018, pp. 30–34).

[8] Brännlund and Axelsson (2011) and Bylund (1956).

[9] Definition of self-governance is "the capacity of communities to organize themselves so they can actively participate in all (or at least the most important) decision processes relating to their own governance" (McGinnis 2011a, p. 171; see also Ostrom 2005).

early modern Sami economy and culture. James Scott argues, on a global level, that a number of difficulties "placed sharp limits on the reach of even the most ambitious states" until the early nineteenth century.[10]

We analyze early modern Sami natural resource use from a self-governance perspective from 1550 to around 1780. The starting point for the study was chosen for two main reasons. First, around 1550, Sami households in interior northwest Fennoscandia relied to a large degree on fishing and hunting, while large-scale reindeer herding had not yet developed. This changed rapidly, and at the end of the eighteenth century, large-scale reindeer herding, or reindeer pastoralism, had become the backbone of the economy for many households. Hence, by studying this period it is possible to investigate how the changes in the economy impacted institutions for governance. Second, the earliest systematically collected written sources, in the form of tax records and trade lists, originate from around 1550.[11] These source materials make it possible to systematically retrieve information about the household economy.

Similarly, there are two main reasons behind why we chose to end the study period around 1780. First, the local court, where many user conflicts over natural resources were settled, changed procedures at the end of the eighteenth century and engaged local Sami lay-judges (see Chapter 3) to a much lesser extent. The number of sedentary settlers had by then increased and it had impacted the court's decision-making considerably.[12] More importantly, however, around this time proceedings concerning land use were moved from the local court to the County Administrative Board, directly under the state government in Stockholm.[13] Hence, Sami users lost direct influence over the court proceedings and were effectively excluded from participation in the settlement of strategic land-use issues.

---

[10] Scott (2009, pp. 3–4).

[11] Göthe (1929), Hultblad (1968), and Lundmark (1982).

[12] Arell (1977).

[13] Lundmark (2006, pp. 108–118).

Common-Pool Resources and Property Rights

Reindeer herding, fishing, hunting, and gathering are activities that imply humans interacting with nature. In order to catch or trap animals, fish, or manage tame reindeer herds, users must have access to land and water. Hence, these activities can be analyzed as uses of CPRs. What characterizes a CPR is that it is difficult, but not impossible, to exclude other users and that the catch or harvest is subtractable.[14] Once an animal or fish is caught, it is not possible for someone else to use or catch it, and there is potential for overuse. Overuse means, for example, that the grazing resources might be impaired if an area is grazed or trampled by too many reindeer. A robust human use of land and water requires institutions with rules that can control users' access rights in different ways. These rules might stipulate who has access, when someone has access, withdrawal amounts, punishments for violations of rules, etc. and are a means to avoid collective-action problems, such as free riding.[15]

Defined property rights were a prerequisite for early modern Sami to engage in reindeer herding, fishing, and hunting, and to use other natural resources, such as plants and berries. In that sense, property rights determined the group's economic performance and development trajectory, and different parties were likely to control different attributes of a resource because of their respective comparative advantages.[16] An economic property right could be described as "the ability to freely exercise a choice over a good or service."[17] This right could be de jure or de facto, based on customary relationships, and exist with or without government enforcements.[18] De facto and de jure property rights can overlap, and a non-state-based property system recognized by all parties involved is de jure.[19] Property rights cannot completely be specified and

[14] Ostrom (1990, p. 90) and Ostrom (2005, pp. 258–270).

[15] Ostrom (1990, 2005).

[16] Lueck (1989).

[17] Allen (1999, p. 898).

[18] Ellickson (1991).

[19] Cole (2015).

strictly defined; there will always be some ambiguity.[20] Property rights are a "bundle of rights" that gives both rights and duties.[21]

Research about management of CPRs has often focused on local users' ability to build their own institutions for governance.[22] Property rights was not only a way to secure and designate harvest; it was also a means to create social justice. However, when it comes to Sami land use, self-governance has been discussed mostly in relation to present-day reindeer husbandry,[23] not so much in an early modern Sami context.[24] The exceptions are two early contributions by Ivar Bjørklund regarding pastoralism and fishing in northern Norway. However, in recent years a few attempts have been made. Gudrun Norstedt's dissertation is titled *A land of one's own*, implying that users had a high degree self-determination, and Bertil Marklund, also in a dissertation, views a Sami village, with its resource in the forest region of Ume lappmark, as its own CPR.[25]

Much of the previous research on Sami's land rights in interior northern Sweden has centered on the institution of *skatteland*, a term known since the mid-seventeenth century as the land equivalent that a Sami paid tax for.[26] Earlier research has assumed that these lands represented an older organization, predating their first appearance in the sources, and that they made up the land that a household (or a small group of households) had exclusive rights to use.[27] Other scholars do not perceive *skatteland* as originally Sami, but rather as the result of the Swedish government's desire to organize taxing by connecting all Sami to specific places.[28] Regardless, in the mid-seventeenth century, *skatteland*

---

20 Penner (1996).

21 Hohfeld (1913).

22 Gibson et al. (2005).

23 Marin and Bjørklund (2015) and Riseth (2004).

24 Bjørklund (1990, 1991).

25 Norstedt (2018, p. 28) and Marklund (2015, pp. 34–38).

26 Holmbäck (1922), Hultblnd (1968), Arell (1977), Korpijaakko-Labba (1994), Lundmark (2006) and N-J Päiviö (2011).

27 Holmbäck (1922, pp. 10–11).

28 Hansen and Olsen (2014, pp. 287–289). Hansen and Olsen argue that *skatteland* is connected to Karl IX's tax reform in 1602, which "shows a strong will to regulate and create stability in the Sámi's land usage" and concludes that "there is good reason to ask whether the influence from Swedish administrative practice might in fact have been decisive in these matters

represented a resource area that was used by individual Sami households. Furthermore, legal scholars have argued that the government gave the same rights to the holders of *skatteland* as it gave to *skattebönder* (freeholding peasants) in the rest of the country during the seventeenth and eighteenth centuries.[29] But while freeholding peasants gained stronger property rights in the nineteenth century, holders of *skatteland* gradually lost their rights and came closer to holding the same rights as Swedish *kronobönder* (crown tenants).

The focus on the development of *skatteland* has, to a large degree, shadowed the larger context of how Sami property rights developed in the seventeenth and eighteenth centuries. Property rights has rarely been recognized as being intricately connected to customary practices that often differentiated between natural resources. Also, early modern Swedish peasants, both freeholders and crown tenants, had different property rights to different resources, implicating how and when a specific resource could be used.[30] When analyzing early modern Sami property rights and land use, it is therefore reasonable to assume that their rights had also developed in accordance with their use of natural resources. Scholars have interpreted almost every change in *skatteland* as the result of the Swedish government's attempt to erode Sami property rights.[31] Although it probably is an accurate interpretation for the nineteenth century, it is too one-dimensional to explain why and how Sami land use changed in the preceding centuries. In Chapters 5–8, we clarify the details of Sami land use and highlight the diversity of Sami property regimes and how they came to change.

Property systems are usually divided into four basic regimes: state, private, common, and non-property.[32] In theoretical models, pastoralist systems are usually defined as common-property regimes. Robert Netting

[creating *skatteland*]." However, it is important to distinguish between the early modern state's ambition and what they actually could do to steer the Sami economy on the ground.

29 Korpijaakko-Labba (1994) and N.-J. Päiviö (2011).

30 Dahlman (1980) and J. Larsson (2014).

31 Most pronounced by Lennart Lundmark (2006) in his book *Samernas skatteland* that gives an overview of the development through 300 years.

32 Bromley (1991).

identified five key variables that he considered most important in differentiating common-property rights from individual rights to land, based on land use: common property is more likely to develop and be sustained if (1) the value of production per unit area is low, (2) the frequency and dependability of use or yield is low, (3) the possibility of improvement or intensification is low, (4) the area required for effective use is large, and (5) the labor- and capital-investment group is large.[33] Although these variables were developed in an agricultural context, they are applicable in a Sami land use context as well. In an economy where many users became more dependent on large-scale reindeer herding, it is likely that common property would benefit these users. It would enable seasonal movements over long distances in search for available grazing. Previous research about Sami use of natural resources has mostly overlooked what role self-governance played in the development of property rights, especially common property.

Problems with the conventional property regimes are that they do not fit many real-world circumstances and policy problems are complex.[34] As pointed out above, property gives both rights and duties. In most private, state, and common-property regimes there are restrictions, or circumscriptions, for what an owner can actually do with his or her property. In an early modern indigenous setting, the components included in the right to use resources are even more elusive. For the users, it was important to be able to take advantage of resources that were essential for household members' well-being, and the rights regulating their use were often well-defined from their perspective, although they might not be straightforwardly comparable to present-day understandings of rights. Consequently, we use the terms *right* and *access* interchangeably as the ability to legally derive benefits that do not presuppose property.[35] We want to understand how land and water were used, how users had access to resources, and how rights to access were created and changed. Users invest time and energy to make a difference in outcome. Hence, it is important to discuss how decisions were made during our study period

[33] Netting (1976).

[34] Cole (2002, p. 6) and Ostrom (2005, p. 256).

[35] Ribot and Peluso (2003).

regarding the right to fish, hunt, and use grazing land for reindeer and who were involved in these discussions and decisions. Beginning with discussions about who had legal property rights is to start from the wrong end. The Swedish state has regarded itself as the legal owner of the land,[36] but as we will show, they were quite clueless about how Sami households' economy came together, how Sami managed land and water, and which users had rights to which resources. Even if there had been tensions between the state and the indigenous population already in the mid-seventeenth century, particularly regarding mining (see Chapter 4), the notion that all land in the Swedish lappmark was state owned actually started in the 1680s but not universally manifested until the nineteenth century.[37]

Before we present the framework, we must point out that common-pool resources (CPRs) and common-property regimes are not synonymous. A CPR is a type of good, or resource, from which it is difficult to exclude people and where one user's harvest depletes it for other users.[38] CPRs relate to the physical qualities of the resource. A common-property regime is an institutional construction where groups of individuals share private rights and duties in relation to a particular resource.[39] To manage the resource, cooperation between individuals who share rights (commoners) are necessary. A common-property regime is thus a way to manage a CPR, although other property regimes are also possible: state and private. They might even be non-property or res nullius. Before the movement to enclose properties, and similar movements, where one of the goals was to shift common property to private or state property, many forests, pastures, and fisheries around the globe were owned or managed by commoners. Since the mid-eighteenth century, starting in Europe and spreading around the world during the nineteenth and

---

[36] Lundmark (2006).

[37] Holmbäck (1922, pp. 44–68) and Lundmark (2006, pp. 15–18).

[38] Ostrom (2005).

[39] Bromley (1990), McKean (1996), and Ostrom and Hess (2010); Swallow and Bromley (1995, p. 100) "consider a *common property regime* to be a set of institutional arrangements that define the conditions of access to, and control over, a range of benefits arising from collectively-used natural resources."

twentieth centuries, more and more common property was dissolved and transformed to private property or state property.

Connecting Variables for Policy Decisions

Reindeer herding, fishing, and hunting all entail human interaction with nature and can therefore be considered parts of social-ecological systems. Since they require access to land or water, they also entail use of CPRs. Two commonly used frameworks to analyze CPRs are Institutional Analysis and Development (IAD) and the later Social-Ecological Systems (SES).[40] Both belong to what has been labeled the Bloomington School of Political Economy with Nobel Laureate Elinor Ostrom as the central creator.[41] However, the development of the original frameworks was a collaborative work with numerous people involved and it is still an ongoing process. This is particularly true for the SES framework that was launched in the fall of 2007.[42]

The emphasis of these frameworks is on the actors' ability to create policy when they manage natural recourses and when they build institutions for governing natural resources. Such approaches have been applied extensively, especially in analyses of self-governing communities, and they correspond very well with our inquiry, which sets out from questions to do with, for example, self-governance, ecology, natural resource management (reindeer herding, fishing, and hunting), property rights, and social justice. The basic idea of the framework is that all decisions in policy processes have outcomes and these outcomes will be evaluated and lead to changes in any stage of the process, including the exogenous variables, or contextual factors, which in turn make it necessary for the users to reevaluate their policies. The reevaluation will thus result in new policy decisions, new outcomes, and new evaluations in a continuous process. At the core of the framework is the action situation where

---

40 Kiser and Ostrom (1982), Ostrom et al. (1993), Ostrom (2005, 2009), and McGinnis and Ostrom (2014).

41 Aligică (2014).

42 Ostrom (2007, 2009) and McGinnis and Ostrom (2014).

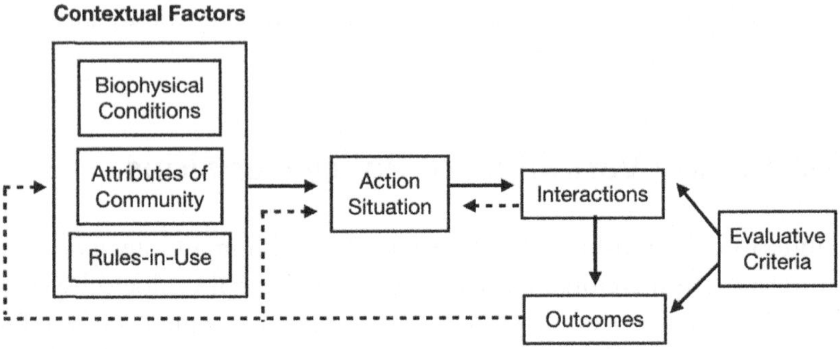

Fig. 2.1 Institutional Analysis and Development (IAD) framework (*Source* Ostrom [2010, p. 646], with permission)

actors are in positions to make choices among available options that affect the outcome. The "action situation" is where policy decisions are made and new institutions are created. However, not all institutions that impact a policy decision are created by the users, some might come with national legislation and others are part of older policy decisions. These will then be part of the exogenous variables that impact the action situation (Fig. 2.1).

From our point of view, the strength of the IAD framework is threefold: first it is process oriented, second it allows for interdisciplinary research tools that recognize complexity, and third, it makes it possible to investigate the process by which institutions emerge and change over time. Critics of the framework pointed out that IAD pays too little attention to the diversity and complexity of the natural systems.[43] So, in response, the SES framework was developed to analyze closely coupled social-ecological systems and to identify and analyze the relationships between multiple levels of these complex systems. In order to do so the exogenous variables had to be expanded, and biophysical conditions in the IAD became the two first-tier variables, Resource system and Resource units in SES.[44] The exogenous variables Attributes of the

[43] Cole et al. (2019) give a short and useful introduction to the two frameworks and provide the most important references to the development of them. For an introduction to IAD, see McGinnis (2011a) and Ostrom (2010).

[44] Ostrom (2007, 2009).

community and Rules-in-use in the IAD framework are almost identical to the first-tier variables Actors and Governing system in SES. Compared to IAD, the SES framework is more formalized, and the first-tier variables are divisible into second-tier and third-tier variables that enable more fine-grained analyses of social and ecological conditions. Criticism of SES has been that scholars can present long lists of variables that may impact the outcome, and that the SES is too static. Cole, Epstein, and McGinnis summarized the problem as "scholars are left to choose between a finely-detailed but ultimately static analysis with the SES framework or a more dynamic but underspecified analysis with the IAD framework," and showed how the two frameworks can be combined.[45]

Both frameworks are centered around actors who make decisions that impact the outcome. We appreciate particularly that the IAD framework recognizes the dynamics of the action situation, and has an articulated feedback loop. Since we have followed users from mid-sixteenth century to the end of the eighteenth century with the ambition to understand how changes in natural resource use impacted Sami society, this dynamic has been essential. The expansion of the biophysical conditions into Resource system and Resource units in the SES has also been useful for our purposes, since the natural conditions were essential for the performance of the system. The labels for the other two exogenous variables are Actors and Governing system. In an early version of the SES framework, the first-tier Actors were called Users. However, it was later changed to Actors since the resource is not restricted solely to the users but can include a third party.[46] In our case, non-Sami tradesmen and state judges would be examples of Actors who are not synonymous to users. The SES framework also offers opportunities to apply second-tier variables. These allow us to dig deeper into the underlying factors that were important for the development of natural resource management in interior northwest Fennoscandia. Even though there has been one attempt to combine the two frameworks, we stuck with the SES framework. Both frameworks have the action situation at the core which potentially gives the SES a

[45] Cole et al. (2019, p. 250).

[46] McGinnis and Ostrom (2014).

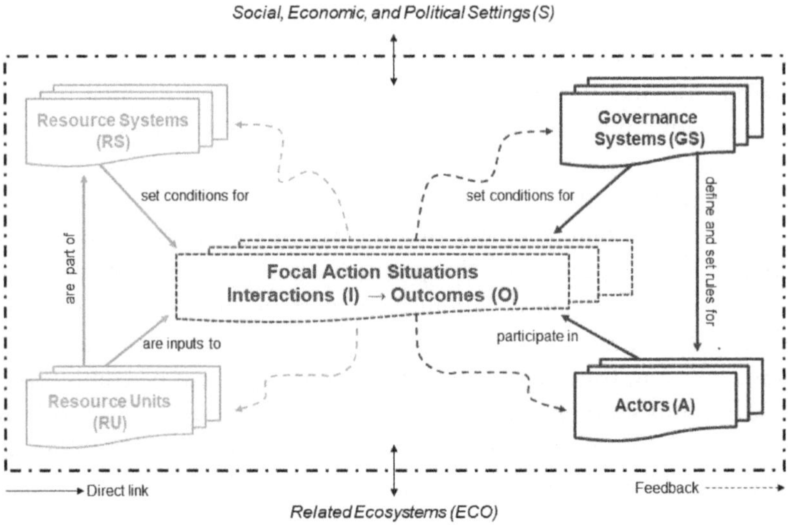

Fig. 2.2 Social-Ecological System (SES) framework with multiple first-tier components (*Source* Adapted from McGinnis and Ostrom [2014, Fig. 2] with permission)

"deeply dynamic orientation."[47] The problem in earlier research is that this dynamic orientation was not used much (Fig. 2.2).

Rules about natural resource management can be established at three levels.[48] There are three types (levels) of action situations.[49] Rules on one level are nested into second-level rules that define how the first set of rules can be changed. The first level is the day-to-day, operational level where users have to make decisions about where to graze reindeer, hunt or fish, what gear to use, who is going to participate, etc. These rules can be changed quite rapidly. In an early modern Sami context, rules on this level are often hard for us today to retrieve at the household level due to lack of sources. However, the accounts we have used as sources provide some of this information, as do the court rulings. At

[47] Cole et al. (2019, p. 250).

[48] Ostrom (2005, pp. 58–62).

[49] Cole et al. (2019, p. 246).

the second, collective-choice level, rules have to be established to determine who has the right to hunt, fish, graze reindeer, or pick berries, where they can do these activities, how to do them, and sometimes when to do them. Thus, they regulate access. These rules change at a slower pace. In an early modern Sami context, the rules on this level were often made by small user groups within a Sami village, *siidas*,[50] or at the village level. Again, it is hard for us today to retrieve information about the decision-making process. However, when users contested or violated rules, and the matter could not be resolved within the *siida* or village, it could be taken to the local court, which was a trusted arena for solving conflicts. Most of the court rulings from these proceedings are preserved in writing, and tell a lot about how local Sami communities treated questions that concerned users' access to land and water and who could use them. The detailed descriptions found in many court rulings also provide evidence of which gears were used, which prey were hunted, who tended and milked reindeer, who participated in fishing, etc.[51] Hence, they offer plenty of information about the first level, operational rules. At the third, constitutional, level, rules are established regarding who has the right to participate in the collective-choice decisions. We touch upon this level only when we describe the function of the local court; for example, who had the right to become a lay-judge, and how they could influence court proceedings. The first two levels give sufficient information to understand and interpret the development of rules concerning early modern Sami natural resource management. To understand why the self-governance structure of Sami decision-making began to diminish at the end of the eighteenth century, one has to take the constitutional level into consideration, and carefully consider how and why Sami were deprived of participation in collective-choice arenas.[52]

The IAD and SES frameworks have mostly been used by social scientists in situations inspired by game theory, where it is possible to control many of the factors involved. When the frameworks are applied in a historical setting, the circumstances that determine the outcome are

[50] The *siida* concept, and its different interpretations, is further elaborated in Chapter 3.

[51] Larsson (2016) and Larsson and Päiviö Sjaunja (2020).

[52] Lundmark (2006, pp. 108–118), N.-J. Päiviö (2011), and Lantto (2010).

often much harder to retrieve due to lack of sources. It is more so in an indigenous setting where sources are especially scarce. Therefore, we cannot fully understand who participated in the actions that led to policy changes, and most situations will probably remain forever hidden. Another difficulty is that the time span comprises more than 200 years of development and changes. In a real-world setting, there is never only one action situation on any of the levels. Instead, the outcome of an action situation is determined by the outcome of preceding actions, and by decisions made on other, adjacent levels. A network of adjacent action situations is "when outcomes generated in one action situation help determine the rules under which interactions occur within the other action situation."[53] Hence, since there are multiple action situations, we must treat them as a process. In a historical setting, it is not possible to wholly grasp all the details that were involved when rules were created and changed in practice. For us, the action situation is more like a figure of thought that can help elucidate how natural resource management came to develop, and the role of local users in that development in an early modern Sami context.

As historians, we only have some of the pieces of the puzzle of how indigenous users formed institutions for governance, and of the motivation behind rules and norms. Notwithstanding the difficulties explained earlier, the SES framework has helped us to dig deeper into early modern Sami self-governance. The framework provides a means of organizing an inquiry into a set of variables to examine. It has assisted in clarifying relevant explanatory factors. Further, it has helped us to recognize that there were actors in certain positions who made decisions about management, and that these decisions had an impact on the outcomes of the systems. We have analyzed these outcomes as both a social performance measure (e.g., efficiency, equity, sustainability) and an ecological performance measure (e.g., overharvest, biodiversity, sustainability).[54] The decisions were evaluated and led to changes in exogenous variables and to new decisions.

[53] McGinnis (2011b, p. 52).

[54] McGinnis and Ostrom (2014, Table 1).

Our purpose is to show how indigenous users, through self-governance, negotiated and developed rules for natural resource management. The SES framework per se was not the focal point of our analyses; we saw it more as a categorization that helped us structure our thinking about indigenous self-governance. For reasons presented above, it is impossible to fully understand every aspect of early modern Sami land use. The framework is very useful in giving us keys to how changes in rules for management of natural resources can be understood. Nonetheless, scarcity of sources and the study's time span make it hard to apply the framework to its full extent. Hence, we will not put up the investigations as a chart where all parts of the framework will be filled out. We used it as a guide for conceptualizing our thinking.

As pointed out in the first part of this chapter, the local management of natural resources is tightly connected to its context. In the SES framework, local management and its context are related to social, economic, and political systems. New trade patterns and government policies certainly played important roles in influencing early modern Sami economy. Sami culture is shaped by its relations to neighbors and, from the sixteenth century, also relations to strong nation-states. In Chapter 4, we present these contextual circumstances and place the area of investigation in a broader context.

References

Aligică, Paul Dragoş. 2014. *Institutional diversity and political economy: The Ostroms and beyond*. Oxford, UK: Oxford University Press.

Allen, Douglas W. 1999. Transaction costs. In *Encyclopedia of law and economics*, ed. Boudewijn Bouckaert and Gerrit De Geest, 893–926. Vol. 1. Chelthenham, UK: Edward Elgar Press.

Arell, Nils. 1977. Rennomadismen i Torne lappmark: markanvändning under kolonisationsepoken i fr.a. Enontekis socken. PhD diss. Umeå, Sweden: Skytteanska samfundet. http://www.diva-portal.org/smash/record.jsf?pid=diva2%3A616377&dswid=6098.

Bergman, Ingela, Olle Zachrisson, and Lars Liedgren. 2013. From hunting to herding: Land use, ecosystem processes, and social transformation among

Sami ad 800–1500. *Arctic Antrophology* 50 (2): 25–39. https://doi.org/10.3368/aa.50.2.25.
Bjørklund, Ivar. 1990. Sámi reindeer pastoralism as an indigenous resource management system in northern Norway. *Development and Change* 12: 75–86. https://doi.org/10.1111/j.1467-7660.1990.tb00368.x.
Bjørklund, Ivar. 1991. Property in common, common property or private property. *North Atlantic Studies* 3 (1): 41–45.
Brännlund, Isabelle, and Per Axelsson. 2011. Reindeer management during the colonization of Sami lands. *Global Environmental Change* 21: 1095–1105. https://doi.org/10.1016/j.gloenvcha.2011.03.005.
Bromley, Daniel W. 1991. *Environment and economy, property rights and public policy*. Oxford, UK: Blackwell.
Bylund, Erik. 1956. Koloniseringen av Pite lappmark t.o.m. år 1867. PhD diss., Uppsala University.
Cole, Daniel H. 2002. *Pollution and property: Comparing ownership institutions for environmental protection.* Cambridge, UK: Cambridge University Press.
Cole, Daniel H. 2015. 'Economic property rights' as 'nonsense upon stilts': A comment on Hodgson. *Journal of Institutional Economics* 11: 725–730. https://doi.org/10.1017/S174413741500020X.
Cole, Daniel H., Graham Epstein, and Michael D. McGinnis. 2019. The utility of combining the IAD and SES frameworks. International Journal of the Commons 13(1):244–275. https://doi.org/10.18352/ijc.864.
Dahlman, Carl J. 1980. *The open field system and beyond*. Cambridge, UK: Cambridge University Press.
Ellickson, Robert C. 1991. *Order without law: How neighbors settle disputes.* Cambridge, MA: Harvard University Press.
Gibson, Clark C., John T. Williams, and Elinor Ostrom. 2005. Local enforcement and better forests. *World Development* 33: 273–284. https://doi.org/10.1016/j.worlddev.2004.07.013.
Göthe Gustaf. 1929. *Om Umeå lappmarks svenska kolonisation: från mitten av 1500-talet till omkr. 1750*. PhD diss., Stockholm University.
Hansen, Lars Ivar, and Bjørnar Olsen. 2014. *Hunters in transition: an outline of early Sámi history*. Leiden, the Netherlands: Brill.
Hohfeld, Wesley Newcomb. 1913. Some fundamental legal conceptions as applied in judicial reasoning. *The Yale Law Journal* 23 (1): 16–59. http://www.jstor.org/stable/785533.
Holmbäck, Åke. 1922. *Om lappskattelandsinstitutet och dess historiska utveckling*. Stockholm: Statens offentliga utredningar.

Hood, Bryan C. 2015. Framing Sámi entanglement in early modern colonial processes. *Arctic Anthropology* 52 (2): 37–56. https://doi.org/10.3368/aa.52.2.37.

Hultblad, Filip. 1968. *Övergång från nomadism till agrar bosättning i Jokkmokks socken*. PhD diss. Uppsala University.

Kiser, Larry L., and Elinor Ostrom. 1982. The three worlds of action: A metatheoretical synthesis of institutional approaches. In *Strategies of political inquiry*, ed. Elinor Ostrom, 179–222. Beverly Hills, CA: Sage.

Korpijaakko-Labba, Kaisa. 1994. *Om samernas rättsliga ställning i Sverige-Finland. En rättshistorisk utredning av markanvändningsförhållanden och -rättigheter i Västerbottens lappmark före mitten av 1700-talet*. Helsinki: Juristförbundets förlag.

Lantto, Patrik. 2010. Borders, citizenship and change. *Citizenship Studies* 14: 543–556. https://doi.org/10.1080/13621025.2010.506709.

Larsson, Jesper. 2014. Boundaries and property rights: The transformation of a common-pool resource. *The Agricultural History Review* 62 (1): 40–60.

Larsson, Jesper. 2016. Conflict-resolution mechanisms maintaining an agricultural system: early modern local courts as an arena for solving collective-action problems within Scandinavian Civil Law. *International Journal of the Commons* 10 (2): 1100–1118. https://doi.org/10.18352/ijc.666.

Larsson, Jesper, and Eva-Lotta Päiviö Sjaunja. 2020. Early modern reindeer husbandry, Sami economy, and grazing rights. *International Journal of the Commons* 14 (1): 91–107. https://doi.org/10.5334/ijc.965.

Lueck, Dean. 1989. The economic nature of wildlife law. *Journal of Legal Studies* 18: 291–324. https://doi.org/10.1086/468149.

Lundmark, Lennart. 1982. *Uppbörd, utarmning, utveckling*. Det samiska fångstsamhällets övergång till rennomadism i Lule lappmark. PhD diss.: Umeå University.

Lundmark, Lennart. 2006. *Samernas skatteland i Norr- och Västerbotten under 300 år*. Stockholm: Institutet för Rättshistorisk Forskning.

Marin, Andrei, and Ivar Bjørklund. 2015. A tragedy of errors? *International Journal of the Commons* 9: 19–40. https://doi.org/10.18352/ijc.586.

Marklund, Bertil. 2015. *Det milsvida folket. Skogssamernas samhälle i omvandling, 1650–1800*. PhD diss., Umeå University.

McGinnis, Michael D. 2011a. An introduction to IAD and the language of the Ostrom Workshop. *Policy Studies Journal* 39: 169–183. https://doi.org/10.1111/j.1541-0072.2010.00401.x.

McGinnis, Michael D. 2011b. Networks of adjacent action situations in polycentric governance. *Policy Studies Journal* 39 (1): 51–78. https://doi.org/10.1111/j.1541-0072.2010.00396.x.
McGinnis, Michael D., and Elinor Ostrom. 2014. Social-ecological system framework. *Ecology and Society* 19 (2): 30. https://doi.org/10.5751/ES-06387-190230.
McKean, Margaret A. 1996. Common property: What is it, what is it good for, and what makes it work? Conference paper delivered at International Conference on Chinese Rural Collectives and Voluntary Organizations: Between State Organization and Private Interest. http://hdl.handle.net/10535/5330.
Netting, Robert McC. 1976. What alpine peasants have in common. *Human Ecology* 4 (2): 135–146. https://doi.org/10.1007/BF01531217.
Norstedt, Gudrun. 2018. *A land of one's own.* PhD diss., Swedish University of Agricultural Sciences, Umeå. https://pub.epsilon.slu.se/15451/1/norstedt_g_180502.pdf.
Ostrom, Elinor. 1990. *Governing the commons, the evolution of institutions for collective action.* Cambridge, UK: Cambridge University Press.
Ostrom, Elinor. 2005. *Understanding institutional diversity.* Princeton, NJ: Princeton University Press.
Ostrom, Elinor. 2007. A diagnostic approach for going beyond panaceas. *Proceedings of the National Academy of Sciences of the United States of America* 104 (39): 15181–15187. https://doi.org/10.1073/pnas.0702288104.
Ostrom, Elinor. 2009. A general framework for analyzing sustainability of social-ecological systems. *Science* 325: 419–422.
Ostrom, Elinor. 2010. Beyond markets and states. *American Economic Review* 100: 641–672. https://doi.org/10.1257/aer.100.3.641.
Ostrom, Elinor, and Charlotte Hess. 2010. Private and common property rights. In *Property law and economics*, ed. Boudewijn Bouckaert, chapter 4. Cheltenham, UK, Edward Elgar.
Ostrom, Elinor, Roy Gardner, and James Walker. 1993. *Rules, games, and common-pool resources.* Ann Arbor: University of Michigan Press.
Päiviö, Nils-Johan. 2011. Från skattemannarätt till nyttjanderätt. en rättshistorisk studie av utvecklingen av samernas rättigheter från slutet 1500-talet till,. 1886. *års renbeteslag*. PhD diss.: Uppsala University.
Penner, James E. 1996. The "bundle of rights" picture of property. *UCLA Law Review* 43: 711.
Ribot, Jesse C., and Nancy Lee Peluso. 2003. A theory of access. *Rural Sociology* 68 (2): 153–181. https://doi.org/10.1111/j.1549-0831.2003.tb00133.x.

Riseth, Jan Åge. 2004. Sami reindeer management in Norway. In *Indigenous peoples*, ed. Svein Jentoft, Henry Minde, and Ragnar Nilsen, 229–247. Chicago, IL: University of Chicago Press.

Robbins, Joel. 2013. Beyond the suffering subject: Toward an anthropology of the good. *Journal of the Royal Anthropological Institute* 19 (3): 447–462. https://doi.org/10.1111/1467-9655.12044.

Scott, James C. 2009. *The art of not being governed*. New Haven, CT: Yale University Press.

Sommerseth, Ingrid. 2011. Archeology and the debate on transition from reindeer hunting to pastoralism. *Rangifer* 31 (1): 111–127.

Swallow, Brent M., and Daniel W. Bromley. 1995. Institutions, governance and incentives on common property regimes for African rangelands. *Environmental and Resource Economics* 6: 99–118.

Wallerström, Thomas. 2018. *Kunglig makt och samiska bosättningsmönster: Studier kring Väinö Tanners vinterbyteori*. Oslo: Novus.

3

Lule Lappmark and Sources

In this chapter, we describe the study area, Lule lappmark, and the sources we used. We discuss how land use was influenced by differences in environmental settings and argue that empirical material from Lule lappmark in northern Sweden can be used to draw valid conclusions about general features regarding Sami land use and property rights in other regions as well. We introduce the reader to our interpretations of some important concepts necessary to understand the development of natural resource governance and argue that some earlier interpretations of the pre-modern Sami organization have led to misconceptions about that development.

Lule Lappmark

We chose Lule lappmark, in interior northwest Fennoscandia, as our main study area. Lule lappmark is located around 66°N latitude, literally on the Arctic Circle, and encompasses approximately 300 km from the eastern boreal forest to the mountains, the Scandes, in the west and 200 km from north to south. The climate is subarctic with long and

J. Larsson and E.-L. Päiviö Sjaunja, *Self-Governance and Sami Communities*,
https://doi.org/10.1007/978-3-030-87498-8_3

typically very cold winters, and short summers with cool to mild temperatures. In the east, the landscape is dominated by boreal forest, known as taiga in Europe, Asia, and North America. It consists of a mix of Norway spruce (*Picea abies*), Scots pine (*Pinus sylvestris*), and downy birch (*Betula pubescenc*), interwoven with innumerable bogs and lakes. The west has mountainous terrain. As in most of Scandinavia, the tree line is formed by arctic downy birch (*Betula pubescens var. tortuosa*), and as the terrain rises, conifers become rare and montane birch forest takes over. In Lule lappmark, the tree line sits at an altitude of 600–800 m. At higher altitudes, alpine tundra spreads out with a mix of montane grasslands, shrublands, rocky terrain, and glaciers. The highest mountain peaks rise just over 2,000 m. There were several reasons for choosing Lule lappmark as our primary research area.

Our research questions revolved around how users built institutions for governance and how the introduction of reindeer pastoralism altered access rights to land. Hence, we were looking for an area where reindeer pastoralism had developed early, since it would make it possible to study change during a longer period of time. One of the areas where the earliest transition from reindeer husbandry to reindeer pastoralism took place in Fennoscandia was the mountain area in interior northern Sweden, including Lule lappmark.[1]

The heterogeneous topography of Lule lappmark makes it possible to study how different ecologies impacted strategies in management of natural resources and the implications for livelihoods. With two distinctive ecological regions, mountain, and boreal forest, it is possible to study the dialectical interaction between humans and the environment. It is possible to study how people who used the different habitats built institutions for governance. What property-rights regimes were best suited for fishing, hunting, and reindeer pastoralism, and how did users respond to changes in the early modern Sami economy?

To succeed in this endeavor, we needed a place where we could study how people had practiced hunting, fishing, and reindeer pastoralism in detail and how institutions for governance of these activities were

[1] Hultblad (1968, pp. 61–63) and Lundmark (1982). The topic is further developed in Chapter 7.

built and changed. The rules and norms that lay the foundation for the property-rights regime were negotiated at the micro level. Hence, we needed to study one area thoroughly and Lule lappmark had the right conditions when it came to sources and previous scholars' work. With detailed knowledge about one region, it is possible to discuss the general features of development in the whole area where reindeer pastoralism emerged and grew. It is also possible to make comparisons with other pastoralists in different environments.

Lappmark, Sami Village, and Siida

The Swedish lappmark is a vast area in interior northern Fennoscandia where the population into the seventeenth century was almost entirely Sami. It stretched from the border with the counties of Jämtland and Ångermanland in the south to the Russian border in the northeast. It included land in today's Sweden, Finland (Finnish Lapland), and northern Norway (Finnmark). However, it is important to remember that not all Sami lived within the borders of the lappmark. There were Sami communities south of the lappmark in Sweden, in northern Norway, and in northwest Russia. In Sweden, Finland, and Norway, Sami also lived among peasants in settled areas (Fig. 3.1).[2]

The lappmark was an administrative area known from the Middle Ages (fourteenth century) that appears frequently in discussions about the organization of Sami land use throughout history.[3] Some researchers say that divisions within the lappmark were established as part of an ambition to tax Sami and facilitate trade, and are thought to roughly correspond to indigenous Sami territories. Their locations and boundaries were defined by the large rivers that flow from the mountains and inland areas down to the Gulf of Bothnia. Each lappmark district had one or two major watersheds, and Lule River was the major water system

[2] Tegengren (1952, pp. 248–268), Svanberg (1981), L.-G. Larsson (2018) and Elenius (2019).

[3] Sommarström (1981 [1956–1978], pp. 320–323).

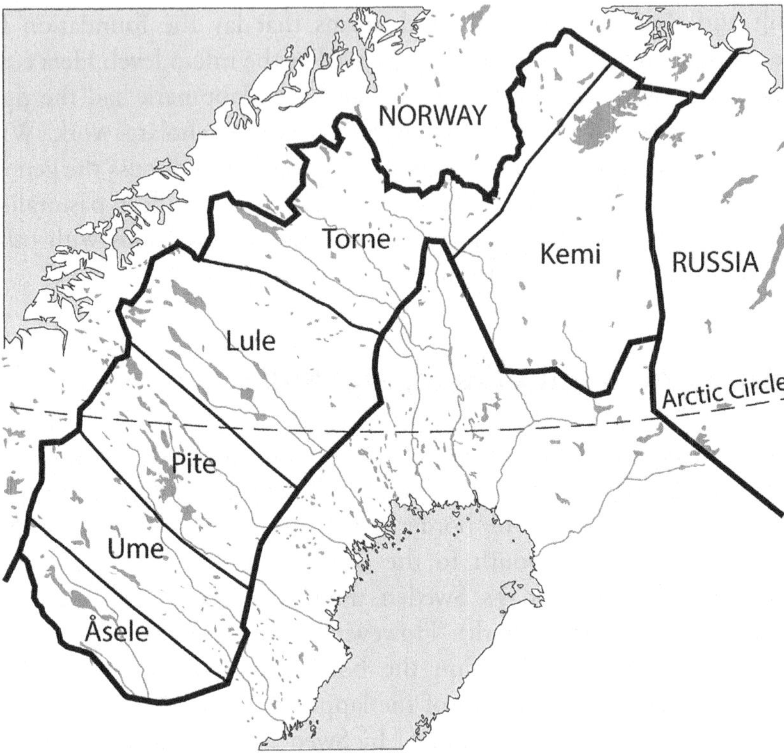

Fig. 3.1 The Swedish lappmark in the eighteenth century (*Source* Authors' adaption of Charta öfver Wästerbotten och Svenske Lappmarkcken, https://commons.wikimedia.org/wiki/File:Västerbottens_län_och_svenska_lappmarken_1796.svg)

in Lule lappmark.[4] During the early modern period, there were six districts, listed here from south to north: Åsele, Ume, Pite, Lule, Torne, and Kemi (Fig. 3.2).[5] The boundaries of each district have changed several times, and units within a district have been shifted to adjacent

[4] Elenius (2019, pp. 16–17). Råne River is also in Lule lappmark, but its watershed is much smaller than Lule River's watershed.

[5] Åsele lappmark is also called Ångermanlands lappmark, and Ume lappmark has been called Lyckselse lappmark. Since 1809, Kemi lappmark has been part of Finland. Into the eighteenth and nineteenth centuries, a large part of Torne lappmark was in Norway and Finland (Norstedt 2018, p. 22).

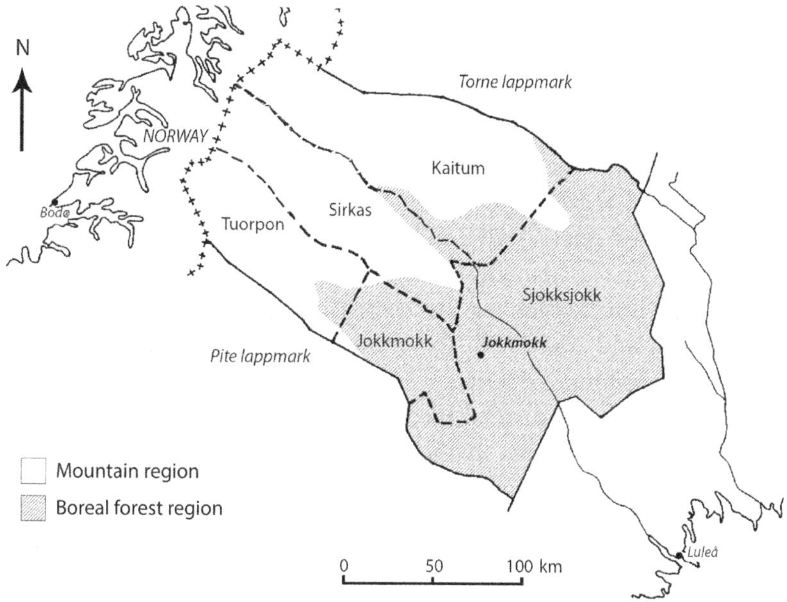

Fig. 3.2 Lule lappmark circa 1760, showing approximate borders between Sami villages Sjokksjokk, Jokkmokk, Tuorpon, Sirkas, and Kaitum. Shaded and white areas represent the boreal forest and mountain regions, respectively (*Source* Authors' adaption of map from Kvist [1989, p. 16])

districts. Lule lappmark had the fewest changes to its outer borders; the border between Lule lappmark and coastal Lule parish was determined in the 1750s. The lappmark administrative division gradually lost its importance as other divisions of land made by the Swedish state and church became more important. However, the borders of the former lappmark districts are still valid as borders between many municipalities, and the concept of the lappmark is used in many historical studies concerning the early modern period.

Until the mid-sixteenth century, *birkarlar* (tradesmen from coastal farming communities) had a monopoly to trade with Sami in Pite, Lule, and Torne lappmark districts.[6] For the right to do trade, they paid a low

[6] Steckzén (1964), Luukko (1980 [1956–1978], pp. 594–597), and Bergman and Edlund (2016).

fee, or lease, to the Swedish king.[7] *Birkarlar* also had the privilege to tax Sami in those regions. From the mid-sixteenth century the Swedish crown decided to be more involved in trade and taxation. The purpose was to tie the area closer into the Swedish realm. The *birkarl* system was gradually replaced with *fogdar* (bailiffs), employed by the King, who traded with the Sami and collected tax. The state's ambition was to get better control of the lucrative and important fur trade. From this time, we have the first systematically retrieved sources, tax collections, that give detailed information of the Sami economy.[8] The organization of tax collection and trade with the Sami was organized according to the division into lappmark districts.

Lule lappmark was divided into four Sami villages (Sw. *lappby*) from the time they first appear in the sources in the mid-sixteenth century to 1647. These four villages were Sjokksjokk, Jokkmokk, Tuorpon, and Sirkas.[9] Sjokksjokk and Jokkmokk were located in the boreal forest region in the eastern part, and Turopon and Sirkas were in the west and had land in the mountains. Sirkas was particularly huge and covered a large area both south and north of Lule River. Hence, it was divided into two villages in 1647: Sirkas in the southern part and Kaitum in the north. Scholars have debated whether the Sami villages were established intrinsically by Sami or if they were tax districts created by the Swedish government, or perhaps the division was created by *birkarlar* and the king's bailiffs took it over for tax and trade purposes.[10]

A problem with the village concept is that it has not been used consistently. In tax records, people are listed according to the village concept we describe, but in court rulings from the eighteenth century, the word *village* has two meanings. The first one is what we describe. The second meaning of *village* (Sw. *by*) has been used to describe a small group of

---

[7] Lundmark (1982, p. 78).

[8] Lundmark (1982) and Phebe Fjellström (1986). The first preserved tax record is from 1553, the same year a special "fur chamber" (Sw. *skinnkammare*) was established at the royal castle in Stockholm, where two scribes worked (Steckzén 1964, p. 322).

[9] Tuorpon was in many early modern sources called Turponjaure, and Sirkas was called Sirkasluokta.

[10] Hultblad (1968, pp. 68–69). *Birkarlar* will be further discussed in Chapter 4.

households living part of the year in the same area. The men who lived there were described as village men, or hamlet men (Sw. *byamän*).[11]

This takes us to the next level of organization in Sami communities, user groups. Each village in the lappmark consisted of many smaller user groups, or local bands, called *siida*–households working, migrating, and residing together. A user group could consist of one to six households, but they usually were one to four households.[12] However, the number of households in a *siida* could adjust according to the season. In reindeer pastoralism, the size of a *siida* could vary according to feeding strategies for the reindeer, larger in the summer and smaller in the winter. As with the word *village*, the *siida* concept has more than one meaning. The differences come from scholars, and some have used the word synonymously with Sami village. That makes it difficult to compare scholarly work; is the scholar talking about a small user group or a large village with numerous households?

To understand why *siida* has been used with different meanings, one needs to look into how scholars have understood the society they have studied. At the core of the word is local cooperation between households. In that respect, it has similarities to how scholars have perceived medieval and early modern cooperation between users in villages all over pre-industrial Europe. Those scholars who have focused on the Sami villages as a unit that worked together and shared a common responsibility have used *siida* in that meaning.[13] Those who have viewed cooperation within small units of households as the foundation of Sami livelihood have used *siida* to mean smaller (subvillage) user groups. The latter has been the most common way to use the word, particularly for scholars focused on the modern and early modern periods and cooperation in reindeer herding.[14]

---

[11] See for example, HRA (1704, p. 820; 1706, p. 49). The distinction between village and hamlet that is made in English is not made in Swedish. The Swedish word *by* could be translated to hamlet or village, depending on the context. A Swedish *by* can consist of as few as two households.

[12] Bergman et al. (2008, p. 101).

[13] See, for example, Tanner (1929), Vorren (1978) and Mulk (1994, pp. 10–11).

[14] Pehrson (1964 [1957], pp. 92–93) and Ingold (1980, p. 268). In *The Saami, a Cultural Encyclopaedia*, the word *siida* is explained as a "lapp village," a Sami community that had "common sources of livelihood and common usufruct territories." With the development of

Winter Villages

If understanding how concepts like village and *siida* have been used is difficult, an even larger problem has been to interpret how Sami societies were governed before the early modern state took charge and organized taxation. Few sources can tell us how Sami organized their society. Nevertheless, a baseline for discussion and a starting point to interpret changes is needed. Such a baseline is found in Väinö Tanner's work about Skolt Sami.

Based on field studies in the 1920s among Skolt Sami in Petsamo on the Kola Peninsula in today's Russia, the Finnish geographer Väinö Tanner argued that their society represented an ancestral, pristine Sami organization.[15] Large groups had gathered in permanent *siida* where they held meetings, local courts, and elected representatives. These places were located in the forest region and were what Tanner called *winter villages*. Tanner claimed that these *siida* groups were original Sami institutions that had been preserved into the early twentieth century through the region's isolation from Tsarist Russia. According to him, equivalent institutions also had existed among Sami in Sweden and Norway but were destroyed in the seventeenth century when Sami society encountered strong central states, the kingdoms of Sweden-Finland and Denmark-Norway.

Tanner used the words *village* and *siida* interchangeably and claimed that members of the *siida* were spread out during summer and gathered in the winter, during the idle season. He argued that the locations of some of these winter villages are known since they are marked on maps made by surveyors Andreas Bureus and Olof Tresk in the first half of the seventeenth century.[16] Moreover, he argued that the household was the most important social unit, while the *siida* was a political unit. The tasks

reindeer husbandry, in the western Sami languages it has come to mean reindeer herding community, including grazing lands, herds, and camping places, while in the eastern Sami area it means a village community (Koponen 2005, p. 392).

[15] Tanner (1929, see particularly pp. 345, 351, 388–389).

[16] Tanner (1929, pp. 388–389). Bureus did not visit the area but created his map in 1611 (Wallerström 2018, pp. 38–39). Tresk's maps, based on fieldwork, are from 1642 to 1643 and were published much later by Ahnlund (Tresk and Ahnlund 1928).

of the *siida* were to ensure that households could take advantage of the rights they had as members and, at the same time, respect the rights of other households and the interests of the *siida* as a whole. In relation to other organizations, i.e., other *siidas*, the *siida* represented the collective as well as its individual members. To govern, senior members gathered and the *siida* was led by an elected president.[17]

Tanner's model of pre-modern Sami society with an overarching Sami organization and gatherings of large groups in winter villages gained many disciples over the years. However, scholars have started to question Tanner's model. Ethnologist Kerstin Eidlitz Kuoljok has convincingly showed that the Skolt Sami society of Tanner's study period did not represent a pristine Sami organization but was the result of changes in Russian society after 1861, when serfdom was abandoned.[18] Kuoljok believed the institutions that Tanner had thought where originally Sami were modeled after Russian village ordinances and governed under Russian laws. In addition, she argues that Skolt Sami were integrated in the Russian realm in many ways; for example, they lived under the same laws as the country's peasants, participated in national and international trade, and were forced to give up major parts of their land to monasteries belonging to the Christian Orthodox Church. This research refuted Tanner's theory that Skolt Sami society had developed in isolation from the Russian government and that it could be used as a blueprint for understanding pre-modern organization in other Sami districts. Furthermore, archaeologists have reinterpreted ancient remains of groups of hearths in the northern boreal forest in Lule lappmark that previously were interpreted as evidence of large Sami winter settlements. They are now understood as overlayered remains of dwelling places from different time periods that have been used by small groups of Sami.[19] Wallerström has lately systematically tested the arguments for winter villages in

[17] Tanner (1929, p. 345).

[18] Eidlitz Kuoljok (1987, 2011). The article from 1987 is a short piece in which she launched the idea that Tanner's model was wrong. Her article did not receive much attention; as a response, she published a book on the subject in 2011 where she thoroughly penetrated the question. See also Wallerström (2018).

[19] Karlsson (2006) and Aronsson (2009).

the Swedish lappmark, and concludes, in accordance with Kuoljok, that Tanner's theory must be rejected.[20]

If Tanner's model is refuted, how was Sami governance organized in the Swedish lappmark before the seventeenth century? Since little is known and there are no signs of a court system, chiefs or other governance structures, it is most likely that the pre-modern Sami society basically lacked overarching institutions. Decisions regarding use of natural resources were made within small, self-organized, and functional user groups. They were called *siida*, which diverges from Tanner's definition of *siida*. They were often based on kinship relations and describe small groups of two to four Sami families who gathered primarily to facilitate hunting, fishing, and reindeer herding, much like modern *siida* groups. Conflicts between *siidas*, or individual members of a *siida*, were solved by the parties involved. In the seventeenth century these small groups shared property rights to clearly defined resources, and the resource area used by one group was called *skatteland*.[21]

Even if we think one would apply the term *siida* to small user groups, for clarity we refrain from using the word, since there is an eminent risk of mixing it up with the other use of the word *siida*, a Sami village.[22] We will instead call it what it was, a *small user group*. When we use the term *Sami village*, we are referring to the division of Sami made for tax purposes. Whether or not this division, in its origin, was intrinsically Sami will have to be solved elsewhere.

By defining these concepts, it is possible to discuss how the changes in economy came to impact small user groups and the division into Sami villages. A fundamental concept in the discussion about the origin of CPRs in medieval Europe is the transition from an economy based on family and kinship to an economy in which neighbor relations grew in importance. In this emerging economy, people started to make alliances with others who had a similar lifestyle.[23] Accordingly, the question is how changes in early modern Sami economy toward more

[20] Wallerström (2018).

[21] Holmbäck (1922), Hultblad (1968), and Norstedt (2011). The concept *skatteland* is discussed in Chapter 2.

[22] See also Wallerström (2018, pp. 43–44) regarding the use of the word *siida*.

[23] de Moor (2015, p. 3).

intense use of CPRs, with the expansion of reindeer pastoralism, required more collaboration between neighbors. Hypothetically, Sami households that developed reindeer pastoralism would thus have developed more elaborate collaborations with actors outside their kinship group. This discussion about reindeer pastoralism is continued in Chapter 7 and in the concluding Chapter 9.

Users in Mountains and Forests

Some early modern sources from the seventeenth century make a distinction between inhabitants in interior northwest Fennoscandia by dividing them into either *Mountain Sami* or *Forest Sami*.[24] In Lule lappmark, this division was linked to the Sami villages Sirkas and Tuorpon, situated mostly in the mountains, and Sjokksjokk and Jokkmokk, situated mostly in the boreal forest. Hence, the members in the former villages were sometimes called Mountain Sami while members in the latter were sometimes called Forest Sami. These concepts primarily reflect the inhabitants' economies and natural resource uses. This division is described in historical sources and, thanks to its apparent distinctness, can sometimes be helpful in analyses of different land-use processes. The concepts also have been much used in research that depict early modern or precolonial Sami livelihoods, especially regarding Sami land use in Ume lappmark.[25] However, we have chosen to define inhabitants with different economic starting points in other terms, since we find the groups to be much more nuanced and open for interpretation than this twofold concept admits.

One argument for choosing other terminology is that practically all early modern indigenous inhabitants in Lule lappmark belonged to the same ethnic group, spoke the same language (Lule Sami), and shared cultural traits. The concepts Mountain Sami and Forest Sami were rather fluid in the sense that inhabitants could change their group from one year to the next, which is evident, for example, in tax registers. Also, the court rulings show how inhabitants were interconnected through

[24] Schefferus (1673), Graan (1899), and Rheen (1897). Some of the seventeenth-century sources use *Gran* Sami (*Gran* is Swedish for spruce) as a synonym for Forest Sami.

[25] Marklund (2015) and Norstedt (2018, p. 60).

kinship ties across these groups.[26] Inhabitants from one group could be employed in households belonging to the other group. The court ruling from the *häradsrätt* (the local court) in Jokkmokk can tell us from which village some servants came and where they worked. That information was mentioned in passing during court proceedings to clarify who a person was.

A case from 1702 tells us that the maid Sigrid Larsdotter from Sirkas became pregnant when working with a male servant from Sjokksjokk in 1693. In 1702 she came in front of court again. The reason for the new trial was that she had given birth to a child in 1701. There were two potential fathers, a servant from Tuorpon and the reindeer owner's son from Sirkas, and the court's task was to find out which of them was the father. After some investigation, they discovered that the reindeer owner's son was the father and that Sigrid probably became pregnant at the market or when they worked together in the boreal forest tending reindeer at night in late January.[27] In 1707, a widow came to court in a case regarding her husband, a 45-year-old man, who had died when he worked as a servant for a reindeer owner. The male servant was from Sirkas and the reindeer owner was from Sjokksjokk. The servant had perished in May 1706 during the migration (*rajd*) of reindeer to the mountains.[28] The two court cases are of value for us for several reasons. They show how servants worked in villages they did not belong to, that there were both female and male servants, that they could be unmarried or married, and that servants were not only young people. They also give insights to the practices of reindeer herding and interconnections between people.

[26] A few examples: In 1704 a man from Sirkas came to court and explained that he was missing his sister, who was married and lived with her spouse in Sjokksjokk (HRA 1704, p. 819). The same year, a man in Sirkas handed over his seven-year-old daughter to a *frände* (relative) in Tuorpon who promised to raise her. The relative and his wife had no children, and the girl would become their legal heir (HRA 1704, p. 825).

[27] HRA (1702, pp. 530–531, 538, 542).

[28] HRA (1707, p. 157). Two additional cases from the early 1700s involved a maid from Jokkmokk working for a reindeer owner in Tuorpon (HRA 1704, pp. 807–808) and a woman from Jokkmokk who had worked five years as a maid in a household in Sirkas (HRA 1705, p. 973).

The fact that people spoke the same language (Lule Sami) is a strong sign of a shared culture. The major differences between inhabitants in different parts of the lappmark had more to do with their respective economic focus, which is a much more dynamic and changeable factor than culture, although livelihood and culture are undeniably interlinked. Moreover, the majority of the historical sources that described inhabitants as Mountain Sami or Forest Sami were produced in the second half of the seventeenth century and the first part of the eighteenth century. As our book shows, this was a period with noticeable economic differences between inhabitants in the mountains and the boreal forest. We use the inhabitants' access to resources in different areas as an explanatory factor: the mountains and boreal forests and how the economy for people using these areas came to impact decisions about natural resource management.

Sources

In common with the majority of indigenous peoples, the Sami produced virtually no historical records of their own before the twentieth century. Information about Sami history must instead be pieced together from a number of sources produced by others, chiefly different branches of the early modern Swedish state or organizations connected to the state, such as the Swedish church and scientific organizations. We have relied mostly on court rulings from the local court in Jokkmokk to cover the eighteenth century and early modern accounts from the mid-seventeenth century to the end of the eighteenth century. To cover the sixteenth and first half of the seventeenth century, when there were no records of court rulings and very few personal accounts are available, we used cadastral records (*jordeböcker*) and tax records as proxies for Sami land use. We also used many of the other printed sources, mostly tax records and other accounts from the Swedish state. However, for the time period from 1550 to the mid-seventeenth century we mostly relied on secondary sources.

Early Modern Accounts

Sources that describe Sami husbandry in the seventeenth and eighteenth centuries consist of accounts by missionaries to the lappmark. Six of these date from the seventeenth century, most of them prepared on behalf of the statesman Chancellor of the Realm Magnus Gabriel de la Gardie and forwarded to Uppsala professor Johannes Schefferus for his book project *Lapponia*.[29] For various reasons, Schefferus did not use all of the accounts in his book, and the complete collection was edited and published, some of it for the first time, in the late nineteenth and early twentieth centuries.[30] All in all, this compilation is made up of accounts by six missionaries: Samuel Rheen,[31] Olaus Graan,[32] Johannes Tornaeus,[33] Olaus Petri Niurenius,[34] Nicolai Lundius,[35] and Gabriel Tuderus.[36] In the early 1740s, another detailed description of Sami life and customs was written and published by the missionary Pehr Högström.[37] Högström had become well acquainted with both Sami livelihood and language through his work as a missionary and priest in Lule lappmark. In his book, he refers quite often to Schefferus' *Lapponia*, commenting on and correcting information that he considers to be wrong.

Even though missionary accounts provide many valuable insights into Sami history, they are also associated with source-critical problems. First, they are inevitably colored by the Swedish context in which their authors were raised and educated, and moreover by the ideals of the Christian Lutheran Church that sent them to the lappmark in the first place. In fact, only one of the missionaries, Nicolai Lundius, was Sami and thereby

---

29 Schefferus (1673).

30 The Royal Skyttean Society republished the accounts in compilation in 1983 (Fjellström et al. 1983).

31 Rheen (1897). Rheen's manuscript was written in 1671.

32 Graan (1899). Graan's manuscript was written in 1671.

33 Tornaeus (1900). Tornaeus' manuscript was written in 1672.

34 Niurenius (1905). Niurenius' manuscript was written in the early 1640s.

35 Lundius (1905). Lundius' manuscript was written circa 1674.

36 Tuderus (1905). Tuderus' manuscript was written between 1672 and 1679.

37 Högström (1747).

also part of the Sami context.[38] The primary task of the many missionaries was to spread the Christian Lutheran faith and customs among the Sami through preaching and traveling in the Swedish lappmark. This would certainly have provided many valuable insights into Sami subsistence, and the missionaries would surely have developed a relatively close, albeit unequal, relationship with the Sami they described. As a result, the strength of the accounts as source material is that the authors actually interacted with the Sami of northern Sweden in the seventeenth and eighteenth centuries. They thereby provide us with a unique window into Sami history, albeit with various problematic filters.

Second, another source criticism is that some missionaries seem to have copied parts of others' texts, incorporating them into their own accounts. This calls for careful reading and analysis in order to identify each author's independent contribution. The third problem concerns how well the priests and the Sami could communicate with one another, given that they spoke different languages. According to contemporary sources, some Sami, at least in the southern lappmark, understood Swedish quite well, and similarly some Sami in the eastern lappmark understood Finnish.[39] These language skills are described as especially good among the Sami who took part in trade. Some accounts indicate there were plenty of interpreters in the lappmark whom priests, for example, could use when preaching sermons. In one account, the author actually mentions his interpreter, which clearly shows that not all priests could speak Sami, and that interpreters were used not only for sermons but also for other forms of contact between missionaries and Sami.[40] All in all, it seems to have been quite possible for missionaries and Sami to bridge the language barrier by using Swedish or Finnish through an interpreter or more rarely speaking Sami.

Missionaries aside, a number of Swedish and foreign travelers in the eighteenth-century lappmark recorded their encounters with Sami. Most famous among these is perhaps Carl Linnaeus who, as a young man in the spring and summer of 1732, journeyed to the lappmark at the behest

[38] Lundius (1905, p. 3). Lundius' background is depicted by K. B. Wiklund and is part of the Foreword to Lundius' account.

[39] Högström (1747, p. 77) and Rheen (1897, p. 52).

[40] Tornaeus (1900, p. 61).

of the Royal Academy of Sciences in Uppsala. On his travels he visited both Ume and Lule lappmark making countless useful observations on Sami livelihood. He noted and illustrated many of his observations in a personal diary that was supposedly never intended for publication. His edited journal first appeared in English in 1811.[41] The Swedish version, which has been edited and republished several times, was published most recently in three volumes by the Royal Skyttean Society in 2003.[42]

Almost a decade later, another young man, Arwid Ehrenmalm, traveled from Stockholm to Åsele lappmark on behalf of the Royal Swedish Academy of Sciences. On his return to Stockholm, he wrote a book about his experiences, its final section describing Sami customs and habits.[43] Both these travelogues contain detailed and useful information, allowing us to understand more about Sami subsistence. These accounts, however, share similar source-critical problems with the missionary accounts described above, some of which will be elaborated in the next section.

The prime objective of the journeys by Linnaeus and Ehrenmalm was to investigate the natural resources of northern Sweden, and to ascertain how the area could best be exploited from a Swedish point of view. As part of their task, the travelers also provided valuable insights into Sami subsistence. However, as with the missionaries described above, the travelogue authors came from a different context to the Sami they described. This sometimes shines through by way of derogatory descriptions, especially related to Sami beliefs, appearances, and manners, and more so for Ehrenmalm than for Linnaeus. Nevertheless, both authors were more objective and matter-of-fact when describing various aspects of Sami trade, reindeer herding, fishing, and their use of other natural resources. As neither of them spoke Sami, one suspects that a great deal of information, as well as the many nuances of Sami culture, became lost in translation. Ehrenmalm mentions using an interpreter, which Linnaeus does not, even though he too certainly would have been accompanied by one.

---

41 Linnaeus (1811a, 1811b).

42 Linnaeus (2003, parts I–III).

43 Ehrenmalm (1743).

An increased scientific activity, and an interest in exploring Sweden's natural resources, in order to promote the country's economy impacted the publication of dissertations and scientific journals during the eighteenth century. This included topics and places from interior northern Sweden, and the authors often had lived in the area they covered. An example of that would be Jonas Hollsten from Lule lappmark, who wrote articles about three animals: beaver, wolverine, and wild reindeer.[44] Table 3.1 contains an overview of accounts used with a biosketch of each author.

The travelogues and missionary accounts are mainly descriptive in character and therefore not particularly suitable for quantitative analyses. However, since the descriptions derive from sources who depict different districts in the lappmark, it is still possible to make comparisons, which in turn strengthen the credibility of the descriptions as source material. One additional source is Anders Holm's account that is part of a map drawn by surveyor Jonas Gedda covering Ume lappmark in 1671 and published by Norstedt in 2011.[45] The map is divided into 37 *skatteland* (tax lands), and Holm systematically describes available resources on each portion of land.[46]

Court Rulings

The other major source material we used are court rulings from the local court (*häradsrätt*) in Jokkmokk in Lule lappmark. The early modern *häradsrätt* was an arena where users could bring unresolved conflicts regarding natural resource management to have them settled.

Scandinavian law is generally regarded as distinct from other legal families. Another name for Scandinavian law is Nordic law since it refers to the law of the five Nordic countries—Denmark, Finland, Iceland,

[44] Hollsten (1768, 1773, 1774).

[45] Norstedt (2011).

[46] Norstedt (2018, pp. 32–34).

Table 3.1 Major early modern accounts used as sources, including biographical information of the authors; listed in alphabetic order by author

Author	Birth	Death	Background	Title (translated from Swedish)	Date written	First published
Arwid Ehrenmalm	1720	1745	Visited Åsele lappmark in 1741 at the behest of the Royal Swedish Academy of Sciences (where he was notary public)	*Journey through Wäster-Norrland to Åsele lappmark district*		1743
Carl P. Fjellström	1732	1772	Defended a thesis on the possibilities to further cultivate the entire lappmark; he grew up in Lycksele in Ume lappmark, where his father Pehr Fjellström was priest	*Thoughts about the possibility of cultivation in the Lappmark*		1760
Pehr Fjellström	1697	1764	Schoolmaster and priest in the parish of Lycksele, Ume lappmark (1718–1764)	*Short story about the Sami bear-hunt, as well as related superstitions*		1755
Olaus Graan	1618	1689	Priest in the parish of Piteå, County of Västerbotten (1656–1689); wrote about Sami in Pite lappmark	*Relation, or a complete description of the origin of the Sami, as well as their entire living conditions*	1672	1899

Author	Birth	Death	Background	Title (translated from Swedish)	Date written	First published
Pehr Högström	1714	1784	Priest in the parish of Gällivare, Lule lappmark (1742–1748)	*Description of Sami districts belonging to the Swedish crown*		1747
Jonas Hollsten	1717	1789	Priest in the parish of Jokkmokk, Lule lappmark (1757–1775)	*Remarks on the beaver, castor* *Remarks on the wolverine* *Dissertation on the reindeer*		1768 1773 1774
Carl Linnaeus	1707	1778	Visited Ume, Lule, and Torne lappmark in the summer of 1732 on behest of the Royal Society of Sciences in Uppsala	*Iter lapponicum*	1732	1811
Nicolaus Lundius	1656	1726	Sami; born in Pite lappmark where his father was priest. Minister (Sw *klockare*) in the parish of Jokkmokk, Lule lappmark, at the time of his death; wrote about Sami in Ume lappmark; he might have attended the Skytteanska school in Lycksele	*Descriptio Lapponiae*	ca 1674	1905

(continued)

Table 3.1 (continued)

Author	Birth	Death	Background	Title (translated from Swedish)	Date written	First published
Olaus Petri Niurenius	1580	1645	Priest in the parish of Umeå, County of Västerbotten (1619–1645); wrote about Sami in Ume lappmark	*Lapland, or a description of the Nordic region inhabited by the Sami in the most remote parts of Scandinavia or Sweden*	ca 1640	1905
Samuel Rheen	1615	1680	Priest assistant vicar (Sw *komminister*) in the parish of Jokkmokk, Lule lappmark (1664–1671)	*A short story about Sami life and customs, superstitions, and in many cases severe delusions*	1671	1897
Johannes Tornaeus	unk	1681	Priest in the parish of Nedertorneå, County of Västerbotten (1639–1681)	*Description of the Sami districts and their conditions*	1672	1900

Norway, and Sweden.[47] The Scandinavian legal tradition goes back to the early medieval period when similar provincial law codes appeared in Denmark, Norway, Iceland, and last in Sweden. This intense period of legislation coincides with a period of political and ideological consolidation of the emerging states.[48] In Sweden, the medieval law code was in place until 1734, when a new national law was introduced to include countryside and towns.[49] However, the new law code did not radically break from legal tradition.[50] The laws of the local community were written by and for the land-holding peasants.[51] The long-term history of jurisdiction in Sweden relates to how the king and the state (the crown) gained increasing control over the process at the expense of local communities. Starting in the seventeenth century, the jurisdiction slowly became more professionalized.

The countryside was divided into judicial areas. The primary unit of jurisdiction was an assembly called *ting*. During the Middle Ages, it became an arena were rural communities convened to manage their legal matters. The court proceedings took place under the leadership of a judge who made decisions with a panel of twelve local men, the *nämnd* or *tolvmanna*, who served as lay-judges, *nämnedmän*. No official could sit on the *nämnd*. The *nämnd* represented the community and its knowledge of local people and circumstances. The participation of the community was essential for the legitimacy of the court. One explanation for the stronger influence of the Swedish peasantry compared to much of contemporary Europe was that peasants constituted one of the four societal estates of the Diet that was standardized in the sixteenth century.[52] Another feature of the Nordic judicial system was that many cases were resolved by settlements in court, not out of court.[53] The courts

[47] Zweigert and Kötz (1998) and Malmström (1969). Scandinavian law tradition also includes three territories with a high degree of self-governance: the Danish Faroe Islands, Greenland, and the Finnish Åland Islands.

[48] Lindkvist (1997).

[49] Sveriges Rikes Lag (1984 [1780]).

[50] Lindkvist (1997, p. 216).

[51] Korpiola (2014).

[52] Korpiola (2014).

[53] Österberg et al. (2000).

have been described as social arenas where the local community met the authorities and together "took part in the exercise of social control,"[54] and as a place where local economic disputes and other relations were settled.[55]

A fundamental feature of the court was its lay dominance, where conflict resolution was a bottom-up process.[56] Lay dominance was a cornerstone in the Swedish legal cultural identity at that time.[57] Since the courts in the Swedish lappmark belonged to the same legal system as the courts in the rest of Sweden, we can assume that the legal culture there was analogous, albeit reflecting local practices in a Sami context. This assumption is reinforced by the fact that the *häradsrätt* in Lule lappmark, at least into the mid-eighteenth century, had twelve Sami lay-judges and one Swedish head judge, like the other local courts in the *lappmark*.[58] The courts in Sweden were inclined to accept the economic reality in the local community and strived to maintain social stability.[59]

However, it is important to stress a few things to put the local court in perspective. The lay-judges were not randomly selected. They represented established taxpaying people. They all had a stake in natural resource management, i.e., reindeer herding, fishing, hunting. An eighteenth-century source described the lay-judge position in the *lappmark* as desired and the lay-judges as honorable, not different from the same position in an agriculture setting.[60] While the court decision in the eighteenth century was a bottom-up process regarding land use where Sami customary rights were taken into consideration, not all cases brought to the court were. In criminal cases and religious matters, it was the Swedish

---

[54] Österberg et al. (2000, p. 252).

[55] Lindkvist (1997).

[56] Ågren (1992), Korpiola (2014), J. Larsson (2016) and Österberg et al. (2000).

[57] Korpiola (2014).

[58] Högström (1747, pp. 240–241), Korpijaakko-Labba (1994, p. 113), Larsson and Päiviö Sjaunja (2020) and Marklund (2015, p. 83).

[59] J. Larsson (2016) and Österberg and Sogner (2000).

[60] Högström (1747, pp. 240–241).

state's view that prevailed. In the seventeenth and eighteenth century it was the Christian Lutheran faith that showed if you were a Swede. Religion was the cohesive force and a glue in society, not the language, since Sweden was a multilingual country. According to Lars-Gunnar Larsson, even Sami-speaking people were seen as good Swedes as long as they confessed to the Lutheran faith, something that changed during the nineteenth century when the Swedish language came to define the country.[61] When the court became aware that Sami had been practicing a pre-Christian faith, they investigated the circumstances meticulously and punished the practitioners severely.[62] In cases regarding land use, the court acted the other way around, with inclusiveness that involved users.

Solving Conflicts in Practice

How policy making regarding land use and grazing rights were shaped is hard to fully understand in an early modern setting, where the users have left no written evidence of how the process evolved. Natural resource governance was complex, and we can assume that users routinely interacted with each other to make policy decisions. These interactions are difficult to research today, but from the late seventeenth century, the local court became a trusted arena for policy discussion and decisions regarding natural resource management policy. To get a sense of how the court worked and the bottom-up perspective used, we present a few court rulings.

In 1732, Anund Larsson in Tuorpon complained to the court that Jon Larsson Hufwa and his father Lars Andersson Kock in the same village, had been fishing in a lake in the mountains. Particularly annoying for Anund Larsson was that they had been fishing in the part of the lake where the fish spawn each year. Since the court was not able to determine who had the right to fish in the lake, they appointed two lay-judges to do an investigation, Tomas Storm from Jokkmokk and Pål Andersson in Sirkas. The lay-judges were told to visit the lake with the plaintiff and the

[61] L.-G. Larsson (2018, pp. 224–225).

[62] Rydving (1995a. pp. 54–68).

defendants and gather all information possible. The court only convened once each year and told the users to share the lake as they had been doing while they waited for a decision regarding the case. One year later, the lay-judges reported back to the court what they had discovered. Based on that information, the court eventually was able to make a decision in the case in February of 1733. The plaintiff and the defendants agreed upon a solution that the lay-judges had suggested and the lake was divided between them. A border between the two parties was determined, and Anund Larsson had the right to fish on the south side and Jon Larsson Hufwa and Lars Andersson Kock on the north, and most likely, both getting half of the spawning area.[63]

As the case shows, a lay-judge was a trusted man and was often appointed to resolve conflicts and suggest solutions to the court regarding disputes among users, usually after he had met the parties involved in the field. In this case, the Sami-speaking lay-judges met with the plaintiff and defendants in Tuorpon to find a solution that the court later confirmed. The lay-judges came to have an important role in determining the outcomes of conflicts regarding land use brought to court. The lay-judges could also be asked to determine if arguments put forward in court were plausible, as a case from 1743, about an *oxren* (ox reindeer) shows.

A week before Christmas, eight reindeer that belonged to Pål Eriksson had merged into Anders Anundsson's reindeer herd. Seven of them had been retrieved, but an ox reindeer was still missing. A few days later, a thirteen-year-old boy, who had herded Eriksson's reindeer during the summer, saw Anundsson slaughter a reindeer and he recognized it as the reindeer Eriksson was missing. When Eriksson was notified, he went over to confront Anundsson and took the reindeer pelt from the slaughtered animal as a proof. Anundsson insisted that the slaughtered reindeer was his own property. The discussion in court came to revolve around the reindeer pelt and if it had belonged to Eriksson's reindeer or Anundsson's reindeer. Eriksson displayed the pelt for the court and argued that his animal could be recognized because "hair" was missing at the neck where a *trälg* (collar) had been attached. When Anundsson told the court that

63 HRA (1732, February 8, pp. 138–139; 1733, February 10).

he too had had a collar on his reindeer, the lay-judges pointed out that it seemed implausible that the reindeer could have lost so much hair since Anundsson had told them his reindeer had not worn the collar for a long time.

The discussion about recognizing a reindeer by the pelt or "hair" continued when Gunilla Pålsdotter took the stand. During the summer she had had Eriksson's reindeer in her herd and she told the court that she *känner således alla renar äldre och yngre, om de än vore ibland tusende främmande renar* (recognize all reindeer, old as well as young, even if they were with thousands of unfamiliar reindeer).[64]When the fur was displayed, Pålsdotter said she knew it was Eriksson's missing reindeer from "the hair," as well from the fact that part of the fur on the neck was worn away. The judge seemed to have a hard time judging Pålsdotter's testimony, and he asked the lay-judges if it was possible for a caretaker of reindeer to recognize a single reindeer out of many. The lay-judges said that it was possible for a person who took care of reindeer to distinguish a reindeer by "the hair," even if the number of reindeer in a herd were large and they look alike in color. Anundsson agreed but added that reindeer pelts could be quite similar.[65]

These two court cases show not only that the lay-judges played an important, and often instrumental, role in determining the outcome of a court case regarding natural resource management, but that the judge from the state often was clueless about how Sami economy and culture worked, especially when it came to the details. One way for the state to keep the faith in the court system was to leave important decisions in the hands of people who actually knew how the economy worked for local users. Since the court only convened once each year, a few days in January or February, and the judge did not live in the area, he had no time to visit contested places. This and the fact that the jurisdiction area was huge made it impossible for the state judge to know details about local circumstances. That district court existed until 1751, when

---

[64] RA SH (1743, p. 505).

[65] RA SH (1743, pp. 504–507); see also Hultblad (1968, p. 426, evidence 1094a).

its jurisdiction of approximately 36,000 km^2 was split basically in half. After 1751, the local court in Jokkmokk covered around 19,500 km^2.

Through the court rulings, we are enlightened by "hearing" the users' own voices in their arguments and attitudes. The rulings were scripted by a clerk (probably non-Sami) who was appointed by the state; however, the written records present only summaries of what actually was said during the court proceedings. Most users spoke only Sami, which meant that an interpreter translated to Swedish all that was said in court before the rulings were recorded. For sure, all of this added the risk of information being lost in the process. The judges often worked for a long time in the lappmark and sometimes they knew a little Sami. When new judges were to be appointed in 1697, an argument for two candidates was that they were fairly good at the language.[66]

Rulings from Lule Lappmark

Filip Hultblad worked more than thirty years on his dissertation *Transition from Nomadism to Farming in the Parish of Jokkmokk*.[67] In his seminal work, he laid the foundation for other scholars working on settlement development in Lule lappmark.[68] His aim was to understand the settling process, but it was only possible to do this as a study of the total development of settlements in the area. Hence, he became involved in Sami history. In order to understand the development in the southern part of Lule lappmark, Jokkmokk's parish, he used the time-consuming method of studying the population person by person, a method he described as genealogical-topographic. He went through almost all available written sources (unpublished as well as published

[66] Göthe (1929, p. 338).

[67] Hultblad (1968, p. 5). The dissertation *Övergång från nomadism till agrar bosättning i Jokkmokks socken* is written in Swedish and has an English summary on pages 436–439.

[68] Lundmark (1982), Kvist (1989), Sköld (1992) and Mulk (1994).

sources) from the early modern period to the end of the nineteenth century, and added some early twentieth-century sources.[69] An important source Hultblad used was court rulings from the *häradsrätt* in Jokkmokk. The court rulings are from the end of the seventeenth century to the second half of the nineteenth century.[70] From the late seventeenth century, it is possible to follow individual people through the sources. Hultblad estimates that he read approximately 20,000 pages of court rulings, an astonishing number. In his book he has a long section of abbreviated court rulings listed according to people involved.[71] Each person was assigned a number, and in another part of the book he has a family register regarding families that were established in the area before 1880. He listed both court rulings and family members according to the Sami village the person belonged to. Settlers, mostly non-Sami, are listed at the farms where they lived or in other settlements. Since Hultblad studied settlement development and wrote a dissertation in geography, the list of court cases he published often involved names of places. Court rulings that are rich in place names are civil court cases regarding, for example, the right to use grazing land, fish, or hunt. Hence, they make up a large part of the abbreviated court rulings Hultblad published.

The court in Jokkmokk encompassed all of Lule lappmark from its inception in the first decade of the seventeenth century to 1751, when the new court was established in Gällivare in the northern part of Lule Lappmark. In Jokkmokk, the villages Tuorpon, Sirkas, and Jokkmokk and the southern part of Sjokksjokk continued as a smaller version of the original court. Hultblad was focused on Jokkmokk parish and excluded court rulings regarding Kaitum village and the northern part of Sjokksjokk that became part of Gällivare court's jurisdiction.

We used Hultblad's compilation of court rulings in Lule lappmark to systematically find cases dealing with reindeer herding, fishing, and hunting as well as other cases related to land use. To validate the cases, we compared a sample of his transcripts to the original court rulings, and our assessment was that they match well in regard to principal content.

[69] Hultblad (1968, pp. 440–441). The investigation covered up to 1910.

[70] Hultblad (1968, p. 41).

[71] Hultblad (1968, pp. 354–435).

Nevertheless, his transcripts are abbreviations of the original records. When we needed more meticulous descriptions of court cases, we used the originals. In total, there were about 280 cases concerning land use between 1699 and 1780. The large number of court cases in a small population (more about population in Chapter 4) is evidence that users used the court to develop policy. The court was a collective-choice arena where policy decisions about rules that defined and constrained operational activities often were made.[72] Decisions about the right to use grazing land and fishing waters were discussed in detail, and the court rulings make it possible to study the gradual changes in the institutions that regulated rights to graze reindeer, fish, and hunt.[73]

A classification shows that around 70% of 280 cases dealt with reindeer grazing or access to land in more general terms, around 24% dealt with fishing, and only 6% dealt explicitly with hunting.[74] These proportions suggest that users were concerned mostly with the expanding reindeer pastoralism during the eighteenth century and that reindeer owners used the court to change policy about grazing rights. At the other end of the spectrum, conflicts over hunting rarely were taken to court. However, the percentages say less about what role hunting played in the household than the cases themselves. Although there are relatively few hunting cases in the court material, the ones that exist provide detailed information.

With fewer cases available, we turned more to the original court rulings to get more meticulous descriptions. In practice, this means that all court rulings regarding hunting have come from the original records. We read about one-third of the cases regarding fishing and about 10% of the rulings regarding reindeer herding. In addition, some court rulings mentioned reindeer, fishing, and hunting in passing, although they mainly dealt with another type of conflict, e.g., theft, assault. We used information from a few such cases, all retrieved from the original records. For hunting, it meant that we almost doubled the number of cases.

72 Ostrom (2005).

73 Streeck and Thelen (2005).

74 Some court rulings involved many activities, such as reindeer herding and fishing or reindeer herding, fishing, and hunting.

To get a sense of how the court worked in Lule lappmark, and to get a feeling of what kinds of other conflicts were brought to the court at the beginning of the eighteenth century, we read all court rulings from 1699 to 1708. They encompass about 130 court rulings and add valuable insights into Sami culture. The court rulings sometimes contain details about practices that can add to or corroborate information in other sources, specifically the priests' and travelers' accounts. Some of these cases are rulings concerned with reindeer herding, fishing, and hunting and are included in the number above. In total, we used around 400 court rulings.

The authors of accounts and court records used Swedish spellings when they transcribed Sami names of users, lakes and streams, grazing land, and other places. Sami language and Sami name traditions are fundamentally different from their Swedish equivalents, which vary considerably in historical sources, and it was probably difficult for contemporary interpreters and authors to get the names right. We transcribed the names in modern Swedish, although we are aware that Lule Sami orthography would have been more accurate and would have added context and familiarity for readers. However, to be useful, such a translation requires a rigorous and systematic approach, which was beyond what is possible to do in this book. An additional problem with place names in the court rulings is that some of them are grossly misspelled or have been misunderstood.[75]

References

Ågren, Maria. 1992. *Jord och gäld: social skiktning och rättslig konflikt i södra Dalarna ca 1650–1850*. PhD diss., Uppsala University.

Aronsson, Kjell-Åke. 2009. Saami societies and the *siida*. In *Máttut – máddagat: the roots of Saami ethnicities, societies and spaces/places*, ed. Tiina Äikäs, 58–67. Oulu, Finland: Giellagas-Instituhtta.

[75] Hultblad (1968, p. 354). See, for example, Rydving (1995b, pp. 36–62), for more about Sami place names.

Bergman, Ingela, and Lars-Erik. Edlund. 2016. *Birkarlar* and Sámi—Intercultural contacts beyond state control: Reconsidering the standing of external tradesmen (*birkarlar*) in medieval Sámi societies. *Acta Borealia* 33: 52–80. https://doi.org/10.1080/08003831.2016.1154676.

Bergman, Ingela, Lars Liedgren, Lars Östlund, and Olle Zachrisson. 2008. Kinship and settlements: Sami residence patterns in the Fennoscandian alpine areas around ad 1000. *Arctic Antrophology* 45 (1): 97–110. https://doi.org/10.1353/arc.0.0005.

de Moor, Tine. 2015. *The dilemma of the commoners*. New York: Cambridge University Press.

Ehrenmalm, Arwid. 1743. *Resa igenom Wäster-Norrland til Åsehle lappmark, anstäld uti julii månad 1741*. Stockholm. Available page by page at http://runeberg.org/resawenoas/index.html.

Eidlitz Kuoljok, Kerstin. 1987. *Den samiska sitan en utmaning*. *Rig*. 70 (3): 74–76.

Eidlitz Kuoljok, Kerstin. 2011. *Den samiska sitan och vinterbyarna. En utmaning*, Dissertations and Documents in Cultural Anthropology, No. 10. Uppsala University

Elenius, Lars. 2019. *Möten mellan olika folk: det mångkulturella världsarvet i Gammelstad*. Luleå, Sweden: Gammelstad Visitor Center.

Fjellström, Phebe. 1986. Samernas samhälle i tradition och nutid. 2nd ed. Stockholm: Norstedt.

Fjellström, Phebe, Israel Roung, and Karl Bernhard Wiklund. 1983. *Berättelser om samerna i 1600-talets Sverige,*1983. Faksemilutgåva av de s. k. prästrelationerna m. m. först publicerade av K. B. Wiklund 1897–1909. Umeå, Sweden: Skytteanska samfundet.

Göthe, Gustaf. 1929. Om Umeå lappmarks svenska kolonisation: från mitten av 1500-talet till omkr. 1750. PhD diss., Stockholm University.

Graan, Olaus. 1899. *Relation, eller en fulkomblig beskrifning om lapparnas ursprung, så wähl som om heela dheras Lefwernes Förehållande*. Uppsala, Sweden: Harald Wretmans tryckeri.

Högström, Pehr. 1747. *Beskrifning öfwer de til Sweriges krona lydande lapmarker*. Stockholm: Salvius. http://urn.kb.se/resolve?urn=urn:nbn:se:umu:eod-114.

Hollsten, Jonas. 1768. *Anmärkningar om bäfvern, Castor.* Stockholm: Vetenskaps Akademiens handlingar.

Hollsten, Jonas. 1773. *Anmärkningar om järfven*. Stockholm: Vetenskaps Akademiens handlingar.

Hollsten, Jonas. 1774. *Afhandling om renen.* Stockholm: Vetenskaps Akademiens handlingar.

Holmbäck, Åke. 1922. *Om lappskattelandsinstitutet och dess historiska utveckling*. Stockholm: Statens offentliga utredningar.

Hultblad, Filip. 1968. *Övergång från nomadism till agrar bosättning i Jokkmokks socken.* PhD diss., Uppsala University.

Ingold, Tim. 1980. *Hunters, pastoralists and ranchers.* Cambridge, UK: Cambridge University Press.

Karlsson, Nina. 2006. *Bosättning och resursutnyttjande: miljöarkeologiska studier av boplatser med härdar från perioden 600–1900 e. Kr inom skogssamiskt område.* PhD diss., Umeå University.

Koponen, Eino. 2005. Siida. In *The Saami: A cultural encyclopaedia,* ed. Ulla-Maija Kulonen, Irja Seurujärvi-Kari, and Risto Pulkkinen. Helsinki: Suomalaisen Kirjallisuuden Seura.

Korpijaakko-Labba, Kaisa. 1994. *Om samernas rättsliga ställning i Sverige-Finland. En rättshistorisk utredning av markanvändningsförhållanden och -rättigheter i Västerbottens lappmark före mitten av 1700-talet.* Helsinki: Juristförbundets förlag.

Korpiola, Mia. 2014. Not without the consent and goodwill of the common people. *The Journal of Legal History* 35 (2): 95–119. https://doi.org/10.1080/01440365.2014.925173.

Kvist, Roger. 1989. *Rennomadismens dilemma, det rennomadiska samhällets förändring i Tuorpon och Sirkas, 1760–1860.* PhD diss., Umeå University.

Larsson, Jesper. 2016. Conflict-resolution mechanisms maintaining an agricultural system: early modern local courts as an arena for solving collective-action problems within Scandinavian Civil Law. *International Journal of the Commons* 10(2):1100–1118. https://doi.org/10.18352/ijc.666.

Larsson, Jesper, and Eva-Lotta Päiviö Sjaunja. 2020. Early modern reindeer husbandry, Sami economy, and grazing rights. *International Journal of the Commons* 14 (1): 91–107. https://doi.org/10.5334/ijc.965.

Larsson, Lars-Gunnar. 2018. *Per Holmberger och sockenlapparnas språk.* Sweden: Uppsala University.

Lindkvist, Thomas. 1997. Law and the making of the state in Medieval Sweden. In *Legislation and justice,* ed. Antonia Padoa-Schioppa, 211–228. Oxford, UK: Clarendon Press.

Linnaeus, Carl. 1811a. *Lachesis Lapponica or a tour in Lapland, now first published from the original manuscript journal of the celebrated Linnaeus,* ed. J. E. Smith. Vol 1. London: White and Cochrane.

Linnaeus, Carl. 1811b. *Lachesis Lapponica or a tour in Lapland, now first published from the original manuscript journal of the celebrated Linnaeus*, ed. J. E. Smith. Vol 2. London: White and Cochrane.

Linnaeus, Carl. 2003. *Iter Lapponicum: Lappländska resan 1732. I.* Dagboken. Umeå, Sweden: Kungl. Skytteanska Samfundet.

Lundius, Nicolai. 1905. *Descriptio Lapponiæ*. Uppsala, Sweden: Harald Wretmans tryckeri.

Lundmark, Lennart. 1982. *Uppbörd, utarmning, utveckling. Det samiska fångstsamhällets övergång till rennomadism i Lule lappmark*. PhD diss., Umeå University.

Luukko, Armas. 1980 [1956–1978]. Birkarl. In *Kulturhistoriskt lexikon för nordisk medeltid*, band 1, 2nd ed., 594–597. Copenhagen: Roskilde og Bagger.

Malmström, Åke. 1969. The system of legal systems. *Scandinavian Studies in Law* 13: 127–149.

Marklund, Bertil. 2015. Det milsvida folket. Skogssamernas samhälle i omvandling, 1650–1800. PhD diss., Umeå University.

Mulk, Inga-Maria. 1994. Sirkas, ett samiskt fångssamhälle i förändring kr.f. – 1600 e.Kr. PhD diss., Umeå University.

Niurenius, Olaus Petri. 1905. *Lappland, eller beskrivning över den nordiska trakt, som lapparne bebo i de avlägsnaste delarne af Skandinavien eller Sverge*. Uppsala, Sweden: Harald Wretmans tryckeri.

Norstedt, Gudrun. 2011. *Lappskattelanden på Geddas karta. Umeå lappmark från 1671 till 1900-talets början*. Umeå, Sweden: Thalassa förlag.

Norstedt, Gudrun. 2018. *A land of one's own*. PhD diss., Swedish University of Agricultural Sciences, Umeå. https://pub.epsilon.slu.se/15451/1/norstedt_g_180502.pdf.

Österberg, Eva, and Sølvi. Sogner, eds. 2000. *People meet the law*. Oslo: Universitetsförlaget.

Österberg, Eva, Malin Lennartsson, and Hans Eyvind Næss. 2000. Social control outside or combined with the secular judicial arena. In *People meet the law*, ed. Eva Österberg and Sølvi Bauge Sogner, 237–266. Oslo: Universitetsforlaget.

Ostrom, Elinor. 2005. Understanding institutional diversity. Princeton, NJ: Princeton University Press.

Pehrson, Robert N. 1964 [1957]. *The bilateral network of social relations in Könkömä Lapp District*. First edition by Indiana University Press 1957. Oslo: Norsk folkemuseum.

Rheen, Samuele. 1897. *En kortt relation om Lapparnes lefwarne och sedher, wijd-skiepellsser, sampt i många stycken grofwe wildfarellsser*. Uppsala, Sweden: Harald Wretmans tryckeri.
Rydving, Håkan. 1995a. *The end of drum-time: Religious change among the Lule Saami, 1670s–1740s*, 2nd ed. Uppsala, Sweden: Almqvist & Wiksell International.
Rydving, Håkan. 1995b. Samiska ortnamn: en litteraturöversikt och bibliografi. In *Ortnamnssällskapets i Uppsala årsskrift*, 36–62. Uppsala, Sweden: Almqvist & Wiksell International.
Schefferus, Johannes. 1673. *Joannis Schefferi Argentoratensis Lapponia,* Francofvrti ex officina Christiani Wolffii typis Joannis Andreæ. Anno M. DC. LXXIII.
Sköld, Peter. 1992. *Samisk bosättning i Gällivare 1550–1750*. Umeå, Sweden: Center för arktisk kulturforskning, Umeå universitet.
Sommarström, Bo. 1981 [1956–1978]. Lappmark. In *Kulturhistoriskt lexikon för nordisk medeltid,* vol. 10, ed. Ingvar Andersson and John Granlund, 320–323. Reprint. Copenhagen: Rosenkilde og Bagger.
Steckzén, Birger. 1964. *Birkarlar och lappar: en studie i birkarleväsendets, lappbefolkningens och skinnhandelns historia*. Stockholm: Almqvist & Wiksell.
Streeck, Wolfgang, and Kathleen Thelen. 2005. Introduction. In *Beyond continuity*, ed. Wolfgang Streeck and Kathleen Thelen, 1–39. Oxford, UK: Oxford University Press.
Svanberg, Ingvar. 1981. *Sockenlappar: en etnologisk studie av bofasta samer och deras nomadiska förfäder i Mellansverige*. Uppsala, Sweden: Etnologiska institutionen., Uppsala universitet.
Sveriges Rikes Lag Gillad och antagen på Riksdagenåhr 1734 [Sweden's Law, approved and passed by the Parliament in 1734]. 1984[1780].
Tanner, Väinö. 1929. *Antropogeografiska studier inom Petsamo-området. 1, Skoltlapparna*. Helsinki: Tilgmanns Tryck.
Tegengren, Helmer. 1952. *En utdöd lappkultur i Kemi lappmark*. Åbo/Turku, Finland: Åbo Akademi.
Tornaeus, Johannes. 1900. *Berättelse om Lapmarckerna och Deras Tillstånd*. Uppsala, Sweden: Harald Wretmans tryckeri.
Tresk, Olof, and Nils Ahnlund. 1928. *Kartor över Kemi & Torne lappmarker 1642 och 1643: av trycket utgivna och tillägnade K.B. Wiklund på 60-årsdagen 15. mars 1928 av vänner*. Stockholm: Nordisk Rotogravvyr.
Tuderus, Gabriel. 1905. *En kort underrättelse om the österbothniske lappar: som under Kiemi Gebiet lyda*. Uppsala, Sweden: Harald Wretmans tryckeri.

Vorren, Ørnulf. 1978. Bosetning och naturesursutntting under veidekulturen og dens differensiering. In *Finnmarksvidda natur–kultur*. Oslo: Statens forvaltningstjeneste. https://www.nb.no/items/a947f2133e81bfcf9a162e9f837b7fe6?page=0&searchText=altajuvet.
Wallerström, Thomas. 2018. *Kunglig makt och samiska bosättningsmönster: Studier kring Väinö Tanners vinterbyteori*. Oslo: Novus.
Zweigert, Konrad, and Hein Kötz. 1998. *Introduction to comparative law*. Oxford, UK: Clarendon Press.

Archival Sources

Härnösand Regional Archive (HRA):
Rulings in Jokkmokks District Court, Sweden, 1689–1780.
Riksarkivet [National Archives of Sweden]:
Svea Court of Appeal (RA SH). 1712–1780. Rulings in Jokkmokks District Court, Sweden.

4

Trade, Taxation, and Population

In this chapter, we present three main variables that impacted how and why Sami land use changed in the early modern period. The first one is trade, which had been important since prehistoric times but gained importance in the seventeenth century with fundamental changes in its infrastructure. Sami households accumulated a surplus in their growing herds of domesticated reindeer. Production for a market thus became a vital part of Sami household economy. The other variable that interacted with Sami land use was taxation. During most of the seventeenth century, the taxation of Sami was a complicated task for the government. They tried different methods for taxing Sami before they finally decided on a collective tax paid in money in 1695. In practice, it meant lowered tax levies and a more predictable tax for individual Sami, which in turn had a positive effect on the household economy as well as on population numbers in the eighteenth century. The last variable to be defined is population size.

J. Larsson and E.-L. Päiviö Sjaunja, *Self-Governance and Sami Communities*,
https://doi.org/10.1007/978-3-030-87498-8_4

Trade

In Chapter 2 we discussed how the early modern period saw the Nordic states' colonial ambition gaining pace and the ambition for both Denmark-Norway and Sweden-Finland was to tie the northern part of Fennoscandia closer to their respective countries and determine who had the right to what area. The colonization process had many parts, and one important feature was how the Swedish state integrated Sami trade into its economic networks.

Trade has been an important part of Sami livelihood since prehistoric time when hunting was the backbone in trade. Hunting has even been regarded as an important factor behind the formation of Sami ethnicity.[1] Scholars have argued that Sami ethnicity in northern Fennoscandia emerged as a result of the interaction between hunting populations and surrounding agrarian societies.[2] An elaborate trade system developed between hunters in the north and traders and producers in the east and south. Hunting was an economic specialization that made the Sami dependent on trade.[3]

Until the seventeenth century, furs from wild game were the main commodity in Lule lappmark, and trade was managed through *birkarlar* who traveled around the inland in winter to trade with groups of six to nine Sami households at different sites.[4] Sami exchanged furs for a great variety of commodities, such as flour, butter, and frieze, but also silver jewelry and coins. Sami also traded and bartered with residents and merchants along the Norwegian coast in summer. There was a great demand for furs on the European market in the sixteenth century, but problems in interior north Scandinavia and changes in the international fur market led to a diminished fur trade in the early seventeenth century.[5] New trade patterns had emerged that increased the fur import to Europe, first from Russia and later from North America.[6] This was also a time

[1] Odner (1983).

[2] Hansen and Olsen (2014, pp. 22–23).

[3] Odner (1983, pp. 85–86), L. Hansen (1990), and Hansen and Olsen (2014, pp. 127–131).

[4] Sandström (1996, pp. 64–68), Bergman and Edlund (2016), and Nurmi et al. (2020).

[5] Lundmark (1982, pp. 120, 135–138).

[6] Brook (2008).

for fundamental changes in how the organization of trade in interior northern Scandinavia was organized, as the government decided that all trade had to be centralized to official marketplaces in each *lappmark*.

In the first decade of the seventeenth century a total overhaul of the Swedish state's governance system of the lappmark took place.[7] A chosen place functioned like a hub in each *lappmark*, where four essential activities took place: church services, tax collection, judiciary, and trade. During the sixteenth century, the church lacked an organization in *lappmarken*, and the few church activities that took place in the area were organized from the parishes along the coast.[8] In the beginning of the seventeenth century, permanent church buildings belonging to the Christian Lutheran state church were being erected near the marketplaces, and local courts (*häradsrätter*) with state-appointed judges were established. At market time, Sami could thus do business, attend church services, and take part in court sessions, during the course of a few days or weeks. Henceforth, the marketplace was also where the government collected the yearly tax from Sami. There was little risk that one activity would interfere with another. During church service no other activities were allowed, and when the court convened, the market was closed. Hence, it was possible for people to attend both church services and court sessions and for the state to use the two arenas to reach people with information. The church and the state were two sides of the same coin. The clergies kept records of people, which facilitated tax collection, and they could even interrogate people before court sessions. Vicars read out loud state information in church and judges or clerks did the same in court before the trials began. At the end of the court session, that year's tax record was read out loud and verified by the court, and tax collection could begin.[9]

The introduction of all these new institutional elements constituted a vital part of the Swedish government's ambition to gain control over interior northern Fennoscandia and its inhabitants.[10] These institutional

[7] Bergling (1964, p. 126) and Hultblad (1968, p. 71).

[8] Bergling (1964, pp. 123–124).

[9] See, for example, HRA (1706, p. 59; 1707, p. 169; 1708, p. 262).

[10] Lantto (2012).

arrangements existed throughout the early modern period. In Lule lappmark, Jokkmokk was the chosen place, and the new organization was instituted between 1605 and 1607.[11] Markets were held twice per year, winter and spring, and the most important was the winter market when the court convened and tax collection took place. The day for the winter market in Lule lappmark to start was Paul the Apostle's day, January 25. The date was moved to February around 1725.[12] Summer and fall markets were held in Norway, and the Norwegian and Swedish seasons for markets complemented each other and created opportunities to visit markets throughout the year.[13]

The Swedish state's institutional arrangements regarding Sami trade did not stop with changes within the lappmark. To facilitate trade, according to the feudal ideological principle in Sweden that people in the countryside were obliged to deliver their products to burghers in towns,[14] new towns were established along the Gulf of Bothnia. In 1621 and 1622, four towns were founded: Umeå, Piteå, Luleå, and Torneå (Fi. Tornio). Each of them corresponded with a lappmark. Torneå served both Torne and Kemi lappmark, and the burghers in Luleå had the right to trade in Lule lappmark; the burghers visited their respective areas during market days.[15] In court records from the eighteenth century, the mayor of Luleå and burghers from the town frequently appear in the proceedings. However, it was hard for the state to contain trade only to the markets and the burghers of the towns because it lacked means to control the trade in the countryside. The Sami often had the ability and the will to take care of their own trade.[16] Hence, trade and barter also took place outside official market days.

---

[11] Bergling (1964, p. 163), Hultblad (1968, pp. 41, 71), and Lundmark (1982, p. 90). The place they chose carried the same name as the Sami village Jokkmokk, but the church was located outside the village boundaries. The first year for the market was 1605, the court's first year was 1606, and the church was built in 1607, the same year a new tax system was introduced.

[12] Rheen (1897, p. 58), Bergling (1964, pp. 254–257), and Hultblad (1968, p. 71).

[13] Bergling (1964, p. 158) and Kvist (1986, p. 23).

[14] Sandström (1996, p. 197).

[15] Bergling (1964, pp. 168–171) and Hansen and Olsen (2014, p. 241).

[16] L. Hansen (1984, pp. 52–53).

Trade requires at least a buyer and a seller. Sami were well situated as sellers and buyers and were good business partners for several reasons. They had a mobile lifestyle and Sami in Lule lappmark traveled from the Norwegian coast in the west to the Gulf of Bothnia in Sweden in the east.[17] The Lule Sami area thus covered a larger area than Lule lappmark. Hence, they could carry goods from one coast to the other. They also traveled to markets in other districts.

Mobility also gave them other benefits. From northern Norway it is known that Sami living along the coast were connected to the Swedish trading system. They also traded with Russian merchants. Copper they acquired in trade in the Norwegian town of Bergen was sold for a higher price in Russia, and they could use the difference in price between areas to their advantage. Sami knew that the Russians paid higher prices for most goods than Swedish traders would.[18] Similarly, Sami could exploit the difference in exchange rates between Norwegian merchants and Swedish tax collectors to their advantage. Sami in Sweden could sell stock fish to Norwegians and use items obtained in return to pay Swedish taxes.[19]

The Sami's mobility also facilitated transportation. The means of transportation was the reindeer, and without knowing how to handle and care for reindeer, transportation in inland circumpolar areas would have been almost impossible. The Sami not only had reindeer for transportation of their own goods, they also provided transport for others and boarded reindeer belonging to burghers in the coastal towns.[20] In the seventeenth century, Sami, especially those living in the mountains, played an important role as middlemen in the transit trade between the Norwegian coast and the Gulf of Bothnia in Sweden, as well as in transporting goods to and from markets in interior northern Fennoscandia. Sami trade provided great value to the Swedish government, because it both contributed to the state's stretched economy and helped to sustain the burghers in the towns that had been established along the coast.

---

[17] Kvist (1986, p. 22).

[18] L. Hansen (2006, p. 71).

[19] L. Hansen (2006, p. 74).

[20] Hultblad (1968, p. 148).

Mobility was not the only advantage Sami had in trade. They also were able to provide goods that were in demand. Until the end of the sixteenth century, their most valuable goods were furs. Sami trade in reindeer products grew in importance in the seventeenth century. By this time, many Sami had enlarged their reindeer herds and thereby had increased surpluses, for example, of cheese, meat, and furs. These products could either be sold at market or bartered with neighboring groups.[21] The Sami where not self-sufficient, and the revenues were often used to buy a wide range of products, such as tobacco, alcohol, copper, steel, iron, fishing gear, needles, wool blankets, clay tobacco pipes, tar, hides from cows and oxen, and silver objects. What goods they exchanged and how they changed through time, and using reindeer for transportation, are discussed in more detail in later chapters, particularly Chapter 8.

Marklund analyzed Sami subsistence and trade in the forest area in Ume lappmark from the seventeenth century to the mid-nineteenth century.[22] He presents a model of trade and subsistence that illuminates the high level of connectedness between Sami in the mountains, Sami in the forest, and peasants along the Gulf of Bothnia. Moreover, Nielssen studied Sami economic adaption around 1700, focusing on coastal Sami in northern Norway. He concludes that economic adaptation varied between regions where sets of subsistence activities played important roles.[23] Historical Sami trade has been studied in detail by Hansen and put in a wider historical Sami context by Hansen and Olsen.[24] The latter see a connection between the changes in trade made by the Swedish government and the introduction of reindeer pastoralism in the area.[25] In these works, the Sami's active and dynamic role in trade systems in early modern northern Fennoscandia is emphasized. Most recent archaeological and historical analysis portrays the Sami mainly as their own historical agents with varying subsistence practices and many contacts with neighboring groups, not least with regard to trade. We agree with this research and interpret the changing trade

---

[21] Hansen and Olsen (2014).

[22] Marklund (2008, p. 345).

[23] Nielssen (1986).

[24] L. Hansen (1990, 2006) and Hansen and Olsen (2014, pp. 232–239, 243–248).

[25] Hansen and Olsen (2014, p. 250).

patterns in interior northern Scandinavia in the seventeenth century as the most important attribute for explaining the development of reindeer pastoralism, a development that spurred changes in property regimes.

Taxation

The second attribute to consider is taxation, which is important for many reasons. What inhabitants paid in tax can tell us about production and how those who imposed the tax viewed production. Hence, changes in taxation might tell us how the state's attitude changed toward production. Tax also tells us about the relation between two parties and how it changed through time. Tax was not only a means for the state to gain income, it was also a means to control goods and people. In a society where much tax was in-kind, tax could benefit the state's needs and give us information about what different groups added to the total revenue from tax. Hence, discussion about new tax codes could unearth ideas the state had about the taxed subjects as well as the tax objects.

Since medieval times, *birkarlar* had the privilege to trade with Sami, sanctioned by the Swedish state. This privilege also included a right to tax them, for which they paid a fee to the crown.[26] From the mid-sixteenth century, the Swedish state wanted a firmer grip on taxation and gradually replaced *birkarlar* with the state's own bailiffs. The use of bailiffs increased control, and the first preserved tax records were recorded in 1553. Almost consecutive numbers of tax records from Lule lappmark are preserved through 1620.[27] These tax records contain what Sami paid in tax and a list of taxpayers (*mantalslängd*). An additional reason for the state to increase control of taxation of Sami was to get more involved in the lucrative fur market in Europe. In the tax records, there is also a list of furs that were purchased by the Swedish state. With the large interest in fur trade, it is not surprising to find that the most frequent tax commodity was furs in Lule lappmark. But dried fish, mainly pike

[26] Lundmark (1982, p. 78) and Bergman and Edlund (2016, p. 53).

[27] Lundmark (1982, pp. 80–83, 189). Tax records from 1557 and 1598 are the only missing records between 1553 and 1620.

(*Esox lucius*), perch (*Perca fluviatilis*), and whitefish (*Coregonus* sp.) were also common. Arctic char (*Salvelinus alpinus*), a species that mainly lived in alpine lakes, was a taxed good only for Sami living in the mountains. According to the tax records, reindeer was an unusual taxed good for members of villages in both the forest and mountain region during the sixteenth century; they appeared for the first time in tax records in the 1570s but in low numbers.[28] All Sami men seventeen years and older were registered to pay tax on an individual basis. It is likely that each of them represented a Sami household.

Tax was not only just a means to get revenue to the early modern state and access to valuable goods like furs. The right to tax people was meant to tie people to a country and had geopolitical consequences for Sami; it was part of the struggle to control the Arctic region. A taxpayer was a citizen in the country where he or she paid tax. Since Sami had a mobile lifestyle, there was a risk that they would pledge their allegiance to another country and pay tax there. To keep Sami within Swedish territory, the state could not tax them too much or they would pack up and leave. From the Swedish government's point of view, these countries were Denmark-Norway and Russia, and some Sami in the borderlands between the countries had to pay tax to more than one state.[29] In the decades around 1600, a struggle involving warfare among the three countries took place to define each country's territory.[30]

In early seventeenth century, the Swedish government reformed the tax code for Sami, making live reindeer and dried fish the primary tax commodities instead of furs. This alteration of the tax base has usually been interpreted as an answer to the government's increased demand for food supplies for soldiers in military campaigns. To be successful in warfare, the Swedish army needed to bring their own food, because it was impossible to buy provisions in a war zone.[31] A contributing factor to the change in tax code might have been that Western Europe's fur market was changing. The taxes were still paid in kind, and from the

---

[28] Lundmark (1982, pp. 87–88).

[29] This was a concern for Sweden throughout the seventeenth century and is mentioned in a letter around 1691 (Fellman 1915, p. 227).

[30] Hansen and Olsen (2014, pp. 257–262).

[31] Lundmark (1982, pp. 88–90).

time of the new tax code, the Swedish government made two attempts to count the number of reindeer that people in Lule lappmark had. Two records are preserved, from 1605 to 1609, and we return to them in Chapter 7. Here we only want to point out that the differences in economies between users in the mountains and the forest were still rather small in the first decade of the seventeenth century, according to the tax records. Users from the two regions paid tax in dried fish and the same number of reindeer per taxpayer, although users in the mountains on the whole had more reindeer than users in the forest. Differences between economies of the two subgroups increased during the seventeenth century, and from the 1670s users in the mountains (with a few insignificant exceptions) ceased to pay their tax in dried fish, while users in the boreal forest continued to do so. Sami had options of how to pay tax, and the development of tax items reflects the orientation of the economy for households.[32] In the mountains, users started to pay tax in cash and in boots made of reindeer fur.

The Swedish government found it hard to understand Sami economy and how to best tax them. With the government's increased interest in interior northern Sweden in the second half of the seventeenth century and the ambition to attract non-Sami farmers to settle in the Swedish lappmark, it issued Royal Ordinances in 1673 and 1695 that offered non-Sami exemptions from taxes and military service for fifteen years if they settled there. It is apparent that the government did not know much about the resources that made up the foundation for Sami livelihood. The government had a list of Sami who paid taxes but did not have records of the land and water they used.[33] Hence, the governor of Västerbotten County, Johan Graan, decided that Ume lappmark should be delineated and resources described. He appointed surveyor Jonas Gedda to make a map and clerk Anders Holm to write descriptions of the resources.[34] The map would make it possible to determine resources used by Sami and determine places where settlers could put up homesteads and farm and keep cattle. Graan's purpose was to create a cadastral book.

32 Lundmark (1982, pp. 168–169).

33 Norstedt (2011, p. 14).

34 Norstedt (2011, pp. 14–18) and Norstedt (2018, p. 32). Gedda's map is also discussed in Chapter 3.

However, there were no continuations of the survey of Ume lappmark in other districts. The lack of knowledge by representatives from the state of early modern Sami natural resource management gives further argument to why a self-governance perspective is a fruitful way to analyze early modern Sami land-use strategies.

As we have seen, during most of the seventeenth century, the taxation of Sami was a complicated task for the Swedish government, especially since the tax consisted of no less than five parts, not including corvée (unpaid labor in lieu of paying tax). In the 1680s, the government again launched the idea of a tax reform. A problem was not only that the tax consisted of many parts, the government also knew that there could be large differences in fortunes among Sami, but that they were taxed almost the same. In 1689, Governor Strijk in Västerbotten County pointed out that the number of reindeer a person owned did not reflect the tax level. In the extreme case, an owner with 1,000 reindeer paid the same in tax as one with ten reindeer.[35] Moreover, a government-initiated investigation in 1695 showed a lack of basic data concerning Sami taxation, which made it hard for the state to know if they had received the right amount of tax.[36] Strijk proposed a progressive tax that was supposed to be based on the number of reindeer per Sami.[37] There were, however, numerous problems connected with this proposal. Governor Douglas, who succeeded Strijk, and Judge Buhre conducted an investigation and pointed out that the number of reindeer often fluctuated greatly between years; a rich Sami one year could be poor the next year, which would make reindeer far too uncertain as a base for taxation.[38] In addition, it would have been very hard for the government to keep track of the number of reindeer. In 1692, officials had already expressed that "*ingen stadig ränta kan läggas på det som i sig självt är ostadigt*" (no steady tax can be imposed on what is in itself volatile),[39] which they repeated after the 1695 investigation. To reach this conclusion, Governor Douglas and Judge Buhre had traveled around in the lappmark and talked to Sami

[35] Fellman (1915, pp. 215–216, 232).
[36] Douglas (1695).
[37] Fellman (1915, p. 216) and Arell (1977, pp. 60–61).
[38] Douglas (1695).
[39] Fellman (1915, p. 234). A conclusion about pastoralism most scholars would agree with.

about the tax proposition; they dismissed the idea about a tax on reindeer. The worry that Sami living close to the Swedish borders would pay tax to Norway or Russia was again brought up, but as a minor argument against the proposal.

In the end, after 1695, the previous five-part tax was reduced to one tax which from then on was based on the resource territory that each Sami household used for reindeer herding, hunting, and fishing.[40] The tax rate for these territories was supposed to be fixed "for all eternity" and correspond to the territories listed in a cadastral book.[41] This was the first time a cadastral book of land in the lappmark was created, and former Governor Graan's idea of 1671 was realized.[42] However, some Sami in the mountain area were assessed fixed taxes although they were not assigned to specific territories.[43] Since land henceforth was the basis for taxation, the new tax code for Sami had similarities with how peasants in Sweden were taxed during that time. In contrast to peasants' lands, though, the exact ranges for Sami lands were never measured. Douglas and Buhres' investigation from 1695 concluded that these kinds of measurements would have been impossible, particularly for the Sami in the mountains since the borders of their mountain territories were so diffuse.[44]

The new tax code from 1695 was a break from the old tax code in another important aspect. From then on, the taxpaying unit was the Sami village, not the household. The tax thus became collective for the members of the village, and the village became a means for tax collection.[45] Each household's share of the total tax was defined in the cadastral book, but it was the Sami villages' responsibility to deliver the right amount of tax to the state. This made it possible for them to adjust the tax levels in view of the households' incomes, but they could also make some households pay more if others did not contribute sufficiently, or

40 Arell (1977, pp. 60–64).

41 Hultblad (1968, p. 79). The tax code from 1695 was in use until 1928 (Hultblad 1968, p. 74).

42 Holmbäck (1922, p. 13).

43 Holmbäck (1922, pp. 16–22).

44 Douglas (1695).

45 Hultblad (1968, p. 74).

if some households moved out of the Sami village. Another big change was that the tax was no longer paid in kind, but in money. All in all, the reforms in 1695 made the tax more predictable and lower, and corvée had been restricted. This tax relief surely had a positive effect on Sami households' standard of living, which probably contributed to the increase in Sami population from the late seventeenth century to circa 1780.

Closely connected to the question about how to tax Sami is the question about the division of land into *skatteland*, introduced in Chapter 2, that has been intensively debated since the 1980s.[46] *Skatteland* was for the first time made "visible" through Geddas's map from 1671, and the tax reform in 1695 listed them as a way to connect user with land. However, as we have seen, even these attempts were insufficient for the government to understand Sami land use. A reading of the tax reform of 1695 shows that the Swedish state did not understand Sami economy or how it was organized. Constructing a tax system that reflected the economy in each household would have required an organization and investigations impossible to carry out. The best way to solve the problem was to ask each village to deliver a fixed sum of money. It was then up to the members of the village, who actually knew the nuts and bolts of the economy, to collect the money from each household.

Population Size

The third, and last, attribute we consider in this chapter is population size. The size of the population is an important factor since it is possible to see available resources in relation to the number of people. However, it is difficult to estimate population in the early modern period. The most reliable estimates for the Swedish lappmark are based on the number of Sami listed in tax records (*skattelappar*), where each person represented a household. One problem is that the number of people in the

[46] Korpijakko-Labba (1994), Lundmark (2006), and N.-J. Päiviö (2011). Kaisa Korpijakko-Labba's seminal dissertation was first published in Finnish in 1989 and had been preceded by other works by her in the 1980s.

records fluctuated between years partly because almost all Sami were non-sedentary and could move either between villages or across national borders, making them hard to keep track of.

Between 1553 and 1570, there were on average 105 people registered in the tax records in Lule lappmark. However, after 1570, the number started to increase, and around the turn of the century there were on average 169. The numbers peaked in the 1610s with an average of 186 in the tax records.[47] Between 1621 and 1660 relatively few tax records were preserved from Lule lappmark, but fragmentary records have shown that the number of Sami was similar to the number in the preceding decades. In the 1660s, the state initiated mining activities in several places in Lule lappmark and tried to force Sami to do corvée in these mines, mostly in transport. To avoid forced labor, many Sami moved away, and when the government's tax collector came to Kaitum in 1667, he wrote that "all had escaped," and that there was no tax to collect.[48] At the same time, in neighboring Sirkas, there were only nine taxpayers left. As a comparison, in 1643 Sirkas and Kaitum, which by that time were treated as one unit in the tax records, had had about seventy registered taxpayers.[49]

In 1667, the Sami population in the whole of Lule lappmark had decreased drastically and by then only fifty-five people were registered in the tax record.[50] According to Hultblad it was almost 200 taxpayers a decade earlier.[51] The stress that the mines evidently brought on the Sami population was not in line with the government's intention for interior northern Sweden, and policies had to be revised.[52] From 1670, the number of people registered in the tax records slowly and steadily increased again, but it was not until after the tax reform in 1695 that the increase gathered real momentum. In 1750, there were 295 Sami

[47] Lundmark (1982, pp. 191–197).

[48] Riksarkivet, Kammararkivet, Mantalslängd (1667).

[49] Riksarkivet, Kammararkivet, Mantalslängd (1643).

[50] Riksarkivet, Kammararkivet, Mantalslängd (1667).

[51] Hultblad (1968, p. 121).

[52] Norstedt (2011, p. 13).

registered as taxpayers in Lule Lappmark, and the number peaked in the 1780s with more than 360.[53]

At the same time mining was promoted, the government tried to attract non-Sami farmers to settle in the lappmark. Despite royal ordinances in 1673 and 1695, the result was disappointing for the state. At the end of the seventeenth century, less than ten farms had been established in Jokkmokk parish (Turpon, Sirkas, Jokkmokk, and the southern part of Sjokksjokk) of Lule lappmark, and colonization continued to be a slow process until the end of the eighteenth century. In 1760, there were still only thirteen settler households in Jokkmokk Parish, and in 1780 they had increased to a mere twenty-two.[54] Seventy years later, in 1850, there were 150 farms. The Sami population dominated in numbers in this region until the nineteenth century.[55]

References

Arell, Nils. 1977. Rennomadismen i Torne lappmark: markanvändning under kolonisationsepoken i fr.a. Enontekis socken. PhD diss. Umeå, Sweden: Skytteanska samfundet. http://www.diva-portal.org/smash/record.jsf?pid=diva2%3A616377&dswid=6098.

Bergling, Ragnar 1964. Kyrkstaden i övre Norrland: kyrkliga, merkantila och judiciella funktioner under 1600- och 1700-talen. PhD diss., Uppsala University.

Bergman, Ingela, and Lars-Erik. Edlund. 2016. *Birkarlar* and Sámi—Intercultural contacts beyond state control: Reconsidering the standing of external tradesmen (*birkarlar*) in medieval Sámi societies. *Acta Borealia* 33: 52–80. https://doi.org/10.1080/08003831.2016.1154676.

Brook, Timothy. 2008. *Vermeer's hat, the seventeenth century and the dawn of the global world*. New York: Bloomsbury Press.

Douglas. 1695. *See* Kungliga biblioteket in Archival Sources.

53 Hultblad (1968, p. 121), gives a higher number for Lule Lappmark, but one needs to subtract the Sami in Jukkasjärvi who had been added to Kaitum in 1742.

54 Hultblad (1968, pp. 330–341, Table 5).

55 Kvist (1987, p. 170).

Fellman, Isak. 1915. *Handlingar och uppsatser angående Finska Lappmarken och lapparne. 4*. Helsinki: Finska Litteratursällskapets Tryckeri.
Hansen, Lars Ivar. 1984. Trade and markets in northern Fenno-Scandinavia A.D. 1550–1750. *Acta Borealia* 1 (2): 47–79. https://doi.org/10.1080/08003838408580312.
Hansen. Lars Ivar. 1990. *Samisk fangstsamfunn og norsk høvdingeøkonomi*. Oslo: Novus.
Hansen, Lars Ivar. 2006. Sami fisheries in the pre-modern era: Household sustenance and market relations. *Acta Borealia* 23 (1): 56–80. https://doi.org/10.1080/08003830600789390.
Hansen, Lars Ivar, and Bjørnar Olsen. 2014. *Hunters in transition: An outline of early Sámi history*. Leiden, The Netherlands: Brill.
Holmbäck, Åke. 1922. *Om lappskattelandsinstitutet och dess historiska utveckling*. Stockholm: Statens offentliga utredningar.
Hultblad, Filip. 1968. *Övergång från nomadism till agrar bosättning i Jokkmokks socken*. PhD diss., Uppsala University.
Korpijaakko-Labba, Kaisa. 1994. *Om samernas rättsliga ställning i Sverige-Finland. En rättshistorisk utredning av markanvändningsförhållanden och -rättigheter i Västerbottens lappmark före mitten av 1700-talet*. Helsinki: Juristförbundets förlag.
Kvist, Roger. 1986. Den samiska handeln och dess roll som social differentieringsfaktor: Lule lappmark 1760–1860. *Acta Borealia* 3 (2): 19–40. https://doi.org/10.1080/08003838608580333.
Kvist, Roger. 1987. Rennomadismens dynamik: Rennomadismen och befolkningsutvecklingen i Tuorpon och Sirkas 1760–1860. *Historisk Tidskrift* 107 (2): 161–181.
Lantto, Patrik. 2012. *Lappväsendet: tillämpningen av svensk samepolitik 1885–1971*. Umeå, Sweden: Center for Sami Research, Umeå University.
Lundmark, Lennart. 1982. Uppbörd, utarmning, utveckling. Det samiska fångstsamhällets övergång till rennomadism i Lule lappmark. PhD diss., Umeå University.
Lundmark, Lennart. 2006. *Samernas skatteland i Norr- och Västerbotten under 300 år*. Stockholm: Institutet för Rättshistorisk Forskning.
Marklund, Bertil. 2008. Skogssamernas ekonomiska rum. In *Människor i Norr: Samisk forskning på nya vägar*, ed. Peter Sköld, 343–448. Umeå, Sweden: Centrum för samisk forskning, Umeå universitet.
Nielssen, Alf Ragnar. 1986. Economic Adaptation among the coast Sami population in Finnmark c. 1700. *Acta Borealia* 3 (1): 21–41. https://doi.org/10.1080/08003838608580328.

Norstedt, Gudrun. 2011. *Lappskattelanden på Geddas karta. Umeå lappmark från 1671 till 1900-talets början.* Umeå, Sweden: Thalassa förlag.
Norstedt, Gudrun. 2018. A land of one's own. PhD diss., Swedish University of Agricultural Sciences, Umeå. https://pub.epsilon.slu.se/15451/1/norstedt_g_180502.pdf.
Nurmi, Risto, Jari-Matti Kuusela, and Ville Hakamäki. 2020. Swedenization of the North: The early medieval Swedish northern expansion and the emergence of the *Birkarls*. *Acta Borealia* 37 (1–2): 1–26. https://doi.org/10.1080/08003831.2020.1757275.
Odner, Knut. 1983. Finner och terfinner. Occasional Paper 9. Oslo: Department of Social Anthropology, University of Oslo.
Päiviö, Nils-Johan. 2011. Från skattemannarätt till nyttjanderätt. en rättshistorisk studie av utvecklingen av samernas rättigheter från slutet 1500-talet till 1886 års renbeteslag. PhD diss., Uppsala University.
Rheen, Samuele. 1897. *En kortt relation om Lapparnes lefwarne och sedher, wijd-skiepellsser, sampt i många stycken grofwe wildfarellsser*. Uppsala, Sweden: Harald Wretmans tryckeri.
Sandström, Åke. 1996. *Plöjande borgare och handlande bönder: mötet mellan den europeiska urbana ekonomin och vasatidens Sverige*. Stockholm: Stads- och kommunhistoriska institutet.

Archival Sources

Härnösand Regional Archive (HRA):
Rulings in Jokkmokks District Court, Sweden, 1689–1780.
Kungliga bibliotektet (National Library of Sweden), Stockholm:
Douglas. 1695. Skrivelse till Kungl. Maj:t ang. lapparna dat 25 mars 1695, X [1695] 281a:1.
Riksarkivet [National Archives of Sweden]:
Kammararkivet, Mantalslängder 1643, 1667.

Part II

Land Use, Livelihood, and Ecological Settings

In the early modern period, people's livelihoods were to a large degree determined by which natural resources were available in their local surroundings. For Sami, as for other people living in the circumpolar north, this primarily meant exploiting pasture lands for domesticated reindeer (*Rangifer tarandus tarandus*); using the sea, lakes, rivers, and streams for fishing; and utilizing the northern boreal forest and the mountains for hunting. They also had a wide range of other income sources, such as gathering, handcrafts, trade, and transport, which contributed to the household economy.[1] However, the dependency on these different sectors of the economy was not constant during the early modern period and it was not the same for all households. Sami subsistence, used synonymously with economy, is defined here as the source or means of obtaining the necessities of life, yet it also includes the production of goods to be used for trade.

The empirical part of the book, Chapters 5–8, provides details about different aspects of fishing, hunting, reindeer pastoralism, as well as other income sources that made up the household economy. Together they form the foundation for a discussion about long-term changes in

[1] Phebe Fjellström (1986) and E.-L. Päiviö (2017).

subsistence, and how it impacted property rights. Fundamental for the analysis is the difference between resources in the mountains and the resources in the boreal forest and how changes in the utilization of these resources impacted households. The shift of their importance came to impact culture, economy, and property rights.

5

Fishing

In this chapter, we describe Sami fishing in interior lakes, streams, and rivers in detail. We look closely at Lule lappmark and include information about neighboring areas. Fishing has specific characteristics for various species and seasons, depending on how and when they spawn and how they behave. The waters in interior Fennoscandia generally are considered low in productivity, but waters in the two regions, forest and mountains, differ. The waters in the boreal forest are nutrient rich and high yielding and have many fish species compared to the nutrient-poor fishing waters in the mountains, which are populated by only a few fish species. The main argument put forward is that users who had access to rivers, lakes, and streams in the boreal forest thus had better possibilities to create a livelihood based on fishing compared to those who lived in or closer to the mountains. To create social and economic stability for the household, fishing was organized as an exclusive right, resembling private property. Rules were necessary because households had to optimize the catch to survive on fishing, and were only achievable if there was some kind of institution in place that regulated each household's access to fishing. At the end of the early modern period, these areas became smaller and it became harder to survive on fishing.

J. Larsson and E.-L. Päiviö Sjaunja, *Self-Governance and Sami Communities*,
https://doi.org/10.1007/978-3-030-87498-8_5

Strategies for Fishing

In the early modern period, many Sami households were fishers as their main occupation. An intriguing question is how it was possible to support a household on fishing in an area with low-productivity waters given the existing, relatively inefficient fishing methods, especially when the catch was not enough for households to be self-sufficient. They also had to amass a surplus of dried fish for paying taxes and trading. What strategies, and thus institutions, did households need to secure a satisfactory fish harvest from year to year?

Despite the fact that water and fishing have been at the forefront of discussions about the management of CPRs since the 1950s,[1] relatively little attention has been paid to inland, or freshwater, fishing. Most research about fish as a CPR has been concerned with large-scale fishing in the open seas. The start of the modern debate about collective-action problems and overharvest of commonly used resources was H. Scott Gordon's seminal work about the fishing industry in 1954.[2] He argued, fourteen years before Hardin made the concept "tragedy of the commons" widely known,[3] that resources will be depleted when "natural resources are owned in common and exploited under conditions of individualistic competition."[4] While open-sea fisheries still face many challenges and the depletion of vital resources is an imminent threat, research about inshore fisheries has shown that in many cases collective-action problems have been solved. One example is James Acheson's studies that show how fishers in Maine, USA, managed to devise institutions for a sustainable inshore lobster fishery.[5] Another example is Ostrom's meta-analysis of CPRs that led to her widely known design principles for sustainable use.[6]

Even though the large-scale fishery has attracted most attention in fisheries science and policy, worldwide small-scale fisheries actually have

[1] Gordon (1954). See also Acheson (2003) and Basurto et al. (2013).

[2] Gordon (1954).

[3] Hardin (1968).

[4] Gordon (1954, p. 124).

[5] Acheson (1988, 2003).

[6] Ostrom (1990, p. 90).

many more practitioners and half of the world's wild-caught fish production.[7] In research on fishing, focus has generally been on the harvest, but to understand and analyze the complexity of a fishery, one needs to include all the work that precedes and succeeds harvest: negotiations of access rights, maintenance of gear, preservation of fish, taking fish to markets, etc.[8] All of these activities include more people than those taking part in the harvest and have an impact on a fishery.

Research about CPRs also has generally paid less attention to freshwater fishing than sea fishing. One reason might be that excluding users in sea fishing is harder than in lakes. Nevertheless, harvests of fish in lakes and streams have been very important for people around the world, especially many indigenous groups who depend on freshwater fishing. For them, the household's subsistence has often revolved around strategies to secure fish harvests.[9] In order to analyze fishing strategies and who had the right to harvest fish, one also needs to understand more about the rules and norms that regulated fishing and how they changed. The rules and the ability of households to rely on fishing were, for example, influenced by the composition of fish species, the conditions in the waters that fisher households had access to, and the processes of fishing as a livelihood. Which species of fish were caught? Which methods were used? Who was fishing? Where and when did they fish? What did they do with the fish they caught?

In a Sami context, research has primarily focused on sea fishing along the coast in northern Norway.[10] Fishing in lakes and streams differs in many ways from fishing in the open sea, yet parallels can be drawn between the two due to certain cultural factors that are shared among Sami households. Some anthologies by anthropologists that describe freshwater fishing by Sami focus mainly on methods and gear from

[7] Smith and Basurto (2019).

[8] Basurto et al. (2020).

[9] Bennett et al. (2018), Needs-Howarth and Cox Thomas (1998), and Rapalje Martin (1989).

[10] Some examples are Bjørklund (1991), Brattland (2010), L. Hansen (2006), and Nielssen (1986). Detailed early modern rules about fishing are known from Sea Sami along the Norwegian coast (Bjørklund 1991).

prehistoric time to the twentieth century.[11] However, they only discuss fishing as an economic strategy in general terms and do not try to define any rights to fish. Hultblad reviewed land use and users' rights to resources in Lule lappmark based on court records from the same time period as our research.[12] Nils Arell did the same for Torne lappmark a decade later.[13] In the last decade some new research has emerged about Sami inland fishing that provides a discussion of fishing as an ecologically strategic resource in pre-colonial households.[14] In these studies, historical and ecological methods are combined to describe the environmental settings for pre-colonial Sami land use. Environmental data were used to learn more about what roles different natural resources played in the inhabitants' sustenance. For us, the results chiefly contribute useful knowledge about the historical-ecological frames for inland fishing.

Fishing can be described as a social-ecological system where users interact with nature.[15] The need for institutions, i.e., rules that regulate access to fishing waters, is necessary, and defined rules are especially important in an environment with low-productivity waters. Rules also were necessary because, in these waters, households had to optimize the catch in order to survive on fishing, and maximum sustainable yields were only achievable if there was some kind of institution in place that regulated each household's access to fishing. Some of these rules were nested in national legislation and, regarding fishing, the most important link was established between taxes and fishing rights.[16] The state had connected the right to use specific land and water to the tax and, as long as the tax was paid, users had the right to fish in certain lakes within these *skatteland*.[17] However, even though the state was authorized to tax the inhabitants, the actual use (proprietorship) of land and water and the rules for and practice of everyday fishing in interior northern Sweden

---

[11] See, for example, Phebe Fjellström (1986).

[12] Hultblad (1968).

[13] Arell (1977).

[14] Norstedt et al. (2014) and Norstedt and Östlund (2016).

[15] Ostrom (2009). See also McGinnis and Ostrom (2014).

[16] Norstedt et al. (2014).

[17] Arell (1977, pp. 67 and 129).

were decided by local users. Even changes in users and new boundaries for fishing districts were made by the local users. Any changes in these rules mainly reflected changes in the households' economy and new power dynamics in the local community.

Lakes, Rivers, Streams, and Fish

There are countless lakes and streams in Lule lappmark, and much of the water begins its journey in the mountain ridge that separates Sweden from Norway before it runs east via streams, lakes, and eventually rivers, to the Gulf of Bothnia. Seventeenth- and eighteenth-century accounts retrieved from different parts of interior northern Fennoscandia mention in total twelve fish species that were caught by the inhabitants: northern pike (*Esox lucius*), European perch (*Perca fluviatilis*), common roach (*Rutilus rutilus*), European whitefish (*Coregonus lavaretus*), grayling (*Thymallus thymallus*), salmon (*Salmo salar*), brown trout (*Salmo trutta*), Arctic char (*Salvelinus alpinus*), whitefish (*Coregonus albula*), burbot (*Lota lota*), ide (*Leuciscus idus*), and common bream (*Abramis brama*).[18] In Ume lappmark, all species but burbot were eaten by the inhabitants[19] (Fig. 5.1).

In Lule lappmark, it was possible to live quite well by fishing in the eighteenth century if the fisher also hunted, according to Högström.[20] At the same time, fishing and hunting seem to have been serious businesses only for households that were "poor in reindeer."[21] Ehrenmalm described in his travel account of Åsele lappmark how fish were plentiful in the lakes and that they were fatter and better than he had seen anywhere else. However, not all species were available in all fishing waters, and some lakes offered no fish at all.[22] Moreover, fishing was generally described as very poor in the mountains, with catches predominantly consisting of

---

18 Bergman and Ramqvist (2017), Ehrenmalm (1743, p. 127), Graan (1899, p. 36), Norstedt et al. (2014), Rheen (1897, p. 53), and Tornaeus (1900, p. 61).

19 Norstedt el al. (2014).

20 Högström (1747, p. 85).

21 Graan (1899, p. 35) and Högström (1747, p. 85).

22 Ehrenmalm (1743, p. 127).

Fig. 5.1 From the top, European whitefish (*Coregonus lavaretus*), salmon (*Salmo salar*), and Arctic char (*Salvelinus alpinus*), depicted in 1695 (*Source* Iter lapponicum, Luefsta MS 92, Uppsala University Library, Sweden. Public domain. https://www.alvin-portal.org/alvin/imageViewer.jsf?dsId=ATTACHMENT-0117&pid=alvin-record:162152)

Arctic char and brown trout,[23] albeit Linnaeus and Rheen recorded that harvests in mountain lakes occasionally were considered very good.[24]

Salmon, and northern pike and Arctic char to lesser degrees, were explicitly mentioned in Lule lappmark court cases regarding rights to fish. Two other species were mentioned indirectly as names of lakes—Lake Abborrträsk (European perch) and Lake Mörtsjön (common roach). Lundius wrote that salmon swam up Lule River all the way to Jokkmokk, approximately 170 km from the coast, and that they continued even farther when water levels were higher than normal.[25] We conclude, based on evidence from contemporary accounts, that salmon was an important species in Lule lappmark. Each salmon fishing site along Lule River was listed in an account from the seventeenth century by priest Samuel Rheen.[26] Tornaeus stated that salmon were also important in Torne lappmark and that users there primarily fished for salmon in northern Norwegian rivers.[27]

According to Lundius, salmon fishing was not an option in Ume lappmark, because the salmon swam no more than about 30 km up Ume River.[28] In their research on Ume lappmark, Norstedt et al. listed the fish species commonly harvested in the 1670s: northern pike, European perch, common roach, and European whitefish.[29] Additionally, Bergman and Ramqvist, when comparing the share of each species in the harvests, showed that northern pike made up 67 percent of the catch, European perch 14 percent, and European whitefish 12 percent.[30] The percentages were based on information from 1550s tax records from all parishes in Västerbotten County.

In Lule lappmark, both reindeer pastoralist and fisher households were mobile during the seventeenth century, moving between temporary settlements to optimize their access to natural resources. Reindeer

[23] Norstedt et al. (2014).

[24] Linnaeus (2003, p. 103) and Rheen (1897, p. 54).

[25] Lundius (1905, pp. 18–19).

[26] Rheen (1897, pp. 64–65).

[27] Tornaeus (1900, p. 61).

[28] Lundius (1905, pp. 18–19).

[29] Norstedt et al. (2014).

[30] Bergman and Ramqvist (2017).

pastoralist households moved seasonally to find good grazing, often over long distances between the mountains in summer and the boreal forest in winter. Fisher households, on the other hand, moved over shorter distances between lakes and streams in the boreal forest.[31] According to the sources, their precise routes were decided by when and where certain species of fish spawned, which could vary in space and time between populations, species, and fishing waters. Moving was thus a way for fisher households to try to optimize their harvests. According to Graan, only exceptionally poor fisher households stayed in the same place year-round.[32]

Some sources described fishers' homes as somewhat permanent hexagonal huts with walls made of boards, brushwood, or peat.[33] These huts were built in abundance, especially along the shores of regularly visited fishing waters. Although permanent buildings were common in some places, Högström, who was especially familiar with Lule lappmark, only encountered fishers in moveable tents with canvases made of frieze, similar to those used by reindeer pastoralist households.[34] He, however, described how fisher households sometimes erected temporary shielings alongside far-off lakes. These shielings were made of peat or brushwood, short-lived construction according to him, and were probably only used to give shelter to a couple of household members for a few days while they fished in the lake.

Sometimes more permanent storage buildings were erected along the households' moving routes, where fishing gear and equipment could be stored.[35] A *stabbur* or *ájtte* (small log building for storage) was, for example, mentioned in a court ruling from Lule lappmark.[36]

Fishing with available methods likely only rendered plentiful catches when the fish were spawning. Accordingly, Linnaeus described that fish harvests were especially good in spring and early summer when northern

[31] Graan (1899, p. 35), Högström (1747, p. 98), Rheen (1897, p. 14), and Tornaeus (1900, p. 61).

[32] Graan (1899, p. 35).

[33] Graan (1899, p. 46) and Rheen (1897, p. 15).

[34] Högström (1747, p. 103).

[35] Niurenius (1905, p. 14).

[36] HRA (1710, p. 457).

pike spawned.[37] He described, for example, that no Sami were present in the church town of Lycksele in Ume lappmark at Pentecost since it coincided with spawning, the Sami's prime harvest time. Lundius indirectly corroborated the importance of spring fishing as he stated that the fishing in Ume lappmark was severely hampered in years when spring floods ran extraordinarily high, which, according to him, happened every 4 to 5 years.[38]

The importance of spring fishing in the northern lappmark is linked to the fact that northern pike made up the bulk of the catch for households engaged in freshwater fishing.[39] Consequently, a poor harvest was probably economically devastating. In years when the conditions for spring fishing were unusually difficult due to high water, the households' harvests of the three economically most important fish species (northern pike, European perch, and common roach) were jeopardized. In Lule lappmark, a poor spring harvest could have been somewhat balanced by good harvests of salmon in summer and fall. Linnaeus described that salmon, starting in the beginning of May, progressively wandered west in Lule River to spawn before returning, often emaciated, to the Gulf of Bothnia in late fall.[40] Summer and early fall were hence the best times for salmon fishing. Another recuperative strategy was probably fishing for European whitefish, which spawned in various rivers and lakes between September and February.

Available Technology

Few descriptions of fishing methods exist in the contemporary sources. Lundius described how all Sami, both poor and rich, had nets for seining (using vertical, weighted nets).[41] And according to Tornaeus, household members in northernmost Kemi and Torne lappmark carried their

---

37 Linnaeus (2003, p. 45).

38 Lundius (1905, p. 29).

39 Bergman and Ramqvist (2017) and Norstedt et al. (2014).

40 Linnaeus (2003, pp. 86, 158).

41 Lundius (1905, p. 19).

nootredskap (seining tools) from one lake to the next, depending on where the fish were spawning.[42] A more detailed description is given by Lundius from Ume lappmark, where he recorded that fisher households prepared to *draga not* (seine) in the evening and fished until sunrise (around 2 a.m. in summer).[43] When they came home in the morning, they hung their fishing gear to dry. Thereafter, they boiled and ate the largest fish in the catch. The rest were, according to Lundius, dried to be eaten when they traveled to "church days," which took place in July each year.[44]

Throughout history, seining has been a fishing technique worldwide. The net is dragged through the water from either the shore or a boat and put together to form a bag-like container where the fish are caught. The net could also be extended across a narrow waterbody such as a creek, stream, or bay and dragged along the shores from both sides. Based on the sources, the term *not* (seine) was apparently used throughout the lappmark in the seventeenth and eighteenth centuries, but in specific cases it is uncertain whether *not* actually meant seine hauling or fishing with stationary gillnets. The terminology seems a bit inconsistent here, albeit stationary gillnets were probably also used extensively during this time. According to a 1709 court case, two users from Sjokksjokk had fished *både med noot och näth* (both with seine and gillnets) when they illegally fished in a lake.[45] In accounts written by priests and travelers, the use of *ljuster* (fish spears) is not mentioned explicitly, but in a court ruling dealing with the distribution of an inheritance from a settler who had been married to a Sami woman, various fishing gear were listed, including *36 famnar* (the equivalent of 64 m) of seine, sixteen nets, one fish spear, and one boat.[46]

Fisher households needed boats to fish. In an account about Ume lappmark, Lundius recorded that boats were both constructed and used by the inhabitants.[47] According to him, the typical boat was light enough

---

42 Tornaeus (1900, p. 61).

43 Lundius (1905, p. 10).

44 Phebe Fjellström (1986).

45 HRA (1709, pp. 343–344).

46 HRA (1701, p. 417).

47 Lundius (1905, p. 9).

for one man to carry on his shoulders. It was made of spruce and jointed by threads from fine spruce roots with a minimum number of nails to keep the weight down. Lundius only mentioned that the boats were used for transport, not for other purposes. However, it seems reasonable to say they also were used extensively for fishing. According to him, the light weight was crucial because the boats had to be carried past rapids. Based on the mobile lifestyle of most fisher households, the light weight was just as important for carrying them to remote fishing waters.[48]

Boats that were left unsupervised sometimes were used illegally by others. In one court ruling from Lule lappmark, a boat left on the south shore of a lake had been used unlawfully by a man traveling to Norway. He had left it on the western shore of the lake, which made it impossible for the boat's owner to harvest gillnets that he had set in the lake. When the owner finally got the boat back, after seven days, his ten old nets had been ruined, together with 20 Arctic chars rotting in them.[49] Nets were made of delicate materials, i.e., hemp and flax, and to last they had to be maintained properly.

From Åsele lappmark, Ehrenmalm described three kinds of fishing gear: (1) *ryssjor* (fish traps), (2) gillnets in four mesh sizes, and (3) three types of seining gear.[50] According to him, fishing with hooks and lures were unheard of there.

There are few descriptions of winter fishing in the early modern sources, although fishing probably was a recurring activity for fisher households year-round. Winter fishing was especially strategic if users wanted to catch European whitefish, which spawn from September to February. Lundius wrote in one account of ice fishing, without going into detail, that fisher households in Ume lappmark caught enough fish throughout winter to survive.[51] In Lule lappmark, Linnaeus described, possibly from hearsay, how *isnot* (ice fishing with nets) was implemented between Andersdagen (Saint Andrew's Day) on November 30 and Christmas.[52] He described how the fishers first made holes in the ice

48 Graan (1899, p. 52).
49 HRA (1699, p. 75).
50 Ehrenmalm (1743, p. 128).
51 Lundius (1905, p. 12).
52 Linnaeus (2003, p. 152).

and then pulled the net with a rod under the ice, primarily to catch European whitefish. In Åsele lappmark, Ehrenmalm described how the winter fishing poles were somewhat longer and much thinner than the ones he had seen in Stockholm, a statement that indirectly gives proof that Sami fished during winter. Also, several court rulings mention fishing during winter.

Labor Division

There is sparse information about who in a household did what with regard to fishing. Nevertheless, many of the work tasks related to reindeer husbandry, such as milking, guarding, and gathering the reindeer, were performed by both men and women. This was true also for many of the household chores, such as food preparation and cooking. Therefore, it seems reasonable that fishing was also carried out by both men and women. Concurrently, at the end of the seventeenth century, the provincial governor of Finnmark, Norway (now part of Troms og Finnmark county), described that one difference between Norwegian and Sami fisher households along the northern coast was that Sami women took an active part in fisheries.[53]

Also, two court rulings in Lule lappmark indicate that fishing was a task that could be performed by women. In the first case, from 1701, a settler was using fishing waters belonging to a peasant in Luleå parish without his permission.[54] The peasant had given a Sami household permission to fish there. When the wife in the Sami household was net fishing in the lake, the settler had assaulted her with a stick and a horse rein resulting in bloody wounds. Afterward, he had taken her nets; when she found them fourteen days later, they were destroyed. A maid who had accompanied her to the lake had witnessed the assault according to the court ruling.

In the second case, from 1712, a man, Olof Anderssson, accused a woman, Karin Andersdotter, in Jokkmokk of not letting him use fishing

[53] L. Hansen (2006).

[54] HRA (1701, pp. 411–412).

waters that he claimed he had the right to use. Additionally, he accused her of having removed four of his nets from the water.[55] These two examples show that the gender division of labor was not as apparent among Sami fisher households as it was among non-Sami households. Seemingly, a woman could go fishing with her maid, as well as remove nets that she saw as an intrusion on her fishing rights. An opportunistic strategy for households to optimize their harvests probably was to engage as much of the available workforce as possible during the peak fishing seasons.

Importance of Resources

Fishing was carried out for many reasons, but perhaps the most important motive was that it was an accessible way to get fat and proteins. Sources describe how fish was the most important foodstuff for users along rivers and lakes in the lappmark. Ehrenmalm wrote, for example, that fisher households in Åsele lappmark got almost all of their nourishment from fish, and that fishing was their only occupation.[56] Furthermore, Linnaeus wondered how the Sami he met outside Lycksele in Ume lappmark could eat just fish and nothing but fish.[57]

Until the end of the seventeenth century, it was important for households to have a surplus of dried fish, especially pike, since it was a tax good.[58] Ehrenmalm described that some of the fish was boiled and eaten fresh, some was dried to support the household during winter, and the rest was sold *till sina utskylders betalande* (to pay their debts).[59] Besides the state tax, inhabitants also paid tax to the church, and this was continuously paid in kind with products like dried fish. Additionally, fisher households preferably wanted a surplus of dried fish to use for trade and exchange as a means to obtain goods that were needed in the

[55] RA SH (1712, pp. 505–506, § 11). See also Hultblad (1968, p. 423 case 1067a).

[56] Ehrenmalm (1743, p. 127).

[57] Linnaeus (2003, p. 55).

[58] Lundmark (1982). See also Niurenius (1905, p. 15).

[59] Ehrenmalm (1743, p. 128).

household. Fisher households exchanged, for example, dried fish with reindeer pastoralist households for reindeer calves, meat, and cheese.[60] There was also an annual winter market in Jokkmokk, where households could trade dried fish for consumer products or money from external tradesmen.

Property-Rights System

The rights to use fishing grounds were put forward by users and the local court during court proceedings. As pointed out in Chapter 2, we use the words *right* and *access* interchangeably, as an ability to legally derive benefits, and does not presuppose property.[61] In an early modern indigenous setting, the ways users could get access to fishing waters were complex.

In the mid-seventeenth century, land within Sami villages in Lule lappmark was by and large divided among households into defined *skatteland*.[62] They were fairly large and contained fishing waters, hunting grounds, and grazing land for one to a few households. In discussions about early modern Sami property rights, focus has been on how to interpret rights associated with these *skatteland* and how these rights developed over time.[63]

Strong land tenure usually indicates the right to sell land and water. We have not found any cases where fishing rights were sold between Sami users. Only one record mentioned someone selling fishing waters: a case from 1699 stated that two Sami had sold a salmon fishery in Lule River in the 1670s to a farmer in Lule parish.[64]

---

60 Rheen (1897, p. 19).

61 Ribot and Peluso (2003).

62 Hultblad (1968, pp. 85, 90).

63 Holmbäck (1922), Korpijaakko-Labba (1994), and N.-J. Päiviö (2011).

64 HRA (1699, pp.86–89).

Inheritance

Inheritance of property is another land right, although not as strong as the right to sell. In most court rulings from Lule lappmark, inheritance is merely implied and is clearly mentioned in only a few of them. However, a popular argument among users was that a close relative had used the fishing waters in question.

Only one court record explicitly mentioned inheritance in relation to legal inheritance in Swedish law. In 1692, four large lakes and a few small ones were divided between two siblings. The brother inherited two-thirds ("brother's share") and the sister one-third ("sister's share") of the fishing waters. In 1705, a man in Tuorpon, who had obtained the "brother's share," complained that three users in Jokkmokk, who were in charge of the "sister's share," used more fishing waters than they had the right to. The court decided to delineate the borders between them by placing marks in nature that distinguished who had the right to what (user rights). Moreover, the court appointed two trusted men from Sirkas to organize the demarcation in collaboration with the involved users the upcoming summer.[65] A year later, back in court, the agreement was recorded with a description of the borders.[66]

Aside from inheritance, fishing waters could also be divided and transferred to relatives while landholders were still alive. An example of this was when a man in Sjokksjokk in 1754 divided his land, including fishing waters, between his son and his daughter's son.[67]

A strong argument for a person to continue using specific fishing waters was that it had been used by him or her for a long time. In 1774, two users were in a conflict over the right to fish Arctic char.[68] In the verdict, the court denied the plaintiff the right to fish at the same site as the defendant, the principal argument being that the defendant, and his

[65] HRA (1705, pp. 972–973).

[66] HRA (1706, pp. 56–57).

[67] Hultblad (1968, p. 398, evidence 736a).

[68] HRA (1774, February 7).

relatives before him, had used the site for several generations. Additionally, it was put forward that the plaintiff had access to other sites in the same river where he could fish instead.

Inheritance was a valid argument for users who wanted to gain fishing rights in court, but interestingly this claim became weaker if the court knew that the fishing waters had not been frequently used by its holder. In such a case, the court sometimes argued that the waterbody would be of better use for someone else, and therefore assigned it to a user who needed it more. A court case from 1770 illuminates how the court considered inheritance with regard to fishing rights. The dispute concerned two lakes in Sirkas that had been co-owned by several people. Two sons of one of the landholders had forwarded the right to fish in the lakes to another man, Anders Nilsson Skubb. The court decided that as long as the rightful proprietors did not use the lakes, Skubb could continue using them. A third lake, for which the sons had not forwarded rights to Skubb, was also discussed in the court case. There the court decided that Skubb had no right to use the lake, since he had never had an interest in it before.[69]

The case highlights that the court could accept arguments to do with both inheritance and necessity for survival as grounds for giving someone access to fishing. It also shows that a lake could be split among users.

Limited Access to Resources

In court, previous use by close relatives was usually a strong argument for giving a user access to fishing waters. However, inheritance was not always enough to gain fishing rights, which the following court case exemplifies. Two users from Jokkmokk, shared the right to use certain land.[70] However, Lars Knutsson from Sjokksjokk claimed that he too could use the land since his relatives had done so before him. In court, the lay-judges stated that the land, with its fishing waters, could sustain only two users and therefore his claim to it had to be discarded. The court thus took limited resources as grounds for rejecting Knutsson's use of the

[69] HRA (1770).

[70] Hultblad (1968, p. 418, evidence 1026a).

land even though he seemingly had valid arguments based on inheritance of rights. What counted most for the court in this case was that the land did not have the capacity to support three users' livelihoods.

In the case from 1712 described earlier, Karin Andersdotter had removed four nets from a lake that belonged to Olof Andersson.[71] Andersson argued that his right to fish there was "ancient" and that part of the lake was included in his *skatteland*. However, Andersdotter could show records from 1708 and 1711 that showed how her household had paid tax for land that included rights to fish in the lake. A settlement was made in which Andersson got the right to fish in one part of the lake, while Andersdotter and her husband got rights to the rest of the lake with their four fishing grounds.

Almost 50 years later, the same lake was again involved in a conflict. In 1761, three users went to court to prohibit two brothers from fishing in the lake.[72] The plaintiffs' main argument was that the defendants had access to another fishing water with a good supply of fish. The defendants could, however, show from a 1712 court record that their father had had the right to fish in the southwestern part of the lake. According to that same record, the rest of the lake had belonged to the plaintiffs' father, who had paid tax for it. The 1761 court ruling prohibited the defendants from fishing in the lake on the grounds that they had access to good fishing elsewhere, which in this case, evidently took precedence over inherited rights.

Since it was most rewarding to fish during spawning, it is no wonder that some court cases dealt with intrusions during the spawning period. In one such case, the plaintiff was a widow who complained that the defendant had been fishing unlawfully at a spawning site that belonged to her family during spawning in spring and fall.[73] She testified that her family had always used the fishing site, while the defendant claimed that he too had a right to fish there during spawning. The court, however, denied the defendant any rights to fishing at the particular site, arguing

---

[71] RA SH (1712, pp. 505–506, § 11). See also Hultblad (1968, p. 423, evidence 1067a).

[72] HRA (1761, February 16).

[73] HRA (1775, February 8).

that he had access to other fishing sites that he could use *mest alla årstider* (practically all seasons).

Users' Obtaining Access to Fishing Waters

In some cases, Sami households that did not have access to fishing waters could obtain user rights by the court. In one such case, a man, Per Jönsson in Jokkmokk, who did not have access to land or fishing waters, was granted access to two *sel* (still waters) in Lule River by the court.[74] Although, the two river stretches already had rightful holders, the court's argument for granting Jönsson access to them was that they were not directly attached to the holders' main property. In fact, they were closer to a land that belonged to Jönsson's father-in-law, and had *av gammalt* (since ancient times) been associated with that property.

Another argument for why the court granted Jönsson access was that he needed the fishing sites more than the holders did. A third argument might have had to do with the collective-tax system that was established in 1695, when Sami villages became responsible for paying state tax instead of the individual households.[75] For the Sami village, it thus became advantageous to have as many members as possible with good incomes that could contribute to the total tax levy. Users without land, or with too little land to support their households, could therefore be granted land or water, assuming of course that the resources were available. Hence, a new user could contribute to the collective tax that the village had to pay.[76]

Delineation of Boundaries Between Users

A common way to resolve disagreements regarding fishing was to determine which waters belonged to whom, and mark the boundaries. In 1732, the plaintiff, a man in Tuorpon, complained in court that two

[74] HRA (1767, p. 179).

[75] Kvist (1990, p. 266. See also Chapter 4).

[76] Arell (1977, p. 63).

users had been fishing illegally in a lake belonging to him.[77] He argued that it was particularly troublesome that the defendants had used a spawning site. Since the court could not easily resolve the matter, two of the lay-judges were assigned to investigate the matter further. They were instructed to visit the lake with the plaintiff and the defendants to gather as much information as possible. Since the court only convened once a year, the plaintiff had to wait a year for the court ruling; meanwhile, the users were told to carry on as before. In the next year's court, the lay-judges reported what they had learned so the court could make its final ruling. According to the court ruling, the plaintiff and the defendants agreed upon a division of the lake based on a solution that had been suggested by the lay-judges. A border was set between the two parties, stretching from the inflow of a creek to an island in the lake. The plaintiff got the right to fish on the south side and the defendants on the north side.

Another example of how land could be divided between users comes from 1726, when two lands in Tuorpon were divided among twelve users.[78] Judging by their names, some of them were probably related. In court, the hostility among them was described as a "slowly growing" conflict and that it was about time each of them got his or her share. The court appointed four trusted men to delineate land and fishing waters and emphasized that it was important that they carefully consider how land and water had been used by the twelve users' ancestors.

The trend in the court rulings was that the division of lands, and thus fishing waters, continued throughout the 1700s and became even more prevalent in the second half of the century.[79] The result of this process was that more households obtained access to fishing waters but the water area per household decreased, which implies that the subsistence base for each household decreased.

Nevertheless, it is important to keep in mind that not all conflicts resulted in division of lands or fishing waters. Often the court had no

---

77 HRA (1732, February 8; 1733, February 10). This case is also mentioned in Chapter 3 under the section heading "Solving Conflicts in Practice" as an example of involvement of lay-judges.

78 HRA (1726, February 7, pp. 409–410). See also Hultblad (1968, p. 356, evidence 18a).

79 Hultblad (1968) and Arell (1977).

problem deciding who was the rightful user, and the intruder could be fined and prohibited from fishing. For example, the court decided in 1700 that a man had to pay 40 silver coins (*dalers*) if he continued to encroach on the plaintiff's fishing waters.[80] According to an older court ruling, from 1696, the defendant was the sole user of the lake. Another example comes from 1702, when the plaintiff, a man in Jokkmokk, complained that another man, from Sjokksjokk, had spent the last two summers fishing in a lake on the plaintiff's tax land.[81] He argued in court that this had impaired his livelihood. The defendant was not present in court, but his son was. He had accompanied his father when they had fished in the lake and he claimed that his father had some sort of inherited right to the lake, but that he did not know any more details about it. When asked if his father had paid tax for the land, he admitted that he had not. The defendant was sentenced to pay 40 *dalers* and was prohibited from returning to the lake until he could prove that he had a right to be there.

Sharing of Fishing Waters

Fishing waters were not always divided among users; some conflicts were solved in other ways. Users sometimes agreed to share waters, while details of the agreement had to be clarified in court. In February 1731, discord arose between two users, Nils Nilsson and Pål Jonson Stoorropare in Sjokksjokk, concerning the right to use certain fishing waters.[82] In court, Nilsson and Stoorropare agreed to share the fishing waters, but *vara rådande över halva noten var* (each would be in charge of half of the seine). In addition, one of them was allowed to use the other's seine in return for a small remuneration. More importantly, neither was allowed to invite others, not even relatives, to fish in the lake.

80 HRA (1700, p. 261).

81 HRA (1702, pp. 536–537).

82 HRA (1731, pp. 88–89).

In 1737, a new argument for not dividing fishing lakes between users was put forward in court.[83] This case also involved Nilsson and Stoorropare from the case above, but included one more person and two additional lakes. As established in court earlier, the first lake was to be used jointly by the two aforementioned users and a second lake was to be used only by Stoorropare. The third lake belonged to a third user, and when Stoorropare fished there, he was sued. In court, Stoorropare claimed that this lake had more fish than the other two lakes, which was confirmed by other rightsholders, and by some of the lay-judges who had knowledge about these lakes. All three users agreed that their ancestors had used the lakes together and that the lakes belonged to a property that their ancestors had held in common. The court therefore decided that all three lakes should be used jointly by the rightsholders, in part because the land had been used in common in the past, but more importantly because the lakes contained unequal amounts of fish. It was thus impossible to divide the fishing rights in these waters in a just way.

Temporal Division of Fishing Rights

Most divisions of fishing waters were made through spatial delineation between users. However, the right to fish could also be divided temporally; users could, for example, be given the right to fish only during a limited period. In 1773, a court case between a settler and a Sami man from Tuorpon regarding fishing in a certain bay resulted in time-based delimitations of their access to fishing there.[84] The court gave the Sami the right to fish in late fall and spring, when it was possible to *racka* (ice fish with gillnets). In practice, this probably meant that he targeted European whitefish, which commonly were caught via ice fishing during the spawning season.[85] In late spring, the right to fish passed to the settler. It meant that he most likely targeted northern pike, which spawn after the ice melts.

[83] Hultblad (1968, p. 413, evidence 959d).

[84] HRA (1773, February 10).

[85] Linnaeus (2003, p. 152).

In this case, the temporal division of fishing rights was an interaction between a settler and a Sami. However, there are at least two examples of temporal division between Sami users. In a case from 1714, two users in Jokkmokk had a conflict over fishing rights in a creek at the western shore of a lake.[86] During the court proceedings they agreed, with a handshake, to share the creek by dividing the use temporally. One of them could fish in the creek from Christmas to mid-February (the end of the market season), and the other could fish there for the rest of the winter, for as long as he could use his *våner* (fish traps). In another case, from Sjokksjokk, a dispute had been developing over time between two users on one side and three users on the other side.[87] The dispute revolved around the division of land as well as *rättigheter* (rights) to two fishing waters. The dispute regarding land was settled by defining an exact border between the users. Regarding the fishing, the users decided to divide the access to the water temporally so that each party could fish every other year. The exception was one particular bay, which the first two users got the right to use exclusively.

Fishing Rights Decoupled from Grazing Rights

From the mid-eighteenth century, court cases show how fishing rights could be separated from rights to use land for grazing. For example, two users, Henrik Jansson and Pål Eriksson Tulpa from Tuorpon, had owned grazing land together that included one larger lake and a few smaller lakes for fishing.[88] In 1756, the court awarded the lakes to Eriksson. Two years later, the court changed that decision so Jansson got the right to fish in the larger lake, with the restriction that he could not allow others to fish there.

In 1771, the court decided that two users in Tuorpon would lose their rights to use land for grazing because they had no reindeer. Nevertheless, they could continue to use the fishing waters.[89] Instead, the grazing

[86] HRA (1714, § 10, pp. 1058–1059).

[87] HRA (1726, February 7, pp. 411–412).

[88] Hultblad (1968, p. 372, evidence 297a).

[89] Hultblad (1968, p. 369, evidence 252a).

rights went to another user, but the court emphasized that he *fick ej tränga dem i fisket* (could not intrude in the fishing). The notion that one property should offer both grazing and hunting lands and fishing waters for a household had obviously disappeared by then. The right to fish was still a defined right, but it could be decoupled from other rights on a particular property.

Survival on Fishing

It is evident from the sources that *skatteland* (the tax lands) in the boreal forest in Lule and Ume lappmark were relatively large in the second half of the seventeenth century, and that they included various sizes of hunting grounds, grazing land for reindeer, and fishing waters.[90] They were fairly large because they roughly comprised the resources a village of households needed to make ends meet in an economy that mostly depended on fishing. Norstedt et al. have shown that the water bodies associated with tax lands in Ume lappmark in the late seventeenth century contained on average five fish species per territory and that the mean was thirteen fishing waters per territory.[91] The mean area per water body was 36 km^2. Since different populations of the same fish species can spawn at different times in different places, their conclusion is that it was beneficial for fisher households to have access to as many fishing waters as possible and to move from one to another. The organization of territories was moreover recognized by the state through taxation. However, *skatteland* gradually became divided among individual users during the eighteenth century. With smaller lands, and thus fewer and smaller fishing waters, it became harder for households to make a living on fishing. The difference in living standards between reindeer herder households and fisher households that existed in the seventeenth

[90] Hultblad (1968, pp. 85, 90), Norstedt (2011), and Norstedt et al. (2014).

[91] Norstedt et al. (2014).

century gradually increased, and the eighteenth-century sources generally described fisher households as poor or very poor. The strategies used to survive on fishing were (1) a mobile lifestyle to optimize harvests, (2) pre- and post-harvest fishing activities that facilitated good harvests, and (3) well-defined institutions that regulated access to fishing waters.

Fishing Strategies in Low-Productivity Waters

In the seventeenth and eighteenth centuries, most fisher households in interior northern Fennoscandia had a mobile lifestyle, which meant that they moved between fishing waters following a year-long route that probably was quite similar from year to year. In some regions, households erected more or less permanent huts to live in by lakes they visited regularly, while households in other regions often lived in moveable tents. All households but the poorest kept small herds of reindeer that they used mainly for transportation and milking. The crucial reason behind this fishing mobility was that it was an opportunistic strategy that allowed inhabitants to optimize resource utilization mainly from low-productivity fishing waters. The spawning periods were principally the only times when these waters had high yields, particularly in view of the available but not especially efficient fishing technics. By moving around, households could adapt their fishing schemes to different fish populations and lifecycles, which varied between different waters.[92]

Extreme spring flooding was an imminent risk that could be devastating for fishing.[93] It was additionally hazardous economically, since spring also corresponded with the spawning period for some of the most important fish species.[94] Spring was thus the only time of year when these species were high-yielding. If spring fishing failed, households undoubtedly had to put more energy into fishing for other species later in the year.

[92] Norstedt et al. (2014).

[93] Lundius (1905, p. 29).

[94] An exception is the salmon that spawned later.

Pre- and Post-Harvest Activities

To survive on fishing, most of a household's work had to revolve around this activity. Hunting was merely a complement, and households did not have large herds of reindeer. Studies of small-scale inshore fisheries in Mexico emphasize the importance of pre- and post-harvest activities.[95] This also was true for fishers of interior Fennoscandia to harvest enough fish in low-productivity waters. Gender division in the household was not strict, and both men and women could engage in fishing. The court rulings describe women fishing, rowing boats, and defending the household's fishing waters from encroachments. The sources contain less information about gender division in pre- and post-harvest activities. However, we know these activities took more time than the harvest, and in a household-based economy, all members needed to contribute. Only one court ruling regarding fishing mentioned a maid. Taking into account that most fisher households are described as poor, it seems likely to conclude that it was unusual for them to have servants and that most of the work was performed by family members. In large-scale reindeer herding, having servants was necessary.[96]

The crafting of fishing gear and boats was an important part of pre-harvest work, which included collecting or purchasing raw materials and constructing fishing equipment, such as binding nets. In the post-harvest phase, maintaining and mending equipment, such as nets and seines, was a time-consuming and ongoing task. Gear that was not properly handled and maintained could easily decay, which in turn would increase costs for the household. Moreover, post-harvest work included taking care of the harvest—preparation of fish to be eaten directly and drying of fish to be used for later consumption, trade/exchange, or paying taxes.

The pre- and post-harvest activities also included negotiations with neighbors about fishing rights, travel to fishing sites and markets, etc. Gathering more detailed descriptions of pre- and post-harvest activities is an important area for further research since they contribute to our

[95] Basurto et al. (2020).

[96] Larsson and Päiviö Sjaunja (2020).

understanding of fishing strategies among Sami and in small-scale fishing communities around the world.

Institutions for Management

Fishing waters are CPRs. Without rules about management, there is a risk of overutilization and fish depletions. The investigation of court rulings from Lule lappmark shows that the users in a self-governing context created rules for sustainable use of the fishing lakes by defining user groups and user areas. However, with access to only low-productivity waters and with low-yielding techniques, the real challenge for most households was to secure sufficient harvests for survival. The problem they had to handle was not primarily the risk of overharvest, but how to limit the number of users. Hence, policy discussions regarding fishing waters concerned boundaries of the resources and who had the right to harvest.[97]

In the eighteenth century, the population increased and most tax lands were divided into smaller units. When fishing waters were assigned to new rights holders, negotiations were made among all presumptive users. Advantageous arguments for users who wanted legal rights to specific fishing waters included inheritance or past use by their relatives. But claiming this was not enough; users also had to back up their arguments if contested. The most effective claim, then, was that he or she relied completely on fishing or lacked access to other fishing waters.

Because the right to use fishing waters could be negotiated in the local court, it became a collective-choice arena,[98] defining *who* could use a certain fishing area and sometimes *when* it could be used. Not only were the users defined, a lot of effort was put into defining the exact boundaries between users if a lake or river had to be divided.

Fishing waters in Lule lappmark became a collective resource in the sense that it was within the power of the local community to decide who had what rights. In this process, the lay-judges were important actors

[97] Ostrom (2005).

[98] Ostrom (2005, 2009).

because they often were familiar with the area and its history. Users got well-defined areas where they could fish, and a household could have the exclusive right to fish in an area. In that sense, the territory used by an individual household had similarities to private property: users had strong tenure, and rights to fishing waters could be passed on to the next generation. Other users were not allowed to fish there unless an agreement was made between the parties. When a fishing area was shared between households, they could be forbidden to allow other people to fish.

This collective activity points to another important norm: trust-reciprocity/social capital within the society.[99] Absence of secure user rights would have undermined trust among the inhabitants and, in the end, trust in the local court as a collective-choice arena. The design of a sustainable fishing regime was to a large extent an internal question for the users. The local strategy consisted partly of excluding other users and defining boundaries between fishing waters, as well as having an arena for solving conflicts. The fishing resource system was under the control of the local users, and distribution of fishing rights was a collective responsibility. Social justice is important for effectiveness in governing CPRs and does not rely solely on distributive outcomes. It also includes institutions and governing, such as involvement in decision-making.[100] The court, as a collective-choice arena, where rules were crafted and enforced, was an important part of social justice. This type of involvement was lost in the late eighteenth century, when many decisions about land use were moved from the local court to a government agency.

[99] McGinnis and Ostrom (2014).

[100] Jentoft (2013).

References

Acheson, James M. 1988. *The lobster gangs of Maine*. Hanover, NH: University Press of New England.

Acheson, James M. 2003. *Capturing the commons: Devising institutions to manage the Maine lobster industry*. Hanover, NH: University Press of New England.

Arell, Nils. 1977. Rennomadismen i Torne lappmark: markanvändning under kolonisationsepoken i fr.a. Enontekis socken. PhD diss. Umeå, Sweden: Skytteanska samfundet. http://www.diva-portal.org/smash/record.jsf?pid=diva2%3A616377&dswid=6098.

Basurto, Xavier, Abigail Bennett, Emilie Lindkvist, and Maja Schlüter. 2020. Governing the commons beyond harvesting: An empirical illustration from fishing. *PLoS ONE* 15 (4): e0231575. https://doi.org/10.1371/journal.pone.0231575.

Basurto, Xavier, Stefan Gelcich, and Elinor Ostrom. 2013. The social–ecological system framework as a knowledge classificatory system for benthic small-scale fisheries. *Global Environmental Change* 23: 1366–1380.

Bennett, Abigail, Pawan Patil, Kristin Kleisner, Doug Rader, John Virdin, and Xavier Basurto. 2018. *Contribution of fisheries to food and nutrition security: Current knowledge, policy and research*. Nicholas Institute Report 18–02. Durham, NC: Duke University. https://nicholasinstitute.duke.edu/sites/default/files/publications/contribution_of_fisheries_to_food_and_nutrition_security_0.pdf.

Bergman, Ingela, and Per H. Ramqvist. 2017. Farmer fishermen: Interior lake fishing and inter-cultural and intra-cultural relations among coastal and interior Sámi communities in northern Sweden AD 1200–1600. *Acta Borealia* 34 (2): 134–158.

Bjørklund, Ivar. 1991. Property in common, common property or private property. *North Atlantic Studies* 3 (1): 41–45.

Brattland, Camilla. 2010. Mapping rights in coastal Sami seascapes. *Arctic Review on Law and Politics* 1 (1): 28–53.

Ehrenmalm, Arwid. 1743. *Resa igenom Wäster-Norrland til Åsehle lappmark, anstäld uti julii månad 1741*. Stockholm. Available page by page at http://runeberg.org/resawenoas/index.html.

Fjellström, Phebe. 1986. *Samernas samhälle i tradition och nutid*, 2nd ed. Stockholm: Norstedt.

Gordon, H. Scott. 1954. The economic theory of a common-property resource: The fishery. *Journal of Political Economy* 62 (2): 124–142.
Graan, Olaus. 1899. *Relation, eller en fulkomblig beskrifning om lapparnas ursprung, så wähl som om heela dheras Lefwernes Förehållande*. Uppsala, Sweden: Harald Wretmans tryckeri.
Hansen, Lars Ivar. 2006. Sami fisheries in the pre-modern era: Household sustenance and market relations. *Acta Borealia* 23 (1): 56–80. https://doi.org/10.1080/08003830600789390.
Hardin, Garrett. 1968. The tragedy of the commons. *Science* 162: 1243–1248. https://doi.org/10.1126/science.162.3859.1243.
Högström, Pehr. 1747. *Beskrifning öfwer de til Sweriges krona lydande lapmarker*. Stockholm: Salvius. http://urn.kb.se/resolve?urn=urn:nbn:se:umu:eod-114.
Holmbäck, Åke. 1922. *Om lappskattelandsinstitutet och dess historiska utveckling*. Stockholm: Statens offentliga utredningar.
Hultblad, Filip. 1968. Övergång från nomadism till agrar bosättning i Jokkmokks socken. PhD diss., Uppsala University.
Jentoft, Svein. 2013. Governing tenure in Norwegian and Sami small-scale fisheries: From common pool to common property. *Land Tenure Journal* 1: 91–115.
Korpijaakko-Labba, Kaisa. 1994. *Om samernas rättsliga ställning i Sverige-Finland. En rättshistorisk utredning av markanvändningsförhållanden och -rättigheter i Västerbottens lappmark före mitten av 1700-talet*. Helsinki: Juristförbundets förlag.
Kvist, Roger. 1990. Beskattningen av samerna i Sverige 1695–1860. In *Älvdal i norr: människor och resurser i Luledalen 1300–1800*, ed. Sune Åkerman, Kjell Lundholm, 264–305. Umeå, Sweden: Umeå Studies in the Humanities, Umeå University.
Larsson, Jesper, and Eva-Lotta Päiviö Sjaunja. 2020. Early modern reindeer husbandry, Sami economy, and grazing rights. *International Journal of the Commons* 14 (1): 91–107. https://doi.org/10.5334/ijc.965.
Linnaeus, Carl. 2003. *Iter Lapponicum: Lappländska resan 1732. I*. Dagboken. Umeå, Sweden: Kungl. Skytteanska Samfundet.
Lundius, Nicolai. 1905. *Descriptio Lapponiæ*. Uppsala, Sweden: Harald Wretmans tryckeri.
Lundmark, Lennart. 1982. Uppbörd, utarmning, utveckling. Det samiska fångstsamhällets övergång till rennomadism i Lule lappmark. PhD diss., Umeå University.

McGinnis, Michael D., and Elinor Ostrom. 2014. Social-ecological system framework. *Ecology and Society* 19 (2): 30. https://doi.org/10.5751/ES-06387-190230.

Needs-Howarth, Suzanne, and Stephen Cox Thomas. 1998. Seasonal variation in fishing strategies at two Iroquoian villages near Lake Simcoe, Ontario. *Environmental Archaeology* 3 (1): 109–120. https://doi.org/10.1179/env.1998.3.1.109.

Nielssen, Alf Ragnar. 1986. Economic Adaptation among the coast Sami population in Finnmark c. 1700. *Acta Borealia* 3 (1): 21–41. https://doi.org/10.1080/08003838608580328.

Niurenius, Olaus Petri. 1905. *Lappland, eller beskrivning över den nordiska trakt, som lapparne bebo i de avlägsnaste delarne af Skandinavien eller Sverge.* Uppsala, Sweden: Harald Wretmans tryckeri.

Norstedt, Gudrun, and Lars Östlund. 2016. Fish or reindeer? The relation between subsistence patterns and settlement patterns among the forest Sami. *Arctic Anthropology* 53 (1): 22–36.

Norstedt, Gudrun. 2011. *Lappskattelanden på Geddas karta. Umeå lappmark från 1671 till 1900-talets början.* Umeå, Sweden: Thalassa förlag.

Norstedt, Gudrun, Anna-Lena Axelsson, and Lars Östlund. 2014. Exploring pre-colonial resource control of individual Sami household. *Arctic* 67 (2): 223–237. https://doi.org/10.14430/arctic4389.

Ostrom, Elinor. 1990. *Governing the commons, the evolution of institutions for collective action.* Cambridge, UK: Cambridge University Press.

Ostrom, Elinor. 2005. *Understanding institutional diversity*. Princeton, NJ: Princeton University Press.

Ostrom, Elinor. 2009. A general framework for analyzing sustainability of social-ecological systems. *Science* 325: 419–422.

Päiviö, Nils-Johan. 2011. Från skattemannarätt till nyttjanderätt. en rättshistorisk studie av utvecklingen av samernas rättigheter från slutet 1500-talet till 1886 års renbeteslag. PhD diss., Uppsala University.

Rapalje Martin, Susan. 1989. A reconsideration of Aboriginal fishing strategies in the northern Great Lakes region. *American Antiquity* 54 (3): 594–604. https://doi.org/10.2307/280786.

Rheen, Samuele. 1897. *En kortt relation om Lapparnes lefwarne och sedher, wijd-skiepellsser, sampt i många stycken grofwe wildfarellsser*. Uppsala, Sweden: Harald Wretmans tryckeri.

Ribot, Jesse C., and Nancy Lee Peluso. 2003. A theory of access. *Rural Sociology* 68 (2): 153–181. https://doi.org/10.1111/j.1549-0831.2003.tb00133.x.

Smith, Hillary, and Xavier Basurto. 2019. Defining small-scale fisheries and examining the role of science in shaping perceptions of who and what count: A systematic review. *Frontiers in Marine Science* 6: 236. https://doi.org/10.3389/fmars.2019.00236.

Tornaeus, Johannes. 1900. *Berättelse om Lapmarckerna och Deras Tillstånd*. Uppsala, Sweden: Harald Wretmans tryckeri.

Archival Sources

Härnösand Regional Archive (HRA):
Rulings in Jokkmokks District Court, Sweden, 1689–1780.
Riksarkivet [National Archives of Sweden]:
Svea Court of Appeal (RA SH). 1712–1780. Rulings in Jokkmokks District Court, Sweden.
Uppsala University Library:
Iter lapponicum, Luefsta MS 92.

6

Hunting

Here we outline which species were hunted in the boreal forest and how they were hunted or trapped, and which animals were hunted in the mountains. The conditions for hunting were better in the boreal forest than in the mountains due to differences in topography, habitats, and species composition. From the sixteenth century to the end of the eighteenth century, hunting led to extinction of wild reindeer and depopulation of fur animals; while small-game hunting for subsistence continued to be important. In the forest region, strong property rights to game developed through the *skatteland*, and hunting was a private enterprise. We suggest that the institution of *skatteland* was a response to changes in Sami economy, and the transition from collective to private hunting was a contributing factor. Hunting in the mountain region developed in the opposite direction and was open access after the wild reindeer was extinct. Hunting became important for social justice, and poor Sami had access to hunting grounds.

J. Larsson and E.-L. Päiviö Sjaunja, *Self-Governance and Sami Communities*,
https://doi.org/10.1007/978-3-030-87498-8_6

Hunting in Research About Sami

While previous research has addressed multiple aspects of early modern Sami fishing and reindeer husbandry, the focus on hunting has been relatively constricted.[1] This is due in part to the relative scarcity of hunting evidence in historical sources. In much research, early modern hunting has been described rather unsystematically, lacking in chronology and context. As described in Chapter 2, Sami historiography was characterized by ethnographic perspectives until the 1970s.[2] According to Hansen and Olsen, "the Sami past did not belong to the academic responsibilities of the historical disciplines."[3] Over the past four decades, the understanding of Sami hunting has increased by highlighting the role of hunting in Sami society and its impact on Sami's relations with neighboring people. However, most researchers have concentrated on time periods before 1600, which is about the time hunting ceased to be the backbone of Sami economy.[4] One of the most intense debates among these scholars has revolved around the question of when, why, and how Sami society transitioned from hunting to herding, but the changes in herding were the overriding factor.[5] The focus on herding has somewhat overshadowed how hunting continued to be an integral part of a more complex household economy for many Sami long after the introduction of large-scale reindeer husbandry.[6] Therefore, for the early modern period, the ethnographic descriptions of hunting dominate the literature.[7]

Although hunting lost economic importance in international trading around 1600, it played a vital role in many Sami households in the seventeenth and eighteenth centuries.[8] This circumstance stands out

[1] Josefsson et al. (2010), Bjørklund (2013), and Norstedt et al. (2014).

[2] Tanner (1929), Tegengren (1952), Manker (1960), Phebe Fjellström (1962), Hvarfner (1965), and Henriksson (1978).

[3] Hansen and Olsen (2014, p. 2).

[4] Lundmark (1982, p. 170) and Hansen and Olsen (2014, p. 230).

[5] Sommerseth (2011) and Bergman et al. (2013).

[6] Bjørklund (2013) and E.-L. Päiviö (2017).

[7] Hvarfner (1965), Phebe Fjellström (1986), and Kjellström (2000).

[8] Bjørklund (2013) and E.-L. Päiviö (2017).

in many contemporary sources, where the topic of hunting frequently appears. What is lacking, and what we will contribute to, is an analysis of early modern Sami hunting from a household perspective that advances beyond descriptions of particular practices toward a more systematic understanding of early modern hunting in interior northern Fennoscandia. This will allow us to integrate hunting with the developments in fishing and reindeer husbandry to better understand changes in the economy and rights to land.

Hunting is the practice of pursuing, capturing, or killing wildlife and can be divided into subsistence, commercial, and recreational hunting.[9] Scholars studying pre-historic and medieval Sami hunting in a wider geographical area have mainly been concerned with four themes. The first theme deals with how wild reindeer became the most important animal to hunt, why mobile settlements were required, and how large pitfall trapping systems were established.[10] The second theme deals with fur trade and how Sami's high-quality furs were the most important factor in the establishment of the northern trade networks in the Viking Age and Early Middle Ages.[11] The third theme deals with collective hunting, where researchers have focused on pitfall hunting until circa 1600.[12] Their empirical findings were underpinned by Ingold's theoretical work.[13] The fourth theme deals with hunting rituals and ceremonies, and scholars have shown that there was a strong link between religion and hunting in societies that depended on hunting.[14] Beyond these themes, there are other aspects of pre-early modern hunting. One example is that small-game hunting must have been common, but lack of sources has made it difficult to analyze.

Around the beginning of the seventeenth century, Sami society went through several major changes: the number of wild reindeer was decreasing, and the use of pitfall hunting declined rapidly.[15] In many

---

[9] Peterson (2019).

[10] Mulk (1994), Vorren (1998), and Sommerseth (2009).

[11] Odner (1983), L. Hansen (1990), and Hansen and Olsen (2014, pp. 127–131).

[12] Tegengren (1952), Vorren (1978), Mulk (1994), and Sommerseth (2011).

[13] Ingold (1980).

[14] Korhonen (2007), Rydving (2011), Hansen and Olsen (2014).

[15] Lundmark (1982), and Mulk (1994).

households, reindeer herding replaced fur hunting and gradually became the backbone of the economy. Scholars who focused on the early modern era thus had less interest in analyzing hunting as a collective enterprise. We conclude that when hunting no longer played an important part in the definition of Sami ethnicity, it became less interesting for scholars. Instead, study of Sami ethnicity, and thus research about Sami history, has focused mostly on reindeer herding and the Sami's relation to the state.[16] Much of our little knowledge about early modern Sami hunting still comes from ethnographic literature.

The ethnographic analyses have nevertheless contributed greatly to our understanding of Sami hunting, especially when it comes to small game. They contain detailed descriptions of how hunting was performed, which hunting methods were used, the seasonality of hunting, and types of hunting gear. However, they often portray Sami pre-twentieth-century practices as rather static, practically unchanged over time.[17]

The transition from a hunter-gatherer economy to a pastoral economy has continued to draw the attention of archaeologists and historians, but the primary focus has been on reindeer husbandry, not on hunting. An example would be two papers published in 2013 that came to very different conclusions about the introduction of reindeer pastoralism. Bergman et al. used archeological traces of so-called *stállo* foundations (arrangements of Sami community structures) as proxy for reindeer nomadism and argue that the shift started as early as 800 A.D.[18] In contrast, Bjørklund argues that after 1750 users started to have reindeer herds large enough to make a living, and that there was "no paradigmatic abrupt change through domestication from a 'hunting society' to a 'pastoral society.'"[19] Bjørklund believes that hunting was part of people's adaption to the environment up to the nineteenth century. The point we make here is that hunting is elusive in the empirical parts of these papers.

[16] Hultblad (1968), Arell (1977), Lundmark (1982), Kvist (1989a), Lundmark (2006), and Sommerseth (2011).

[17] Tanner (1929), Tegengren (1952), Manker (1960), Henriksson (1978), Phebe Fjellström (1986), and Kjellström (2000).

[18] Bergman et al. (2013).

[19] Bjørklund (2013, p. 186).

Päiviö takes an approach similar to Bjørklund's when she discusses hunting as part of the household economy.[20] To understand that economy, she argues, one has to include hunting in addition to reindeer herding, fishing, gathering, handcraft, trade, and transport. She uses early modern accounts as sources and applies a broad description of hunting, also used in this chapter, to include grabbing, trapping, pursuing, and tracking.

Research that has analyzed people's adaptations to early modern environmental settings in interior northern Sweden mentions hunting in general terms but gives few details about methods and prey. Josefsson et al., for example, estimated the number of people that a particular territory could support and provided only a short list of animals that were hunted for fur.[21] Norstedt et al. quantified the resources controlled by households in the Ume lappmark district.[22] According to their results, fishing was the only resource that showed any correlation to taxation, underscoring the importance of fishing in the boreal forest. However, in their study, hunting comprised only an estimation of the number of wild reindeer in the region. At that time, wild reindeer were in decline, but more important, the study downplayed the significance of other hunted animals, including small game, which are mentioned in the sources.[23]

Methods and Sources

In Chapters 2 and 3 we described methods and sources, but a few things that are specific to hunting will be touched upon here. In many of the early modern accounts, unlike reindeer pastoralism, hunting was described with few words and almost in passing. Bear hunting was more meticulously described, probably because it was connected to ceremonies that the authors found fascinating. Given the irregular and seasonal

[20] E.-L. Päiviö (2017).

[21] Josefsson et al. (2010, p. 147).

[22] Norstedt et al. (2014).

[23] Norstedt (2011).

nature of hunting, authors who paid only short visits to local households seldom had the opportunity to take part in hunts, particularly for large game. It is therefore doubtful whether they actually witnessed the procedures they described, and it is more likely that their reports were based on hearsay and retelling of hunting stories. For the narrator, it was probably both easy and tempting to choose a spectacular story instead of a more typical one. Hence, it is possible that the accounts give us a slightly embellished picture of hunting.

It is plausible that the visitors actually might have witnessed some of the small-game hunting, which was done more frequently and in the vicinity of the household areas. For example, Linnaeus described that he had seen traps for capercaillies everywhere when he traveled in Ume lappmark in 1732.[24] Other trapping devices that must have been easily recognizable for visitors were bird houses used for gathering eggs, as well as snaring devices for various land fowl, which are commonly mentioned in the accounts.

The anecdotal hunting descriptions make it difficult to systematically assess if a certain hunting practice was common, or to what degree a prey contributed to a household's economy. To try to compensate for the risk of exaggerating sketchy evidence, we have compared accounts describing Sami hunting from several parts of northern Sweden, and combined the information with evidence in court rulings.

A special challenge in regard to hunting regulations is that animals wander in the landscape and can move between areas with detailed regulations and areas with few or no regulations. Rules for early modern hunting ranged from extreme control to total lack of control, or open access. A user's right to prey could be linked either to his or her control over the area where the animal was killed, or to the effort he or she put into the hunt. The issue of who possesses the game has been widely discussed by users, courts, and legal scholars.[25]

In seventeenth-century southern Sweden, most hunting was limited to nobility and resembled legislation in continental Europe, but in northern Sweden, including the Swedish lappmark, which encompassed

---

24 Linnaeus (2003, p. 62).

25 Rose (1985, p. 76).

two-thirds of the country, hunting was available to common people.[26] Availability did not mean the absence of institutions, only that rules were created in a local context with a bottom-up perspective, i.e., users developed their own institutions for regulating, monitoring, and implementing resource use.[27] The first royal ordinance that regulated hunting in the Swedish lappmark was introduced in 1749 and was aimed at limiting settlers' hunting rights to one-half of a Swedish mile, or 5,344 m, from their homesteads. The ordinance reinforced that hunting rights across the lappmark belonged to the Sami. The second ordinance, initiated in 1766, also targeted settlers and made it clear that it was strictly forbidden to hunt domestic reindeer.[28] The ordinance stipulated punishment for illegal hunting of domestic reindeer and looked for ways to prevent it by introducing rules for selling and buying reindeer furs. The ordinance required hunters to keep the ears on the reindeer pelt so the owner could be identified. Both the buyer and seller were responsible and could be fined if the ears were missing.

Hunting in Interior Fennoscandia

The most noticeable physical divide, when it came to early modern hunting practices in Lule lappmark, was the ecological difference between the eastern boreal forest and the western Scandinavian Mountains. For early modern hunters, as for hunters today, ecology set the premise for hunting, foremost by determining which prey could be hunted, and where. In our analyses of different aspects of early modern hunting in Lule lappmark, we used the division between boreal forest and mountains as a starting point. In this section, we present each landscape type and describe how the settings interconnected with early modern hunting.

---

[26] Korpijakko-Labba (1994) and Nyrén (2012).

[27] Ostrom (2005). See also Chapter 2.

[28] Stiernman (1747–1775).

Hunting in the Mountains

Hunters in northern Fennoscandia have depended on reindeer for food, clothing, and shelter since the end of the last Ice Age. There are traces of trapping systems in the mountains in Lule lappmark, which tell us that wild reindeer were hunted there. According to Hollsten, who resided in Jokkmokk parish in the eighteenth century, there were mountain reindeer, forest reindeer, and wild reindeer.[29] He argued that the tame reindeer were mountain reindeer, which spent spring, summer, and autumn in the mountains and winters in the forest, and forest reindeer (*skogs-renar*), which stayed year-round in the forest. Wild reindeer resided in the lowlands east of the lappmark, toward the Gulf of Bothnia. No wild reindeer appeared to be in southern Lule lappmark in the 1770s. However, in the northern part of the Swedish lappmark, including Kaitum in northern Lule lappmark, wild reindeer were present into the nineteenth century.[30]

In 1672, Tornaeus described hunting of wild reindeer in the mountains of neighboring Torne lappmark during winter.[31] In his description, hunters departed in pairs on hunting expeditions that could last for eight to ten weeks. They stalked herds of wild reindeer before crawling behind a rock or snowpack, close enough to shoot a designated animal using rifles. Further evidence of wild reindeer in the mountains comes from a 1731 court case in Torne lappmark in which a user complained about repeated trespassing on his tax land *uppåt på fjället* (in the mountains) by a user from another village.[32]

On the organization of hunting, Tornaeus wrote that either *antingen går hela byn gemenligen* (the whole village [went] together) or only a couple of villagers, and after the hunt, the prey was divided among the villagers.[33] However, those who did not pay tax did not get a share, so it appears that reindeer hunting in the mountains took place on lands held in common by the tax-paying members of the Sami village. In the court

29 Hollsten (1774, p. 128).

30 Læstadius (1832, pp. 344–345) and Ekman (1910, pp. 7–12).

31 Tornaeus (1900, pp. 55ff).

32 Arell (1977, p. 154).

33 Tornaeus (1900, pp. 55ff).

case described by Arell, the defendant had shot four reindeer of which two had been accrued to the proprietor of the tax land.[34] This suggests that hunting of wild reindeer in the Torne lappmark mountains could be organized on private lands with the consent of the landholder. We did not find any evidence in the early modern accounts or in the court rulings of reindeer being hunted in the mountains of Lule lappmark.

Other animal species also were hunted in the mountains, namely arctic fox (*Vulpes lagopus*), wolverine (*Gulo gulo*), and ptarmigan (*Lagopus sp.*). The arctic fox is native to the alpine tundra and well adapted to life in a cold climate thanks to a dense, insulating, and multilayered pelage that changes color seasonally between light grey in summer and white in winter, or stays dark blue, brown, or grey year-round. When Rheen listed Sami trade articles in 1671, he included pelts from black and red foxes (both *Vulpes vulpes*) as well as skins from blue and white foxes (both *Vulpes lagopus*).[35] According to Rheen, who mostly described Lule lappmark, arctic foxes were found only in the mountains.[36] He moreover described that fox hunting was more difficult in years when there was an influx of Norway lemmings (*Lemmus lemmus*). In such years, the foxes feasted on lemmings and did not as willingly seek out carrions that hunters deployed, which suggests that traps were a common method for catching foxes. The method seems rational, as furs certainly must have been priced higher if they were unmarked by bullets, and as foxes, according to Linnaeus, were not hunted for human consumption.[37] We have found only one court ruling from Lule lappmark that concerns hunting in the mountains.[38] The particular case involved two brothers in Sirkas who disputed who had the right to the furs from two foxes and one wolverine. The defendant argued that he alone had caught the animals, while the plaintiff claimed they had hunted *i samma wånher* (in the same traps). Since they had shared the traps, the plaintiff claimed that they both should have a right to the prey. The court proceeding ended by their agreeing to sell the coats and split the reward between them.

---

[34] Arell (1977, p. 154).

[35] Rheen (1897, p. 58).

[36] Rheen (1897, p. 54).

[37] Linnaeus (2003, p. 58).

[38] HRA (1704, p. 804).

Another prey animal was the gamebird ptarmigan. The rock ptarmigan (*Lagopus muta*) was native to the mountains but not the forests. The willow ptarmigan (*Lagopus lagopus*) resided in both lower mountain terrain and boreal forest. For early modern hunters, their feathers and meat were attractive returns. Linnaeus described how all households engaged in reindeer herding in Lule lappmark moved to the boreal forest in winter, and that only some of the poorest inhabitants stayed in the mountains to snare ptarmigans.[39] He described that hunters could snare up to 40 or 50 birds during one night. Högström likewise wrote that poor Sami in Lule lappmark sometimes stayed in the mountains during winter, surviving on abundant catches of ptarmigan.[40] Even so, he described that hunters had to combine the ptarmigan diet with other meat since bird meat allegedly was not nutritious enough to survive on. Niurenius (around 1640), Rheen, and Tornaeus also described snaring of ptarmigans in winter.[41] Both Linnaeus and Högström described that users who owned large reindeer herds were not especially engaged in hunting and not particularly accomplished hunters, and specified that few of the households they visited in the mountains owned rifles or steel bows (cross bows).[42] According to them, reindeer herders' hunting efforts were directed toward either squirrels with wooden bows in the forest in winter, or ptarmigans with snares. Holm described that in the mountains of Ume lappmark there were few bird species to eat other than ptarmigans.[43] (Fig. 6.1).

Hunting in the Boreal Forest

Many more species of prey animals were native to the boreal forest than to the alpine tundra, and early modern sources mentioned several in accounts and court cases regarding forest hunting. Furthermore, forest inhabitants were generally portrayed as proficient hunters, skilled in both

---

[39] Linnaeus (2003, pp. 106–107).

[40] Högström (1747, p. 97).

[41] Niurenius (1905, p. 19), Rheen (1897, p. 53), and Tornaeus (1900, p. 60).

[42] Linnaeus (2003, pp. 101–138) and Högström (1747, p. 86).

[43] Norstedt (2011, pp. 105–108).

Fig. 6.1 Willow ptarmigan (*Lagopus lagopus*) with egg, depicted in 1695 (*Source* Iter lapponicum, Luefsta MS 92, Uppsala University Library, Sweden. Public domain. https://www.alvin-portal.org/alvin/imageViewer.jsf?dsId=ATTACHMENT-0137&pid=alvin-record:162152)

making traps and shooting. Högström described hunting as fundamental for all households in the forest of Lule lappmark.[44] Linnaeus similarly described the inhabitants as skilled marksmen.[45] Several animal species were mentioned in lists of traded goods in the lappmark: otter (*Lutra lutra*), wolverine, lynx (*Lynx lynx*), marten (*Martes martes*), fox (red and black), beaver (*Castor fiber*), grey skin (or red squirrel [*Sciurus vulgaris*]), wolf (*Canis lupus*), and bear (*Ursus arctos arctos*).[46]

The sources told us that wild reindeer were present in the boreal forest of Lule lappmark in the seventeenth century. Wild reindeer there were hunted with snares, spears, rifles, or bows and arrows.[47] The use of bows, snares, and spears was also corroborated by two court rulings from Lule lappmark.[48] In 1672, Graan described how seventeenth-century hunters in Ume lappmark got plenty of food from wild game, such as wild reindeer, which, according to him, were hunted in the forest, rarely in the mountains.[49] The hunt for wild reindeer was described as year-round, especially around St. Matthews Day in September, which was the rutting season, in early spring when the snow cover was deep, and in summer. In fall, hunters stalked herds of wild reindeer in the forest and used a tame *vaja* (female reindeer) to attract bulls and kill them with rifles or bows. The winter hunt was performed on skis; while the hunters stayed on top of the snow, the reindeer sank into the snow, which made it relatively easy to catch up and kill it. Hunters had the most luck in snow-rich winters as a thick snow cover favored hunting of most forest animals.[50] Lundius mentioned how a hunter in one single day had felled 16 wild reindeer. Inhabitants in Ume lappmark were also said to have stalked wild reindeer in the forest in summer, equipped with rifles or bows.[51] However, Holm described how hunting wild reindeer in the summer was

[44] Högström (1747, p. 85).
[45] Linnaeus (2003, p. 138).
[46] Rheen (1897, p. 58) and Tornaeus (1900, p. 63).
[47] Rheen (1897, p. 23).
[48] HRA (1699, pp. 76–85); RA SH (1741, p. 784).
[49] Graan (1899, p. 42).
[50] Lundius (1905, p. 26).
[51] Niurenius (1905, p. 17).

not customary, since meat and skins were destroyed by insects.[52] Further, Holm's account describes how some *skatteland* had many wild reindeer and some had few.[53]

Aside from hunting with rifles or bows, seventeenth-century sources from Ume lappmark described how inhabitants there used trapping pits to catch wild reindeer.[54] The pits were set up in narrow gorges, delimited by steep cliffs or other impassable terrain, where the wild reindeer usually passed in winter. In the midst of the gorge, several deep pits were dug and covered with fine twigs and mosses. On top, loose snow was shuffled to hide irregularities. The hunters either waited for the reindeer's voluntary passage, or actively startled them so they moved toward the pits.

After Linneaus had traveled in Ume lappmark in 1732, he stated that "*willrenar finnas sällan i Lapmarken, förnämligast finnas någre på Almänningen emällan Granöen och Lyksele*" [wild reindeer are seldom found in the lappmark, mostly they reside on a common land between Granön and Lycksele], located at the eastern border.[55] He also wrote that reindeer herders sometimes lost tame reindeer to wild herds but that they usually got them back the following year. The tame reindeer would then be herded back to the flock by its owner or, if it did not comply, it would be shot. If reindeer traps were used, they could have easily become a hazard for tame reindeer and cause problems for reindeer herders.[56] The last evidence we found about wild reindeer hunting in Lule lappmark came from a court case in 1741.[57] The court decided that a settler who had deployed a wild reindeer trap in the eastern part of Sjokksjokk had to reimburse the owners whose reindeer got caught in his trap.

The distribution of moose or elk (*Alces alces*) is hard to interpret. According to Lundius, there were normally no moose in Lule lappmark, but Ume lappmark had both moose and wild reindeer in abundance.[58] However, in Holm's detailed descriptions of game in each *skatteland*,

---

[52] Norstedt (2011, p. 84).
[53] Norstedt (2011, pp. 65–73).
[54] Lundius (1905, p. 22) and Niurenius (1905, p. 17).
[55] Linnaeus (2003, p. 44).
[56] Arell (1977, pp. 99–101).
[57] RA SH (1741, p. 784).
[58] Lundius (1905, pp. 12, 40).

moose are not mentioned in Ume lappmark.[59] Holm's task was to assess the value of resources of each *skatteland*. Since he did not mention moose, he could not have seen it as a reliable asset for landholders. The moose must have been absent or at least very rare. In Torne lappmark, Tornaeus (1900:55) described that moose had existed in past times.[60]

The wolverine is native to both the arctic tundra and the boreal forest. In a text about wolverines in Lule lappmark, Hollsten stated that the animal resided in forests near a mountain with rugged terrain to which they could flee when they were hunted.[61] Wolverines have dark-colored, dense, water-repellant greasy fur. Their coats showed up in early modern trade lists from Lule lappmark, which suggests they were hunted there.[62] According to Holm in 1671, wolverines were common in Ume lappmark, but hard to catch, and were hunted to prevent them from breaking into storage places, such as buildings and mountain crevasses.[63] Hollsten described them as a great nuisance because they ate food people had stocked to use during their return to the mountains in spring.[64] Hunting methods included trapping with steel-jawed leghold restraint traps that were heftier than ordinary traps and hunting on skis with a spear for the final killing. Lundius corroborated trapping wolverines in his account from 1674 of practices in the boreal forest in Ume lappmark.[65]

Sami considered bears to be the most prominent creatures in the forest due to their superior strength compared to other animals.[66] This probably contributed to numerous rituals that surrounded bear hunts, and the subsequent preparation and disposal of meat and bones, described by several authors.[67] Linnaeus described bear hunting in Lule lappmark as stalking by a single man with a dog who eventually crawled close

[59] Norstedt (2011, p. 39).
[60] Tornaeus (1900, p. 55).
[61] Hollsten (1773, p. 232).
[62] Lundmark (1982, pp. 198–203).
[63] Norstedt (2011, p. 72).
[64] Hollsten (1773, p. 235).
[65] Lundius (1905, p. 28).
[66] Rheen (1897, p. 43).
[67] Högström (1747, p. 209), Rheen (1897, pp. 43ff.), and Niurenius (1905, p. 18).

enough to shoot the bear.[68] The hunts took place in fall when bears were busy eating berries. Rheen described a more collectively organized hunt in Lule lappmark, where a person who had found the hibernating bear's den gathered family and friends to help wake and kill it.[69] Killings were performed with either spears or rifles. The bear hide was reserved for the person who had located the den, and the meat was divided among all participants in the hunt. Niurenius specified the time period for bear hunting in Ume lappmark as March and April, when the bear was still in its den but right before it normally awoke.[70]

The priest Pehr Fjellström wrote about the rituals surrounding bear hunting and described a common law among inhabitants wherein the proprietor of a *skatteland* where a bear had been killed got a share of the meat, regardless of whether or not he or she had participated in the hunt.[71] If the proprietor had participated, he or she got to choose the first share, then received the share due to each participant.

Several court rulings from Lule lappmark dealt with bear hunting and gave a different picture. In one case from 1709, two bear hunters from Jokkmokk were the plaintiffs.[72] They claimed to have woken a hibernating bear and thereafter encircled it on their own *skatteland*. However, before they could kill the bear, it had run off to a neighboring *skatteland* where it eventually had been killed by the defendants. In court, the plaintiffs demanded a share of the bear's fur from the defendants, but since the court was not convinced that it was the same bear, the verdict went in favor of the defendants, and the plaintiffs were left empty-handed.

A parallel case was brought to the court just a few days later. In that case, two men in Sjokksjokk had encircled a bear on another user's *skatteland* and then shot it.[73] Thanks to the effort of the men at the beginning of the hunt, the court decided they had rights to one-third of the value of the bear's coat. Even if it was not made explicit in the verdict, it seems reasonable that the remaining two-thirds accrued to the landholder.

---

[68] Linnaeus (2003, p. 148).

[69] Rheen (1897, pp. 43ff).

[70] Niurenius (1905, p. 18).

[71] Pehr Fjellström (1981 [1755], p. 9).

[72] HRA (1709, p. 343).

[73] HRA (1709, p. 357).

In 1742 and 1744, two more court cases dealt with bear hunting. The first involved a dispute between a user in Jokkmokk and a user in Sjokksjokk.[74] The second case involved a user from Jokkmokk and a user from Sirkas.[75] In both cases, the verdicts had been postponed: in the first case, the court needed to find out who owned the land where the bear had been killed; in the latter case, the defendant never appeared in court. Neither of these cases seems to have been reopened, probably because the parties reached settlements outside court.

The court rulings show that the meat and coat from a killed bear belonged to the holder of the *skatteland* where it had been shot.[76] Yet, it was possible to get a share if a person had participated in the bear hunt before the bear fell, even though it was not on his or her land. In court rulings that explicitly mentioned the number of hunters, they always hunted in pairs. This also goes for a case from 1707 where a father and son from Sjokksjokk stood accused of reindeer theft.[77] In defense, they argued they could not have stolen any reindeer since they were out hunting bear at the time.

Between 1572 and 1615, 77 beaver pelts from Lule lappmark were sold or paid in tax to the Swedish crown.[78] According to an account from the seventeenth century, there were beavers in Ume but not in Lule lappmark.[79] In the mid-eighteenth century, Hollsten described how he had taken care of an orphaned beaver kit and, according to him, that beavers had been so rare by then in Lule lappmark that many older inhabitants had never seen a beaver while growing up.[80] Beavers were favored prey for their valuable castoreum, which probably was the main reason beavers became extinct throughout Sweden. Carl Fjellström wrote that castoreum was so expensive in the pharmacies in Sweden that Sami should have sold it to Swedish merchants instead of taking it to markets

---

[74] RA SH (1742, p. 254).

[75] RA SH (1744, p. 289).

[76] Korpijaakko-Labba (1994, pp. 260–261) and Korhonen (2007).

[77] HRA (1707, pp. 145–149).

[78] Lundmark (1982, pp. 191–203).

[79] Lundius (1905, p. 12).

[80] Hollsten (1768, p 286).

in Norway.[81] Because the beaver skins were already being sold to Swedish merchants, they should have been able to offer as much for the castoreum as the Norwegians did.

The source materials reveal little to no information about hunting of many species of small game. Squirrel hunting was especially important for many households in the lappmark, and we know that Sami in Lule lappmark paid taxes in squirrel pelts, which represented the bulk of traded furs.[82] Linnaeus described squirrel traps made of logs that had been split in two.[83] He previously had described, in an account from the mountains, how efficiently Sami handled wooden bows when they hunted squirrels in the forest. In Holm's account, squirrels and other small game are listed for almost all *skatteland* in Ume Lappmark.[84] For some land in the boreal forest, squirrels are listed as rather abundant.[85] In the court rulings from Lule lappmark, we found two cases concerning squirrels.[86] Both were from Sjokksjokk and pointed out that squirrels belonged to the holder of the land. Coats from martens are mentioned in early modern trade lists, and Niurenius described that martens could be killed with arrows while they were up in trees, but that the most common hunting method was to use fire to smoke them out of their hiding places in mountain caves and crevasses.[87] They were then caught in nets that were tied in front of the entrance.

Forest inhabitants also engaged in hunting fowl for meat, feathers, and eggs. The feathers were used in the household and for trade, while the meat and eggs mostly were consumed within the household. Other materials from the birds also were used, such as skins for water-tight containers.

Rheen listed land fowl that resided in the boreal forest in Lule lappmark, such as western capercaillie (*Tetrao urogallus*), black grouse (*Lyrurus tetrix*), and hazel grouse (*Tetrastes bonasia*). Both Tornaeus and

[81] C. Fjellström (1760, p. 21).
[82] Lundmark (1982) and Phebe Fjellström (1986, p. 182).
[83] Linnaeus (2003, p. 61).
[84] Norstedt (2011, p. 39).
[85] Norstedt (2011, pp. 89–114).
[86] HRA (1711, pp. 759–760) and RA SH (1757, pp. 496–497).
[87] Niurenius (1905, p. 19).

Rheen listed several species of water fowl that were present in northern Fennoscandia during summer, such as whooper swan (*Cygnus cygnus*) and various species of geese and mallards, such as common golden eyes (*Bucephala clangula*), Swartor (probably velvet scoter [*Melanitta fusca*]), black-throated divers (*Gavia arctica*), red-throated divers (*Gavia stellata*), and goosanders (*Mergus merganser*).[88] Several methods were used in bird hunting. Linnaeus wrote that he had seen traps for capercaillie along paths all over Ume lappmark and that these traps were deployed in fall.[89] At least in Ume lappmark, traps were also used to catch water fowl, such as geese and swans.[90] Moreover, both Ehrenmalm and Lundius described that inhabitants hunted forest fowl with rifles.[91] Ehrenmalm specified that Sami in the boreal forest shot plenty of birds in spring. Linnaeus described how he nearly had been hit by a misdirected bullet fired by a bird hunter when he was out picking wild strawberries in the mountains in northern Norway, just across the border from Lule lappmark.[92] Sources also mentioned that water fowl were caught in nets but did not specify if hunters were trying to catch birds or if it happened as a bycatch in fishing nets.[93]

We have not found any particular bird species mentioned in court rulings from Lule lappmark. However, bird hunting in general can be affirmed, for example, in a case where plaintiffs and defendants used bird traps.[94] Bird hunting was also stated in several disputes over rights to use specific tax lands, where the court saw long-term use of bird traps as a valid argument for the bird hunter to obtain continuous user rights.[95] All cases regarding bird trapping in Lule lappmark that we found had unfolded in the boreal forest. We learned that users in the mountains snared ptarmigans, and probably trapped other birds, although it is not noticeable in the court records. The lack of court cases regarding bird hunting in the mountains is probably because there were fewer bird

88 Tornaeus (1900, p. 60) and Rheen (1897, p. 53).

89 Linnaeus (2003, p. 62).

90 Lundius (1905, p. 17).

91 Ehrenmalm (1743, p. 128) and Lundius (1905, p. 18).

92 Linnaeus (2003, p. 118).

93 Tornaeus (1900, p. 60).

94 RA SH (1777, pp. 45–46).

95 RA SH (1772, p. 485).

species there than in the boreal forest in the winter, thus less hunting. Also, and maybe more important, because the institution of *skatteland* was more widespread, providing the opportunity for more disputes over rights.[96] Court records from Lule lappmark by and large described trapping of birds, whereas only one court ruling mentioned *fågelskjutande* (bird shooting).[97]

Aside from bird hunting for meat and feathers, Sami also gathered birds' eggs. There were specially built nesting places for gathering eggs.[98] These bird houses were made of hollow trunks with a manmade hole in the middle and ends plugged with moss. The bird houses were attached to trees, and as soon as the birds laid their eggs in them, they were emptied. Hunters also collected swan eggs on mires and tufts after the birds had been snared.

The only evidence we found that revealed anything about the extent of hunting in Lule lappmark came from a court case in 1737. The defendant, a man from Sjokksjokk, was charged for unlawfully using a tax land. The right to the land had originally belonged to the father of the current user, and he had given the defendant provisional rights to hunt there, but only until his son, the plaintiff, had come of age to use it. The court decided that the defendant no longer could use the land, and thus approved the plaintiff's demand. As a consequence, the defendant wanted to be compensated for traps he had deployed on the land. This was approved by the court, and he was compensated for a total of two hundred traps, divided equally between *flakar* (log traps) and *giller* (cage traps). The traps were described as well functioning, and therefore worth a total of 12 *daler* copper coins.[99] It was obviously problematic to remove the traps, and subsequently reasonable for the plaintiff to reimburse the defendant for their worth. Although this evidence concerns one specific case, it suggests that one land parcel could contain hundreds of traps. Besides the 200 traps, the defendant might have had other, less complicated traps made of wires and ropes that easily could have been removed and might have hunted small game with bow and rifle.

96 Hultblad (1968).

97 HRA (1709, p. 352).

98 Tornaeus (1900, p. 60) and Lundius (1905, p. 16).

99 RA SH (1737, p. 682).

Small-game hunting seems to have been a particularly important income source for the poor. This was highlighted in a court ruling from 1701 where the plaintiff, a man from Jokkmokk, accused two maids, who were also sisters, of having destroyed a couple of *fågelflakar* (log traps for birds) and the floor of an *akkja* (sledge) that belonged to him. According to the sisters, it was instead the plaintiff who had acted unlawfully, both by destroying several of their bird traps, and by striking them with rods and twigs. All in all, the court argued that the offense was minor but that the plaintiff nevertheless had a greater liability. The court's main argument was that the plaintiff had acted unjustly toward two simple-minded women, and that he should have been able to handle the situation differently. Moreover, the court stated that since the two sisters lived in great poverty, the plaintiff should compensate them with six *daler* copper coins, or a *vajren* (female reindeer). They also had the right to continue using bird traps on his land. The court emphasized that the plaintiff should *icke förtaga dem deras närings och lifsuppehälle* (not take away their livelihood and life support) and that the sisters, for their part, had to show respect and good manners toward the plaintiff.[100] From Pite lappmark, Öhrling wrote that those who were very poor sought their livelihoods solely from hunting and fishing.[101]

Ecological Differences

With regard to ecological settings, the most important natural conditions that impacted decisions regarding hunting in Lule lappmark between 1660 and 1780 were the differences between mountains and boreal forest. While the forest had many species of mammals and birds, the mountains did not. The same observation was made by Holm in his account of Ume lappmark in the 1670s.[102] The compositions of species of prey animals in the two regions were stable during the study period,

[100] HRA (1701, pp. 406–408).

[101] Öhrling (1970 [1773], p. 11).

[102] Norstedt (2011, pp. 105–107).

but some important changes occurred that impacted hunting strategies and outcome.

The sixteenth century saw an increased demand for expensive furs and a trade that flourished until it peaked in the 1570s. Fur trade declined rapidly in Lule lappmark in the beginning of the seventeenth century.[103] Lundmark suggested that it was caused by an overharvest of fur animals, but another possible explanation was that new trade patterns had emerged that increased the fur import to Europe, first from Russia and later from North America.[104] However, it is likely that the slow, long-term decrease occurred for three reasons: (1) Furs continued to be sought-after goods in local trade even after they lost importance in international trade. Hunters could easily see how incomes from fur trade would improve the household economy, especially in the boreal forest where fur animals were abundant at the time. (2) The human population increase in the eighteenth century led to increased hunting pressure. (3) Some wild animals were a nuisance to people—stealing their stocked food or attacking their domestic reindeer—and were therefore killed.

The developments surrounding wild reindeer are more lucid than for other wild game. It is difficult to pursue reindeer herding in areas with wild reindeer. Vorren established a temporal correlation between the decline of wild reindeer and the emergence of reindeer pastoralism in the Finnmark region of northern Norway during the first half of the eighteenth century.[105] Lundmark argued that a similar development occurred in Lule lappmark and that the extinction of wild reindeer was intentional.[106] It began in the mountains and ended in the easternmost boreal forest of Sjokksjokk, where wild reindeer were rare by the mid-eighteenth century. We know relatively little about how wild reindeer were distributed in the mountains in early modern Lule lappmark. In fact, wild reindeer were mentioned in only one source from 1608,[107] and their presence was indirectly confirmed by the remains of pitfall

103 Lundmark (1982, p. 120).

104 Lundmark (1982) and Brook (2008).

105 Vorren (1978, 1980).

106 Lundmark (1982, pp. 162–163).

107 Lundmark (1982, pp. 163).

systems.[108] When inhabitants with access to mountain grazing developed reindeer pastoralism, wild reindeer would have had no place in the mountains, explaining their rapidly decreasing numbers. According to Holm, there were no wild reindeer in the mountains of Ume lappmark in 1671, although they were abundant in some of the *skatteland* in the boreal forest.[109] Pitfalls thus became useless and hazardous for domestic reindeer, and from the mid-seventeenth century, at the latest, wild reindeer must have been extinct or at least very rare in the mountains.

Some court rulings from the first decades of the eighteenth century contain information about wild reindeer being present in the forest in Lule lappmark. The last one was dated in 1741 and mentioned a trap for hunting wild reindeer. According to Hollsten, wild reindeer were rare in Lule lappmark but remained in the forests between Lule Lappmark and the farming districts in the east.[110] The disappearance of forest reindeer coincided with the introduction of large-scale reindeer pastoralism around 1750.[111]

Small-game hunting for international trade lost importance in the seventeenth century. However, small-game hunting for subsistence was still important. It reinforced the boreal forest as the primary arena for hunting. The boreal forest offered an abundance of animals, while the mountains offered relatively few. Hence, households in the forest had more opportunities to hunt.

Importance of Prey Animals

The source materials give insights into the major reasons why households in Lule lappmark hunted in the seventeenth and eighteenth centuries. First, people needed fat and protein from wild animals for consumption. Second, households needed products for trade and paying

[108] Mulk (2005, p. 48).

[109] Norstedt (2011, p. 38).

[110] Hollsten (1774).

[111] Hultblad (1968).

taxes—for example, skins from a wide range of animals, such as squirrels, foxes, bears, and martens, and feathers from wild fowl. Third, people wanted to prevent predators, particularly wolverines, bears, and wolves, from damaging their stored food and tame reindeer.[112] Besides these three practical and functional motives for hunting, there was surely a fourth, intangible motive: the feelings of excitement, joy, and reward that continue to entice modern-day hunters.

Property Rights

Two central questions are: Who had the right to hunt? and Where could they hunt? The answers for forest hunting were connected to proprietorship of *skatteland*, meaning that rules for access were well defined among users. In the mountains, on the other hand, distribution of tax lands was less clear, and users often had open access to hunting.

In the forest, users were more dependent economically on hunting, and having as much control as possible over the resources was key. There was a strict division into *skatteland* on which individual households had private rights to grazing land, fishing waters, and hunting grounds. The boundaries between them were usually well known, and if not, the local court helped to set the borders. As soon as a wild animal dwelled on a *skatteland*, it was seen as private goods, and the property of the proprietor of that land. Ownership of the animal shifted when it strayed to another person's *skatteland*. In Lule lappmark, all but one of the hunting disputes taken to court took place in the boreal forest. Hultblad showed that most of the forest in Lule lappmark was divided into *skatteland*. Arell conveyed that most court cases regarding hunting in Torne lappmark dealt with uncertainties over boundaries in relation to the natural resources that were disputed.[113]

The formation of hunting rights in the forest followed many of Ostrom's design principles for sustainable use of CPRs.[114] Well-defined

[112] Högström (1747, p. 85) and Linnaeus (2003, p. 138).
[113] Arell (1977).
[114] Ostrom (1990, p. 90).

user groups and resource areas made it possible to control the amounts of resources that were withdrawn from each land, which in turn reduced the risk of overuse. If the use of a resource was contested, or if trespassing occurred, the local court functioned as a collective-choice arena that mediated between users, clarified boundaries between lands, and penalized someone who violated the rules. Clear boundaries between users' lands made it easier to monitor regulations, even though very large *skatteland* still might have been difficult to control fully.

Small-game hunting favored lands that were used individually for two reasons. First, hunting small game often entailed traps, which in turn became investments in the land; for example, fixed log traps took time to construct and were difficult to move. A household could have had several hundred such trapping devices on its land. Second, small-game hunting required users to have great knowledge about the whereabouts and behavior of prey animals in order to deploy the right trap in the right place. The traps also had to be monitored regularly, which required hunters to deploy them near their living grounds. Many aspects of hunting were thus facilitated if users had detailed knowledge about and easy access to land. If a *skatteland* was used by more than one household, each household had its own traps, and the prey animals accrued to the household that had deployed them. Trapping is for the most part an extensive hunting method and many traps are required for it to be rewarding. The probability of catching a prey animal increases if the hunter has large numbers of traps deployed in as many strategic places as possible. Therefore, the division of *skatteland* into smaller units, which became common in the eighteenth century, was disadvantageous for the hunting economy. It decreased each households' catch area and eventually made trapping economically inviable. The smaller land units affected the household fishing economy in the same way.[115]

Large prey animals in the boreal forest also accrued to the proprietor of the *skatteland* where it was felled, but this rule could be set aside by mutual agreements between involved parties. If someone had been instrumental in the pursuit of a bear prior to the killing, it was possible for him or her to get a share even without belonging to the household

115 Chapter 5.

of the landholder. Opposite to the rest of Sweden, where pest animals could be killed and claimed by anyone, in the lappmark they belonged to the landholder.[116]

There were no such strict regulations regarding access to hunting or to whom a felled wild animal belonged in the Lule lappmark mountains. However, where wild reindeer were present in Torne lappmark during the seventeenth century, the hunt was regulated by the villages. Since there were fewer species of wild animals in the mountains than in the forest, hunting played a less important role in the household economy. Early modern sources were vague when it came to the organization of hunting in the mountains, but there was no clear evidence of it being tied to *skatteland* in Lule lappmark, and it seemed as if users were allowed to hunt freely.

Hunting was often described as a collective enterprise organized and regulated by the Sami village and where the wild animals were a CPR.[117] However, seventeenth- and eighteenth-century sources told us that hunting in the forest was organized individually or at the household level, and that wild animals belonged to the holder of a *skatteland* where they appeared. Hunting in the mountains, after the disappearance of wild reindeer, was also organized individually, and wild animals were most likely seen as CPRs.

As discussed in Chapter 2, earlier research assumed that *skatteland* represented an older organization, predating their first appearance in the sources from the seventeenth century.[118] Other scholars did not perceive tax lands as originally Sami, but rather as the result of the Swedish government's desire to organize taxation by connecting all inhabitants to specific lands.[119] The origin of *skatteland* is complex; however, the organization of land into well-defined user parcels makes sense when we consider the organization of fishing and hunting in the boreal forest from the mid-seventeenth century to the second half of the eighteenth century. Norstedt argues that *skatteland* were created "to achieve a satisfactory

---

116 Korpijakko-Labba (1994, p. 263).

117 Ingold (1980), Mulk (1994), and Bergman and Ramqvist (2018).

118 Holmbäck (1922).

119 Hansen and Olsen (2014).

division of predictable and dense resources" and points to fishing as the determinant factor.[120] Well-defined tax lands made it possible for landholders who relied on fishing and hunting to gain control over resources that were fundamental for their survival. The idea of hunting as a collective enterprise or of wild animals as a CPR does not fit with the way land was actually organized in the early modern period. Hence, it is likely that the organization into *skatteland* was a response to changes in the Sami economy, and that changes in the organization of hunting, from collective to private, was one of the contributing factors in that development.

Participation in Hunting

Before 1600, hunting in the lappmark was described, albeit from sketchy evidence, as a task performed mostly by men. Men left home to hunt wild reindeer or bears and returned with the prey and shared it within a group of neighbors and relatives. It is probably an exceedingly one-dimensional description of medieval and pre-historic hunting,[121] but due to the sources, and the dominating portrayals of hunting therein, little else is known about who actually hunted historically. The shift from portraying hunters as main characters to not describing them at all coincided with the expiration of wild reindeer hunting and the increased importance of reindeer pastoralism, which led to the portrayal of Sami after the sixteenth century as foremost reindeer herders.

The fundamental change in hunting in the early modern period, from producing a surplus of furs for trade to a subsistence mode, might have changed who participated. In the early modern accounts, young boys, for example, were said to have practiced squirrel hunting with bows from an early age. And it is fair to conclude that the authors' own views of gender division of labor, from childhood to adulthood, relatively uncritically transferred into their descriptions of Sami customs. Men moved around, chasing and hunting large animals, and women were mostly invisible

[120] Norstedt (2018, p. 65).
[121] Mulk (1994).

or stayed at home. An example would be accounts that present a vivid picture of men being part of ritual bear hunting,[122] although Kuhmunen has shown that women participated in the rituals when the bear was brought home.[123] The use of weapons— rifles, bows, and spears—were associated with men.

Accounts and court rulings gave plenty of evidence of small-game hunting that took place close to the living grounds, and it seems reasonable that both men and women participated. Common tasks were to build, place, and monitor the traps to catch small game. Since one household could have had several hundreds of traps, it would have been a time-consuming endeavor and thus a shared responsibility for several household members. For most species of small game, there was also a seasonal variation in the number of prey animals, and during the high season all the available work force in the household must have been needed, regardless of gender or age. Catching water fowl must have required the same workforce whenever households had to optimize harvests of meat, eggs, and feathers during the few summer months before the birds migrated. Moreover, many of the work tasks related to fishing and reindeer husbandry were performed by both men and women.[124] This was true also for many of the household chores, such as food preparation and cooking. There was thus a tradition of sharing labor. Small-game hunting became the major hunting activity and was more predictable than large-game hunting. Hence it contributed to subsistence. Hunting was not gender neutral, but women's and children's roles in early modern small-game hunting have largely been invisible.

Social Justice

Small-game hunting for subsistence played an important part in upholding social justice among inhabitants in Lule lappmark. Poor people could, for example, stay in the mountains in winter to hunt

[122] Tornaeus (1900, p. 59–60) and Niurenius (1905, p. 14).

[123] Kuhmunen (2015).

[124] Chapters 5 and 7.

ptarmigans, where users had open access to hunting. Despite this, there was probably little risk of overharvest since there were few hunters on relatively vast lands. Hunting by poor people was not limited to the mountains; they also could hunt small game on tax lands in the boreal forest. If landholders claimed that people's hunting was an intrusion, the court could decide that they had rights to continue hunting because they were underprivileged.[125]

Small-game hunting likely increased in importance in the early modern period, even though the scarcity of information from previous centuries makes it impossible to prove. Small-game hunting was possibly motivated by a growing population that made people search for alternative incomes, especially inhabitants who in the beginning of this period did not participate in reindeer pastoralism. The larger picture implies that the gap between wealthy and poor inhabitants in Lule lappmark increased during the early modern period due to population growth and expansion of reindeer pastoralism, which yielded great surpluses for pastoralist households.[126] Hunting was one way to alleviate poverty for those who remained on the wrong side of the gap, and to prompt social equity, the poor's right to hunt was often confirmed by the local community via the local court.

References

Arell, Nils. 1977. *Rennomadismen i Torne lappmark: markanvändning under kolonisationsepoken i fr.a. Enontekis socken*. PhD diss. Umeå, Sweden: Skytteanska samfundet. http://www.diva-portal.org/smash/record.jsf?pid=diva2%3A616377&dswid=6098.

Bergman, Ingela, Olle Zachrisson, and Lars Liedgren. 2013. From hunting to herding: Land use, ecosystem processes, and social transformation among Sami ad 800–1500. *Arctic Antrophology* 50 (2): 25–39. https://doi.org/10.3368/aa.50.2.25.

125 HRA (1701, pp. 406–408).

126 Kvist (1989a).

Bergman, Ingela, and Per H. Ramqvist. 2018. Hunters of waters: Late Iron Age and medieval subsistence and social processes in coastal northern Sweden. *Acta Borealia* 35 (1): 1–28. https://doi.org/10.1080/08003831.2018.1456765.

Bjørklund, Ivar. 2013. Domestication, reindeer husbandry and the development of Sámi pastoralism. *Acta Borealia* 30 (2): 174–189. https://doi.org/10.1080/08003831.2013.847676

Brook, Timothy. 2008. *Vermeer's hat, the seventeenth century and the dawn of the global world*. New York: Bloomsbury Press.

Ehrenmalm, Arwid. 1743. *Resa igenom Wäster-Norrland til Åsehle lappmark, anstäld uti julii månad 1741*. Stockholm. Available page by page at http://runeberg.org/resawenoas/index.html.

Ekman, Sven. 1910. *Norrlands jakt och fiske*. Uppsala, Sweden: Almqvist & Wiksell.

Fjellström, Carl P. 1760. *Tankar om upodlings möjelighet i Lappmarkerne*. PhD diss., Uppsala universitet. http://urn.kb.se/resolve?urn=urn:nbn:se:kb:eod-2554964.

Fjellström, Pehr. 1981 [1755]. *Kort berättelse om lapparnas björna-fänge, samt deras der wid brukade widskeppelser*, Facs.-utg. Umeå, Sweden: Två förläggare.

Fjellström, Phebe. 1962. *Lapskt silver: Studier över en föremålsgrupp och dess ställning inom lapskt kulturliv*. Stockholm: Almqvist & Wiksell.

Fjellström, Phebe. 1986. *Samernas samhälle i tradition och nutid*, 2nd ed. Stockholm: Norstedt.

Graan, Olaus. 1899. *Relation, eller en fulkomblig beskrifning om lapparnas ursprung, så wähl som om heela dheras Lefwernes Förehållande*. Uppsala, Sweden: Harald Wretmans tryckeri.

Hansen. Lars Ivar. 1990. *Samisk fangstsamfunn og norsk høvdingeøkonomi*. Oslo: Novus.

Hansen, Lars Ivar, and Bjørnar Olsen, 2014. *Hunters in transition: An outline of early Sámi history*. Leiden, the Netherlands: Brill.

Henriksson, Heidi. 1978. *Popular hunting and trapping in Norrland*. Stockholm: Kungl. Vitterhets Historie och Antikvitets Akademien.

Högström, Pehr. 1747. *Beskrifning öfwer de til Sweriges krona lydande lapmarker*. Stockholm: Salvius. http://urn.kb.se/resolve?urn=urn:nbn:se:umu:eod-114.

Hollsten, Jonas. 1768. *Anmärkningar om bäfvern, Castor*. Stockholm: Vetenskaps Akademiens handlingar.

Hollsten, Jonas. 1773. *Anmärkningar om järfven*. Stockholm: Vetenskaps Akademiens handlingar.
Hollsten, Jonas. 1774. *Afhandling om renen*. Stockholm: Vetenskaps Akademiens handlingar.
Holmbäck, Åke. 1922. *Om lappskattelandsinstitutet och dess historiska utveckling*. Stockholm: Statens offentliga utredningar.
Hultblad, Filip. 1968. *Övergång från nomadism till agrar bosättning i Jokkmokks socken*. PhD diss.: Uppsala University.
Hvarfner, Harald, ed. 1965. *Hunting and fishing*. Luleå, Sweden: Norbottens Museum.
Ingold, Tim. 1980. *Hunters, pastoralists and ranchers*. Cambridge, UK: Cambridge University Press.
Josefsson, Torbjörn, Ingela Bergman, and Lars Östlund. 2010. Quantifying Sami settlement and movement patterns in northern Sweden 1700–1900. *Arctic* 62 (2): 141–154. https://doi.org/10.14430/arctic970
Kjellström, Rolf. 2000. *Samernas liv*. Stockholm: Carlssons förlag.
Korhonen, Olavi. 2007. Jägaren och björnceremonierna. *Svenska Landsmål Och Svenskt Folkliv* 333: 27–49.
Korpijaakko-Labba, Kaisa. 1994. *Om samernas rättsliga ställning i Sverige-Finland. En rättshistorisk utredning av markanvändningsförhållanden och -rättigheter i Västerbottens lappmark före mitten av 1700-talet*. Helsinki: Juristförbundets förlag.
Kuhmunen, Anna Westman. 2015. A female perspective on bear hunting. *Journal of Northern Studies* 9 (2): 73–94.
Kvist, Roger. 1989. *Rennomadismens dilemma, det rennomadiska samhällets förändring i Tuorpon och Sirkas, 1760–1860*. PhD diss.: Umeå University.
Læstadius, Lars Levi. 1832. Om vilda renen. *Tidskrift för jägare och naturforskare* 11 & 12: 344–347.
Linnaeus, Carl. 2003. *Iter Lapponicum: Lappländska resan 1732. I*. Dagboken. Umeå, Sweden: Kungl. Skytteanska Samfundet.
Lundius, Nicolai. 1905. *Descriptio Lapponiæ*. Uppsala, Sweden: Harald Wretmans tryckeri.
Lundmark, Lennart. 1982. *Uppbörd, utarmning, utveckling. Det samiska fångstsamhällets övergång till rennomadism i Lule lappmark*. PhD diss.: Umeå University.
Lundmark, Lennart. 2006. *Samernas skatteland i Norr- och Västerbotten under 300 år*. Stockholm: Institutet för Rättshistorisk Forskning.
Manker, Ernst. 1960. *Fångstgropar och stalotomter: kulturlämningar från lapsk forntid*. Stockholm: Geber.

Mulk, Inga-Maria. 1994. *Sirkas, ett samiskt fångssamhälle i förändring kr.f. – 1600 e.Kr*. PhD diss., Umeå University.

Mulk, Inga-Maria. 2005. Bosättningsmönster, vildrensjakt och tamrenskötsel i Lule lappmark - 100 e.kr–1600 e.kr. *Fra Villreinjakt til Reindrift* 1: 33–59.

Niurenius, Olaus Petri. 1905. *Lappland, eller beskrivning över den nordiska trakt, som lapparne bebo i de avlägsnaste delarne af Skandinavien eller Sverge*. Uppsala, Sweden: Harald Wretmans tryckeri.

Norstedt, Gudrun. 2011. *Lappskattelanden på Geddas karta. Umeå lappmark från 1671 till 1900-talets början*. Umeå, Sweden: Thalassa förlag.

Norstedt, Gudrun. 2018. *A land of one's own*. PhD diss., Swedish University of Agricultural Sciences, Umeå. https://pub.epsilon.slu.se/15451/1/norstedt_g_180502.pdf.

Norstedt, Gudrun, Anna-Lena Axelsson, and Lars Östlund. 2014. Exploring pre-colonial resource control of individual Sami household. *Arctic* 67 (2): 223–237. https://doi.org/10.14430/arctic4389

Nyrén, Ulf. 2012. *Rätt till jakt, en studie av den svenska jakträtten ca 1600–1789*. PhD diss.: Gothenburg University.

Odner, Knut. 1983. *Finner och terfinner*. Occasional Paper 9. Oslo: Department of Social Anthropology, University of Oslo.

Öhrling, Samuel. 1970 [1773]. *Historisk-ekonomisk avhandling om Arjeplogs församling i Lappland*. Arjeplog, Sweden: Silvermuseet.

Ostrom, Elinor. 1990. *Governing the commons, the evolution of institutions for collective action*. Cambridge, UK: Cambridge University Press

Ostrom, Elinor. 2005. *Understanding institutional diversity*. Princeton, NJ: Princeton University Press.

Päiviö, Eva-Lotta. 2017. Livelihood diversification in early modern Sami households in northern Sweden. In *Integrated peasant economy in a comparative perspective: Alps, Scandinavia and beyond*, ed. Aleksander Panjek, Jesper Larsson, and Luca Mocarelli, 137–159. Koper, Slovenia: University of Primorska Press.

Peterson, M. Nils. 2019. Hunting. In: *Encyclopedia of ecology*, 2nd ed., vol. 3, ed. B.D. Fath, 438–440. Amsterdam: Elsevier Science. https://doi.org/10.1016/B978-0-12-409548-9.11168-6.

Rheen, Samuele. 1897. *En kortt relation om Lapparnes lefwarne och sedher, wijd-skiepellsser, sampt i många stycken grofwe wildfarellsser*. Uppsala, Sweden: Harald Wretmans tryckeri.

Rose, Carol. M. 1985. Possession as the origin of property. *The University of Chicago Law Review* 52 (1): 73–88. https://doi.org/10.2307/1599571.

Rydving. Håkan. 2011. The "bear ceremonial" and bear rituals among the Khanty and the Sami. *Tementos* 46 (1): 31–52. https://doi.org/10.33356/temenos.6940.

Sommerseth, Ingrid. 2009. *Villreinfangs og tamreindrift i indre Troms*. PhD diss.: University of Tromsø.

Sommerseth, Ingrid. 2011. Archeology and the debate on transition from reindeer hunting to pastoralism. *Rangifer* 31 (1): 111–127.

Stiernman, Anders Anton von. 1747–1775. *Samling utaf kongl. bref. [...] angående Sweriges rikes commerce,* [...] Del 1–6. Stockholm: Kongl. Tryckeriet.

Tanner, Väinö. 1929. *Antropogeografiska studier inom Petsamo-området. 1, Skoltlapparna*. Helsinki: Tilgmanns Tryck.

Tegengren, Helmer. 1952. *En utdöd lappkultur i Kemi lappmark*. Åbo/Turku, Finland: Åbo Akademi.

Tornaeus, Johannes. 1900. *Berättelse om Lapmarckerna och Deras Tillstånd*. Uppsala, Sweden: Harald Wretmans tryckeri.

Vorren, Ørnulf. 1978. Bosetning och naturesursutnytting under veidekulturen og dens differensiering. In *Finnmarksvidda natur–kultur*. Oslo: Statens forvaltningstjeneste. https://www.nb.no/items/a947f2133e81bfcf9a162e9f837b7fe6?page=0&searchText=altajuvet.

Vorren, Ørnulf. 1980. Samisk bosetning på Nordkalotten, arealdisponering og resursutnytting i historisk-økologisk belysning. In: *Nord-skandinaviens historia i tvärvetenskaplig belysning. förhandlingar vid symposium anordnat av Humanistiska fakulteten vid Umeå universitet den 7-9 juni 1978*, ed. Evert Baudou and Karl-Hampus Dahlstedt, 235–261. Umeå, Sweden: Almqvist & Wiksell.

Vorren, Ørnulf. 1998. *Villreinfangst i Varanger fram til 1600–1700 årene*. Tromsø Museums skrifter 28. Stronglandseidet, Norway: Nordkalott-Forlaget.

Archival Sources

Härnösand Regional Archive (HRA):

Rulings in Jokkmokks District Court, Sweden, 1689–1780.

Riksarkivet [National Archives of Sweden]:

Svea Court of Appeal (RA SH). 1712–1780. Rulings in Jokkmokks District Court, Sweden.

7

Reindeer Pastoralism

In this chapter, we give a brief overview of the relationship between humans and domesticated reindeer, and show how it changed over time. We focus on intensive reindeer husbandry or reindeer pastoralism, which was a tenure system that emerged in the early modern period. Reindeer pastoralism and grazing are deeply interconnected and, in this chapter, we therefore illuminate the ecological settings for reindeer grazing. A large part of the debate about governing CPRs has dealt with pastoralists and their grazing lands.[1] We continue with a general description of the development of reindeer pastoralism from the late Middle Ages to the end of the early modern period. Important features of reindeer pastoralism are described, including a discussion about how the number of tame reindeer developed in the early modern era. The chapter ends with a portrayal of and a discussion about individual households' rights to use certain areas for grazing, chiefly based on descriptions of contemporary court rulings from the local court in Jokkmokk.

[1] Hardin (1968), Ostrom (1990), and Moritz (2016.)

J. Larsson and E.-L. Päiviö Sjaunja, *Self-Governance and Sami Communities*,
https://doi.org/10.1007/978-3-030-87498-8_7

The Development of Reindeer Herding

Reindeer have been used by inhabitants in northern Fennoscandia throughout history, both as prey animals in hunting and as tamed animals to decoy wild reindeer, for transports, and for milking. It is not coincidental that humans and reindeer developed a strong and complex relationship over time. Inhabitants in the north quickly learned to take advantage of the reindeer's presence, and its exceptional ability to survive in a cold climate with short growing seasons and long winters. In summer, reindeer feed on fresh vegetation, and in winter they survive on last year's vegetation, or on lichens under the snow that they dig out by using their front hooves. Reindeer also have characteristics that enable domestication, such as the right social structure, the proper ease and speed of attachment to parents after birth, enough tolerance and flexibility in habitats and diet, a reduced flight response, and tolerance of humans and other outer stimuli.[2] The questions of when and how reindeer were introduced and domesticated in Fennoscandia are under debate.[3] The earliest written indication of tame reindeer dates back to 890 AD.[4] Wild reindeer continued to be an important prey animal even after the introduction of tame reindeer (read more in Chapter 6) (Fig. 7.1).

The use of tame reindeer in interior northern Fennoscandia from its introduction to present day can be divided into three sequential tenure systems: (1) small-scale reindeer husbandry as a complement in a predominantly fishing- and hunting-centered economy; (2) more specialized and intensive reindeer husbandry, or reindeer pastoralism, with large herds for production of milk, meat, and blood; and (3) extensive reindeer husbandry, or reindeer ranching, primarily for production of meat. In the first phase, most or all households had small numbers of tame reindeer they used to carry loads and haul sledges, or as decoys when they hunted

---

[2] Zeder (2012).

[3] Bjørnstad et al. (2012).

[4] Norwegian chieftain Ottar visited King Alfred the Great in England in 890 AD and explained that he was in possession of six tame reindeer and 600 unsold, probably his food and trade supply from wild reindeer (Bjørklund, 2019, p. 91).

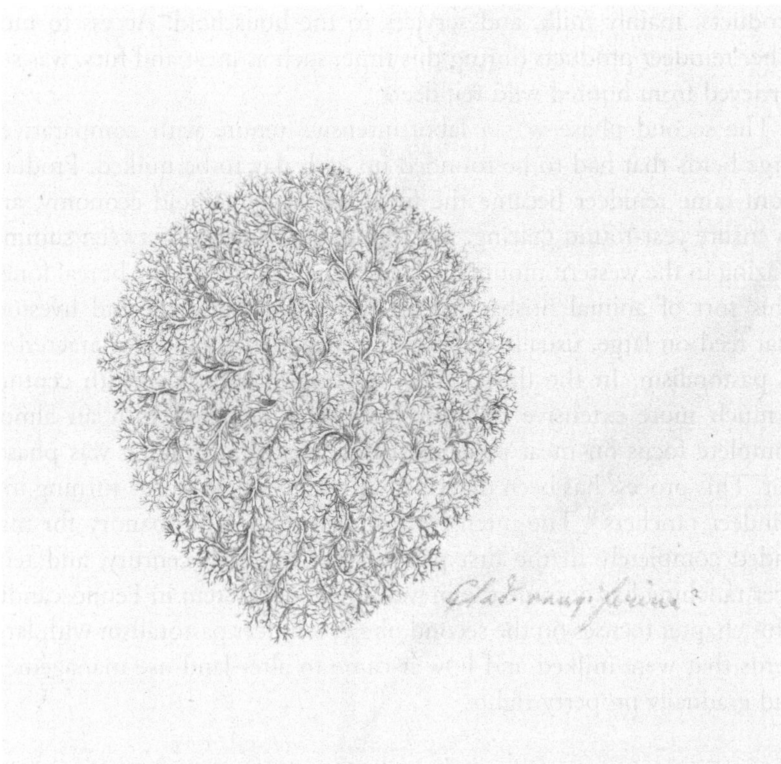

Fig. 7.1 Grey reindeer lichen (*Cladonia rangiferina*), depicted in 1695. *Note* The original image has been cropped (*Source* Iter lapponicum, Luefsta MS 92, Uppsala University Library, Sweden. Public domain. https://www.alvin-portal.org/alvin/imageViewer.jsf?dsId=ATTACHMENT-0057&pid=alvin-record:162152)

wild reindeer.[5] Reindeer milking was depicted in two illustrations by Olaus Magnus in his book *A Description of the Nordic Peoples*, published in 1555.[6] However, milking reindeer probably has a much older history; the oldest historical milking ground known dates to 1350.[7] During the entirety of this phase, hunting and fishing made up the backbone of the households' economy, although tame reindeer provided many essential

[5] Aronsson (1991, pp. 10–12).

[6] The pictures of reindeer milking are dated 1518–1519, when Olaus Magnus traveled the area.

[7] Egelkraut et al. (2018).

products, mainly milk, and services to the household. Access to most other reindeer products during this time, such as meat and furs, was still retrieved from hunted wild reindeer.

The second phase was a labor-intensive tenure with comparatively large herds that had to be rounded up each day to be milked. Products from tame reindeer became the focus of the household economy, and to ensure year-round grazing, most households moved between summer grazing in the western mountains and winter grazing in the boreal forest. This sort of animal husbandry with moveable lifestyles and livestock that feed on large, usually unfenced, grazing lands can be characterized as pastoralism. In the third phase, starting in the nineteenth century, a much more extensive reindeer husbandry emerged with an almost complete focus on meat production for sales, and milking was phased out. This process has been described as reindeer pastoralists turning into reindeer ranchers.[8] The intensive form of reindeer husbandry for milk ended completely in the first part of the twentieth century, and reindeer ranching has become the prevailing tenure system in Fennoscandia. This chapter focuses on the second phase, reindeer pastoralism with large herds that were milked and how it came to alter land-use management and gradually property rights.

What Is Pastoralism?

Pastoralists generally own large herds of grazing animals that they manage by long-distance movements between areas where the grazing is currently good. Their household economy is based on the use of many different products such as milk, blood, and meat from the animals, and for trade with external groups.[9] Since pastoralists typically have access to extensive or low-yielding lands, sizeable territories are a prerequisite if animals are to proliferate. Most types of grazing animals that pastoralists use are slow-growing species of herbivores that roam in herds searching for grazing.

---

[8] Ingold (1980). Tim Ingold's seminal book about circumpolar people's relationship with reindeer is called *Hunters, Pastoralists and Ranchers*.

[9] Galaty and Johnson (1990) and Khazanov (1994).

The animals are naturally adapted to varied and at times quite nutrient-poor feed. Pastoralists benefit when production rates increase, and herds enlarge if the animals are actively steered to areas with more nutritious or energy-rich grazing and drinking water or fresh snow. One can therefore say that grazing is the core resource that all pastoralists primarily have to manage. To be successful, the herder has to have a lot of experience and knowledge of environmental settings, weather conditions, risk aversion, and animal behavior.

In the seventeenth and eighteenth centuries, Sami were nomadic and moved with their herds to find suitable grazing based on the seasons. This lifestyle is sometimes referred to as *reindeer nomadism.*[10] We, however, have chosen to use the term *reindeer pastoralism* for two reasons. First, almost all households in interior northern Fennoscandia, even those that lived on fishing and hunting and accordingly had few reindeer, had a more or less mobile lifestyle in the early modern period (see Chapters 5 and 6). In its scholarly sense, the term *nomad* cannot be confined to those inhabitants who moved around in search of reindeer grazing but also includes nomadic fisher and hunter households. Second, pastoralism is a well-established concept worldwide that describes similar systems of animal husbandry. Use of the concept hence makes it possible to associate with pastoralist systems elsewhere around the world. However, one limitation is its all-inclusiveness, and that it sometimes is interchangeable with, for example, transhumance.[11]

The Debate About the Shift from Fishing and Hunting to Pastoralism

In recent decades, the shift from fishing and hunting to large-scale reindeer pastoralism has been an intensely studied topic among scholars in archaeology and history. The discussion has revolved around questions like When did it take place? Where did it start? Was it a slow

[10] Khazanov (1994, pp. 43–44).

[11] Transhumance is a specialized branch of an agricultural economy; it implies a division of labor and a settled form of agriculture with fixed dwellings. Shepherds take animals to pastures far away from the settled areas (Khazanov 1994, p. xxxvii).

or a sudden process? What were the driving forces behind the transition?[12] One of the problems with the debate itself is that it applies the concept of pastoralism too indiscriminately. Bjørklund summarizes it well: "this debate unfortunately, has not always made a distinction between 'husbandry' and 'pastoralism', the latter being used synonymously for any kind of reindeer husbandry."[13] In other words, many scholars have used the term *pastoralism* for both small-scale and large-scale reindeer husbandry.

Nevertheless, the debate centers on two contending interpretations of the timing of the transformation, where some scholars argue that it took place during the Viking Ages (800–1000 AD),[14] while others argue that it took place in the early modern period (1500–1800).[15] Members of the latter group have moreover interpreted the transition as occurring at a rather fast pace,[16] while the first group believes that it was a more gradual development that lasted until the end of the eighteenth century.[17] With regard to the question of what pushed the transformation to happen, many scholars have pointed to external factors, more specifically trade, and that reindeer pastoralism was the inhabitants' response to new opportunities for trade. Lundmark points instead to a crisis within the local society that forced the inhabitants to quit hunting and change to reindeer pastoralism.[18] According to this theory, the crisis was caused by the Swedish state's introduction of a new tax system combined with several years of harsh climate. By that note, the causes were partly self-imposed, through an increase in hunting pressure and rapid decline in prey animals, which resulted in a collapsing fur trade in the early seventeenth century (Fig. 7.2).

---

12 See Hansen and Olsen (2014, pp. 195–206), for an overview of different perspectives on the questions.

13 Bjørklund (2019, p. 91).

14 Storli (1993) and Bergman et al. (2013).

15 Hultblad (1968), Arell (1977), and Lundmark (1982).

16 Most pronounced by Lundmark (1982), who argued that it happened in Lule lappmark in the first decades of the seventeenth century.

17 Most pronounced by Bjørklund (2013), who argued that it was not an abrupt change: reindeer hunting and fishing were important up to the nineteenth century.

18 Lundmark (1982).

Fig. 7.2 Mountain reindeer (*Rangifer tarandus tarandus*), depicted in 1695 (*Source* Iter lapponicum, Luefsta MS 92, Uppsala University Library, Sweden. Public domain. https://www.alvin-portal.org/alvin/imageViewer.jsf?dsId=ATTACHMENT-0112&pid=alvin-record:162152)

Our position in this debate is that Bjørklund's distinction between husbandry and pastoralism is a key to understanding the transition.[19] Based on the written sources, we conclude that many households in interior north Fennoscandia had kept tame reindeer in small numbers since at least the ninth century. It is reasonable that the increase in tame reindeer began in the sixteenth and seventeenth centuries, and that it continued into the eighteenth and nineteenth centuries.[20] Hansen and Olsen emphasize that it is "important to keep in mind that the extent of reindeer herding even in the sixteenth century generally seems to have been very modest in relation to later levels of 'full nomadism.'"[21] There is also complementary evidence that supports the introduction of reindeer pastoralism in the early modern period: (1) the number of tame reindeer increased considerably (see section "Number of Reindeer"); (2) wild reindeer decreased rapidly, showing a strong correlation between the introduction of reindeer pastoralism in an area and almost simultaneous elimination of wild reindeer[22]; (3) the use of pitfall systems ended due to a combination of the decreasing number of wild reindeer and harm being done to tame reindeer; (4) a genetic shift occurred that separated wild and tame reindeer from each other.[23] To these arguments we add several institutional changes that took place in the early modern period that affected how rules and norms regarding land use developed. Our results show that the introduction of reindeer pastoralism brought alterations to older institutions for land use.

Number of Reindeer

The number of reindeer was officially counted twice in the seventeenth century, in 1605 and 1609. Results from the 1609 survey, which is the most thorough of the two counts, shows the number of reindeer

---

19 Bjørklund (2019, p. 91).

20 Hultblad (1968) and Bjørklund (2013).

21 Hansen and Olsen (2014, p. 194).

22 This development is described in Chapter 6.

23 Bjørnstad et al. (2012).

for each of the 177 taxpaying inhabitants in the four villages in Lule Lappmark, and the distribution of male and female reindeer and calves. Users in Tuorpon and Sirkas, situated mostly in the mountains, had on average twenty-seven and twenty-eight reindeer, respectively, including calves, while users in Sjokksjokk and Jokkmokk, situated mostly in the boreal forest, had on average thirteen and fifteen reindeer, respectively, including calves.[24] Only five users in the tax records had sixty or more reindeer, and the user with the most reindeer had seventy. Overall, the taxpayers in the two mountain villages had more reindeer than the taxpayers in the two forest villages, but the differences were not especially pronounced.

Unfortunately, there are no surveys of the number of reindeer available from the second half of the seventeenth century. There are, however, several contemporary descriptions from the late seventeenth and the eighteenth centuries that describe how inhabitants in the mountains by then had developed an economy that was heavily reliant on reindeer pastoralism.[25] According to Rheen, who was a priest in Lule lappmark in the 1660s, many inhabitants owned a hundred or a thousand reindeer, and some even more. He wrote that inhabitants had to take care of the reindeer "night and day, winter and summer."[26] Around 1675, another priest, Lundius, wrote that a rich inhabitant in the mountains could have more than a thousand reindeer.[27] Linnaeus described how he, in the morning of July 7, 1732, saw "some thousand reindeer" coming back from the pastures to be milked in the mountains in Lule lappmark.[28] In 1747, Högström, described how the inhabitants in Lule lappmark could own a few thousand reindeer and that they counted their fortune in reindeer.[29] According to him, one Sami village could hold 30,000 reindeer in total, and if these reindeer were distributed among the approximately 100 households in the village, they would average 300

[24] Lundmark (1982, pp. 211–215).

[25] Ehrenmalm (1743), Graan (1899), Linnaeus (2003), Lundius (1905), and Rheen (1897).

[26] Rheen (1897, p. 23).

[27] Lundius (1905, p. 20).

[28] Linnaeus (2003, p. 100); our translation.

[29] Högström (1747). Högström's description is mostly based on evidence from Kaitum.

reindeer per household. In 1741, Ehrenmalm traveled through the southernmost lappmark of Åsele and described that a medium-sized herd for inhabitants in the mountains there consisted of 150–200 reindeer.[30] In a dissertation from 1773, Samuel Öhrling, who grew up in Pite lappmark, wrote that it was difficult to say anything for sure with regard to the number of reindeer, and even more so because it was *ovisst för ägaren själv hur många renar han har* (uncertain for the owner himself how many reindeer he has).[31] Nonetheless, Öhrling estimated that inhabitants in the mountains in Pite lappmark owned at least 200 reindeer on average since many of them had 1,000 or 2,000 reindeer.[32] Much like in Lule lappmark, he described that inhabitants there counted their fortunes in reindeer.

It is difficult to estimate the number of reindeer in a herd correctly by just looking at it. None of the early modern accounts from interior northern Fennoscandia offer independent estimations performed by people looking at the same herd at the same time, which could have made the estimations more assertive. Just to illustrate the hardships of telling the number of animals in a livestock herd, we use the notes from a Danish scientific expedition to the Arabian Peninsula in the eighteenth century. On the expedition, three members, independent of each other, registered the size of the camel herd they had traveled with to Cairo.[33] The first person stated that there were between 1,500 and 1,600 camels in the caravan, the second person estimated "many thousand camels," while the third one stated that there were more than 400 camels. We do not know which of them came closest to the right answer, but the example shows how difficult it is to make good estimations of livestock herd sizes by just looking at them. It also indicates that the estimations

[30] Ehrenmalm (1743).

[31] Öhrling (1970 [1773], p. 10). It might have been that the owners knew how many reindeer they had but did not tell when asked by outsiders. In the late nineteenth century, the Swedish government made attempts to count reindeer, but according to Hultblad (1968, p. 141), the Sami neither wanted to nor could tell how many reindeer they had.

[32] Öhrling (1970 [1773], pp. 10–11).

[33] T. Hansen (2000 [1962], pp. 131–132). [Arabia Felix: The Danish Expedition of 1761–1767].

of reindeer numbers in the early modern accounts must be handled with some caution.[34]

Even so, it is evident from the reported numbers that there had been a dramatic shift in the seventeenth century and that many inhabitants then owned larger herds than before. However, it is also important to understand that not all animals in a herd had the same owner; each household member, which could also include servants, owned their own reindeer. Herds might also have included reindeer belonging to other households, since it was common for reindeer herder households to take care of so-called *skötesrenar*—reindeer that belonged to residential, often non-Sami, inhabitants.[35]

Many of the narrators in the early modern accounts, described how households in the mountains lived primarily on reindeer herding while households in the boreal forest lived primarily on fishing and hunting. The use of different resources impacted the households' economic possibilities, and mountain households were described as richer than those in the boreal forest.[36] According to the commissioner of the 1695 tax reform, more people lived in the mountains than in the boreal forest.[37] It is apparent that inhabitants in the mountains had more reindeer than inhabitants in the boreal forest but that reindeer pastoralism eventually became more widespread in the latter group. In the mid-eighteenth century, reindeer pastoralism spread to the easternmost parts of Lule lappmark, as discussed in Chapter 6.

Use of Reindeer

The written sources describe a versatile use of the reindeer that illuminates how important they must have been for inhabitants. Reindeer were

[34] T. Hansen (2000 [1962], p. 132) thinks the third person's estimation was closest to the actual number of camels in the herd.

[35] Hultblad (1968, pp. 146 ff.) has studied all the preserved probate inventories from Jokkmokk parish dating from 1799 to 1860. The average number of reindeer per owner was 148, and the four richest Sami had 1,054, 810, 760, and 602 reindeer.

[36] Graan (1899, pp. 32–49).

[37] Douglas (1695).

used as pack and draft animals to carry or pull loads. Apart from transport, reindeer also provided foodstuff, such as milk, blood, intestines, and meat. Reindeer were milked from summer to early fall. Milking was an elaborate task in which all the reindeer were first herded into pens, with the females separated and tethered, four by four, to special milking poles.[38] Reindeer were milked once or twice a day, which is described as a task for both men and women, young and old. It was time-consuming work, especially for households with many reindeer, which explains why all available labor was needed for milking. Some milk was drunk immediately but most of it was processed into cheese. The milk yield was relatively small and to make one cheese the size of a plate, the milk from at least ten reindeer was required. Households with few reindeer produced very small amounts of milk, and could only produce and trade reindeer cheese on a small scale. For households with many reindeer, on the other hand, cheese is described as a common form of merchandise, which they sold at market and bartered with neighboring groups. Each round of cheese had a high value and was therefore branded with the owner's personal mark. Many of the court rulings that dealt with theft highlight how cheeses were theft-prone due to their high value.[39]

Almost every part of the reindeer was taken care off in the household.[40] Antlers and bones were used for making tools and utensils, such as spoons and knife handles.[41] Sinews were skillfully handcrafted into twine and rope. Stomachs and intestines were cleaned and used as containers for storing blood and milk. The traditional slaughter time started in September, and continued as required until market time in January and February. Some of the meat was consumed immediately, cooked over an open fire, but it was also dried or otherwise preserved to be eaten in winter and spring. Reindeer meat was more important, in terms of diet, for households with many reindeer. Moreover, for

[38] Awebro (2000), Graan (1899, pp, 51, 56); Linnaeus (2003, p. 105), Rheen (1897, pp. 24–25), and Ruong (1969, ch. 10).

[39] One example would be a court ruling from 1706 when a man had stolen reindeer cheese from three persons: One man lost 48 rounds of cheese, another man lost 20, and a third man lost 5 (HRA 1706, pp. 54–55).

[40] Phebe Fjellström (1986, pp. 262–268) and Högström (1747, p. 120).

[41] Högström (1747, p. 84).

them, reindeer meat was an important trade good they sold to Swedish and Norwegian merchants at market. It was also bartered with non-Sami settlers and Sami households with few reindeer, on an everyday basis in return for dried fish or other products. Not least, the reindeer hides were either de-haired and tanned, or stretched out to dry with the hair in place. Reindeer fur, with its tremendous insulating property, was essential for surviving the winters in interior northern Fennoscandia and was thus an indispensable product in every household for both parkas and blankets. Additionally, furs were a tax good and a popular form of merchandise. Households used reindeer for all the above, albeit to varying degrees depending on numerous factors: spatial, temporal, number of reindeer owned, etc.

Grazing Conditions

Most pastoralist households in Lule lappmark in the seventeenth century stayed in the mountains in summer and in the boreal forest in winter. In summer, reindeer feed primarily on fresh vegetation, such as herbs, grasses, and sedges. Fresh vegetation has a high nutritive value and contains much energy, especially early in summer, and promotes both growth and milk production, as well as fat deposition in the animals.[42] The mountains offer especially rich grazing in summer, mostly on widespread alpine heaths and grasslands, willow thickets, and alpine birch forests.[43] The boreal forest also offers vegetation with high nutritive and energy value in summer, albeit not across as coherent and widespread areas as in the mountains. In the boreal forest, there is usually a dense tree layer of conifers under which little field vegetation grows. Suitable grazing is thus primarily located in more open terrain, such as on open

[42] Danell and Nieminen (1997, pp. 21–25).

[43] Today trees do not grow higher than about 800 m above sea level in Lule lappmark. From around 650 m above sea level, there is only mountain birch forest, and thereunder the boreal forest, dominated by spruce and Scots pine, begins. However, the treeline, for both birch and conifers, varies locally due to local climate and soil fertility. The treeline has also varied quite a lot over time.

mires, along shores of lakes and streams, and in terrain with deciduous trees.[44]

In winter, reindeer feed either on last year's vegetation, and on lichens growing on the ground or on trees. Old coniferous forests, especially those containing Scots pine, are often relatively rich in lichens, which makes them favorable locales for winter grazing.[45] Even if there is a lot of snow, reindeer are able to dig out ground lichens with their front hooves as long as the snow is relatively soft. The porousness of the snow depends on several factors, such as openness, forest structure, wind, temperature, and snow depth.[46] Conditions that favor soft snow are generally more prevalent in the boreal forest than they are in the mountains. The openness of alpine heaths, in combination with wind, tend to create a hard, ice-covered snow crust, which is unsuitable for grazing. Only windswept upland terrain in the mountains that is free from snow offers ground lichens and vegetation that reindeer can easily access in winter. According to Hultblad, the inaccessibility of winter grazing in the mountains first became a problem when households increased their reindeer herds in the seventeenth century.[47] The dearth of winter grazing invoked them to move to the boreal forest in winter. Wild reindeer, which were common before the introduction of reindeer pastoralism, stayed year-round in the mountains, and migrated to the boreal forest only when grazing conditions there became extremely severe.[48]

During the short growing season in northern Fennoscandia, reindeer must have as much time for undisturbed grazing as possible. It is necessary both for growth and to amass a reserve of body fat to survive the upcoming winter. Mosquitoes and heat have been considered a major nuisance for reindeer in summer. Deviant behavior among reindeer due to insects was described by Linnaeus in 1732. He noted that one single fly could upset a whole herd:

---

44 Axelsson Linkowski (2015).

45 Danell and Nieminen (1997, p. 23).

46 Roturier and Roué (2009).

47 Hultblad (1968, pp. 53–54, 123).

48 Ekman (1910, p. 9). See also Hultblad (1968, pp. 50–54).

> I remarked with astonishment how greatly the reindeer are incommoded in hot weather, insomuch that they cannot stand still a minute, no not a moment, without changing their posture, starting, puffing and blowing continually, and all on account of a little fly. Even though amongst a herd of perhaps five hundred reindeer there were not above ten of these flies, every one of the herd trembled and kept pushing its neighbor about. The fly meanwhile was trying every means to get at them; but it no sooner touched any part of their bodies, then they made an immediate effort to shake it off.[49]

Linnaeus clarifies that the turmoil was caused by the insect *Oestrus tarandi*, known today as the warble fly (*Hypoderma tarandi*, *Oestridae*). Furthermore, he concluded that heat and gnats/mosquitoes disturb the reindeer and stop them from eating:

> When these animals are permitted to face the wind, they run very fast and without intermission, in hopes of finding a place to cool themselves. Indeed, I observed one of the herds crowding close together under the shadow of a hill, on a spot covered with snow, to avoid the heat caused by the reflection of the sun from the snow in other places. These animals will eat nothing in hot weather, especially as the gnats are then very troublesome.[50]

In modern research of reindeer behavior during summer grazing, Hagemoen and Reimers have shown that parasitic oestrid flies, especially the warble fly and nose bot fly (*Cephenemyia trompe*, *Oestridae*), set off all the observed behavioral deviances among the studied reindeer.[51] Contrary to general opinion, neither mosquitoes nor heat seemed to have any substantial effects on the reindeer in the study. The oestrid flies' activity is tightly linked to air temperatures as they are unable to fly if it is colder than 7 °C in clear skies and 11 °C in cloudy skies. Moreover, wind has a negative effect on their activity. Blustery weather cools the air and

[49] Linnaeus (1811b, p. 22).
[50] Linnaeus (1811a, p. 308).
[51] Hagemoen and Reimers (2002).

creates turmoil, which makes it difficult for the fly to maneuver properly. Furthermore, no signs of heat stress were recorded in the studied reindeer, even on the hottest summer days. Opposite popular belief, it seems that reindeer do not run against the wind, or seek out northern slants, snow patches, or glaciers, primarily to cool down but rather to try to avoid oestrid flies. Even on blustery days, the air temperature above snow-covered surfaces is too cold for the oestrid fly to pass over, at least at the heights that the fly operates.

The optimal summer grazing condition for reindeer seem to be cold (below 7 °C), overcast, and windy weather, which minimizes the activity of the oestrid fly. In fact, in the absence of oestrid flies, weather parameters or mosquitoes had no influence on the conduct of the studied reindeer.[52] All in all, mountain regions offer more favorable settings for reindeer pastoralism in summer compared to the boreal forest, thanks to its rich grazing over widespread areas, occurrences of snow patches and glaciers, and cold and windy weather that decrease the activity of oestrid flies. In the boreal forest, favorable summer grazing is confined to open terrain where the vegetation is lusher, and where recurrent winds hinder oestrids from flying. The study concludes that oestrid flies can cause a significant decrease in reindeer's feeding and resting time, and a significant increase in time spent walking, running, and standing. Altogether, the cutback in grazing and resting time compromises the reindeer's physical condition at the end of the growing season.

Two Trajectories

When we look more closely into the development of reindeer herding in Lule lappmark, it is good to keep in mind that the majority of Sirkas and Tuorpon Sami villages were situated in the mountains while Sjokksjokk and Jokkmokk were situated in the boreal forest. In the early seventeenth century, the average number of reindeer per household in Sjokksjokk and Jokkmokk were eleven to twelve adult reindeer. Some households had very few reindeer, while others had many more than average, but

[52] Hagemoen and Reimers (2002).

no one had a particularly large herd.[53] For poor households, the relatively low animal number had to suffice for transport and some milking. These households either kept the herd close to their temporary location or, according to some sources, left it unattended for most of summer to graze freely in the boreal forest.[54] The average number of animals did not change much during the seventeenth century. The written accounts differentiated between households in the mountains, which generally had more reindeer, and households in the boreal forest, which generally had no or fewer reindeer. In the latter group, fishing and hunting were described as fundamental for survival.[55] Any surplus that the latter produced came from fishing, hunting, gathering of eggs and feathers from wild birds, or from collecting berries or shoe hay (to line soft leather shoes or boots for warmth and stability).[56] Nonetheless, the economic characterization of households into either of these two categories in the seventeenth century clouds the fact that important changes in animal numbers also ensued among households in the boreal forest. Starting in the westernmost parts, some inhabitants began to amass more reindeer and migrate to the mountains in summer to access beneficial grazing.[57] In the mid-eighteenth century, many households in the eastern part of Sjokksjokk had likewise developed reindeer pastoralism. Although these eastern households had reindeer herds as large as western pastoralists, they seem to have initiated a more stationary tenure system that was based in the boreal forest year-round.[58]

By considerably enlarging the reindeer herds between the sixteenth and eighteenth centuries, most households in Sirkas and Tuorpon entered onto an economic path apart from most households in Sjokksjokk and Jokkmokk. For the former, the enlargement of the herds was achievable primarily through having easy access to lands for summer

53 Lundmark (1982, pp. 211–212).

54 Högström (1747, p. 85).

55 Hultblad (1968, p. 141).

56 Chapters 5, 6, and 8.

57 In a court ruling from 1707, reindeer had been stolen from three users from Sjokksjokk in September when they were grazing in the mountains (HRA 1707, pp. 145–149).

58 Hultblad (1968, pp. 141–142). In Chapter 6, we discuss the correlation between the extinction of wild reindeer and introduction of reindeer pastoralism in the eastern part of Sjokksjokk.

grazing in the mountains. Already in the sixteenth century, these users had had more reindeer than the users in the boreal forest, and rather swiftly this had developed into an economy based wholly on the tenure of many hundreds of reindeer moving between mountains and forests. There was a correlation between the number of reindeer and the need to relocate: the more animals a household owned, the farther they had to move to find grazing.[59] As discussed in more detail later in this chapter, the new moving patterns caused some tension between users in Jokkmokk and Sjokksjokk on the one hand and users in Sirkas and Tuorpon on the other hand.

Almost within one century, all households in the mountains had become reindeer pastoralists, and the more animals they accumulated, the less time they could spend on fishing and hunting. It was a shift to a more efficient, high-yielding production system with a higher degree of specialization, which decidedly would turn out to be fortunate for the economic development of these households. The reindeer became an important capital or cash asset for the household, and by producing a surplus of reindeer products, such as meat, cheese, and furs, that could be sold at market or bartered with neighbors, households made substantial profits. These profits were in turn invested in a variety of commodities, such as silver jewelry, tobacco, steel, wool, or alcohol.[60] Still, the new tenure system, where some households accumulated several hundreds of animals, led to more pronounced inequalities between rich and poor households.[61]

Mobility, Flexibility, and Reciprocity

With regard to land use, especially for grazing, reindeer pastoralists require mobility, flexibility, and reciprocity much like other pastoralists do.[62] Since grazing varies spatially and temporally, habitual relocation

[59] Hultblad (1968, p. 135).

[60] Phebe Fjellström (1986, pp. 75–76).

[61] Kvist (1989, p. 100).

[62] Fernández-Giménez (2002).

became the strategy that reindeer pastoralists applied in order to optimize the use of largely erratic resources. Moreover, moving patterns depended on many factors, not least weather, winds, and vacant pastures. Moves often could be performed with only a little forward planning, such as when the winds suddenly turned or when the grazing conditions changed, which called for a highly flexible herding strategy. With a growing number of reindeer came an augmented focus on grazing, so mobility and flexibility inevitably had to become integrated features of the tenure system.

Fernández-Giménez remarks that pastoralists also have to be sure of access to natural resources and therefore identifies a paradox between their simultaneous need for both security and flexibility.[63] In addition to being flexible, reindeer pastoralists needed some degree of predictability to achieve food security for their household members. It therefore became customary for households to return to roughly the same locations every year, and to travel along approximately the same routes between summer and winter grazing. The routes also included several predestined locations for spring and fall grazing. In the eighteenth century, a recurring topic for the local court was to decide which inhabitants had the right to stay where with their reindeer during the seasonal migrations, and sometimes to decide for how long they could stay at specific locations. One of the keys to understanding land-use strategies among early modern reindeer pastoralists is to analyze the balance between flexibility and predictability, and how inhabitants negotiated to maintain this steady state.

Reindeer pastoralism has always been a precarious business, especially due to recurring menaces, such as animal pests, predators, and starvation due to lack of grazing. For most households, the principal strategy for coping with uncertainties, was to strive for the herds to be as large as possible. Owning a large herd increased a household's chances of having at least a few animals left after a crisis. Another strategy was to establish robust relationships with relatives, neighbors, and other households that could lend a helping hand if some misfortune suddenly hit your herd. Good relations worked as a kind of insurance scheme and

[63] Fernández-Giménez (2002, pp. 50–51).

was founded on services and reciprocal services. The establishment of social relations was, among other things, tightly connected to marriage patterns.[64] Strategic marriages were a way of creating coalitions that knit families together, in good times and bad times. Households gained from cooperation, especially during migration when they formed more or less transient alliances depending on grazing conditions and migration routes. Large herds required a lot of manpower to perform the many time-consuming work tasks, such as guarding, gathering, and milking. Wealthier households, with many reindeer, had to have employees, often young men and women from other households who lived with the family and worked with both herding and domestic chores. Another strategy that rich households used in order to get more manpower was to create partnerships with poor households. For the latter group, cooperation with rich households primarily offered enhanced food security.

Three Steps

The development of pastoralism from the seventeenth century onward, which focused on milk and meat production from many animals, gradually evoked a redistribution of the rights to winter grazing lands in the boreal forest in eastern Lule lappmark. Reindeer pastoralism also led to the introduction of a new property regime for summer grazing in the western mountains. During the eighteenth century, the tenure of reindeer grazing in Lule lappmark had been transformed into a well-established common-property regime. As it turned out, all inhabitants in the Sami villages had well-regulated rights to grazing lands. A household, or a group of households, could have rights to use a specific location, but the use could also, if needed, be renegotiated in and confirmed by the local court. The development of a common-property regime for inhabitants with large reindeer herds can be described as taking place in three stages: the first step involved households in the mountains that used winter grazing in the boreal forest, the second step invoked increased competition over grazing between users in villages in the mountains, and

[64] Nordin (2009).

the third step was when users in villages in the boreal forest started to use grazing lands in the mountains.

As households in Tuorpon and Sirkas started to have more reindeer in the seventeenth century, they began to move with the reindeer to the boreal forest in the southeastern part of Lule lappmark in winter to access lichen. This was part of the first stage described above. The rights to winter grazing lands belonged to inhabitants in Sjokksjokk and Jokkmokk, and their access to natural resources was mostly organized within *skatteland*. The migration has left relatively few traces in the court material, mostly because the main resource that inhabitants from Tuorpon and Sirkas needed in the boreal forest—winter grazing—was not so much in demand by the rights holders there. Thus, it seldom resulted in conflicts that had to be taken to court. Moreover, visiting households often paid rent to the rights holders for letting them graze their reindeer.[65] Almost all available information about this early phase of reindeer pastoralism instead originates from mid-eighteenth-century court rulings where inhabitants refer to prior circumstances as evidence in ongoing conflicts over grazing rights. For example, a ruling from 1765 shows how three users were prohibited from letting their reindeer graze on land that belonged to six other users, all nine of them were from Sjokksjokk. As it was made clear in court that the three defendants really needed more grazing in spring and summer, the court concluded that they should be allowed to use grazing in Sirkas. The principal argument being that users in Sirkas had to tolerate intrusion from users in Sjokksjokk on their lands since the former spent their winters in Sjokksjokk in great numbers.[66] The tradition to pay lease for grazing

[65] The tradition to pay a lease, in cash or in kind, for grazing rights in the forest is also known to have occurred in Ume lappmark (Norstedt et al. 2014, p. 234). When inhabitants from Pite lappmark used grazing lands belonging to users in neighboring Lule lappmark, they had to pay rent (Hultblad 1968, p. 93 and p. 399, evidence 768a). Regarding the abundance of winter grazing, Norstedt et al. (2014, p. 232) conclude that users in the boreal forest in Ume lappmark during the 1670s controlled much more winter grazing than they used. According to their extrapolations, users in the boreal forest had less than 500 reindeer combined. The boreal forest received about 6,600 reindeer from the mountains for winter grazing each year. In spite of this, they estimate, users had enough grazing resources left to feed an additional 32,000 reindeer.

[66] Hultblad (1968, p. 397, evidence 715a).

seems to have disappeared by then, and it was now a reciprocal agreement where users from different villages could stay on each other's lands. Gradually, users in Sjokksjokk had acquired rights to use lands in Sirkas, and vice versa. The case described above does not suggest that there was a general consent that let all inhabitants freely use lands belonging to other village members for grazing. It rather shows that it once had been common for users in Sami villages in the mountains to use winter grazing on lands belonging to users in Sami villages in the boreal forest. We assume that the organization of grazing, in the majority of cases, was agreed upon between users without involvement of the court. The case also shows that the jurisdiction of the court went beyond the single village. Obviously, the court could decide that users in one village had the right to use lands in another village. It demonstrates that the court considered and treated grazing like a CPR, and that the inhabitants had developed a common-property regime regulating who had access.

The second step in the development of a common-property regime in Lule lappmark was characterized by users in Sirkas and Tuorpon seeking both flexibility in mountain grazing and secure grazing rights. It could seem contradictory, on the one hand, to be working for the right to roam freely in search for grazing and on the other hand to be working for the right to use specific locations. There are few historical sources that can tell us about land use in the mountains before the seventeenth century or how it was organized. The organization of inhabitants in Sami villages is mentioned for the first time in tax records from the sixteenth century.[67] However, from the seventeenth and eighteenth centuries there are several historical sources that can give more detailed insights into how the use of land was organized. There are court rulings from the local courts, a tax record (*jordebok*) from 1695, and notes citing local inhabitants as part of the assignment to delineate the Swedish-Norwegian border in the 1740s.[68] These records point to the fact that the land division was not very strict between the villages in Lule lappmark's mountains. A court ruling from 1751 described how grazing lands in the mountains

[67] Hultblad (1968, p. 38).

[68] Wiklund and Qvigstad (1909) published the minutes written by border engineers during their work to delineate the Swedish-Norwegian border in 1745, and it was used by Holmbäck (1922) in his inquiry about *lappskatteland*.

were used alternately by users from Sirkas and Tuorpon.[69] Another court ruling from the same court in 1770 described how grazing lands in the mountains in Tuorpon and Sirkas were distributed randomly between users.[70] The overlap suggests that the grazing was organized more or less collectively. This assumption is strengthened by the tax record from Lule lappmark in 1695, which among other things tells us that eighteen out of forty-three users in Sirkas could not be connected to a specific plot of land.[71] This in turn suggests that they used the grazing land in common within the village. A similar conclusion can be drawn from Tuorpon, where the tax record from 1695 do not state anything about inhabitants being connected to specific lands. Nonetheless, court records from the eighteenth century show that individual lands existed in Tuorpon, and that they in fact were connected to specific users. Holmbäck, though, concludes that the division into individual *skatteland* in Tuorpon could not have been strict.[72] It is backed up by a source from 1745 in which a couple of users in Tuorpon told engineers doing preparatory work for the demarcation of the Swedish-Norwegian border that the Sami villages in the mountains (*fjällsamebyarna*) Sirkas and Tuorpon often overlapped "since Sami belonging to both of these villages mostly *ligga om varandra* (lay on each other) as good friends."[73] The engineers were also told that grazing land in the mountains was used as the inhabitants pleased (*efter behag*), even if there were more users from Sirkas farther to the north.[74]

Another example that corroborates a collective organization of grazing in the mountains comes from neighboring Pite lappmark. In the tax record from 1695, only one of thirty-two inhabitants in Norrvästerby Sami village in the mountains of Pite lappmark could be connected to a specific location, while the remaining thirty-one were described as being without land and as moving about in the mountains.[75] There is a similar example in the tax record for Ume lappmark from 1695 that described

[69] Hultblad (1968, p. 368, evidence 213a).

[70] Hultblad (1968, pp. 370–371, evidence 270a).

[71] Holmbäck (1922, p. 18) and Hultblad (1968, p. 89).

[72] Holmbäck (1922, p. 19).

[73] Holmbäck (1922, p. 19).

[74] Wiklund and Qvigstad (1909, pp. 17–18).

[75] Holmbäck (1922, p. 20).

that only two of twenty-one inhabitants in Ran Sami village in the mountains could be connected to specific lands. In the tax record, next to the name of one of the inhabitants from Ran, it is clearly written that he did not have a specific plot and that he moved about in the mountains as did all his neighbors. Holmbäck concluded that this remark was valid also for eighteen other inhabitants in Ran who were listed in the tax record.[76]

At the same time, court rulings from the eighteenth century tell of an increasing competition over grazing in the mountains, especially between users from Tuorpon and Sirkas. The goal was to formally secure locations where households could stay in the summer, and during migrations between winter and summer grazing. Users needed to make sure that the tenure system was as predictable as possible in an otherwise unpredictable setting. Some of the formal institutions that were instigated by the court in the first half of the eighteenth century might have gone back to older, more informal institutions, and might even have been codifications of rights to locations that were already in use. But according to the court rulings, most of the rules were new and illustrated how fast land use in the mountains transformed into a more intensive tenure system. The seventeenth century had seen an increase in the number of reindeer, but a relatively stable number of people in Lule lappmark. The eighteenth century on the other hand, saw both an increase in the number of people and more and more people owning many reindeer. Hence, the competition over grazing became more salient, and the desire to attach user rights to specific locations became a more frequent topic for the local court to handle.

In the eighteenth century, more strict rules developed in the mountains regarding which grazing lands could be used by whom, and for what time periods. By then, many of the lands that were particularly sizeable had also been divided between several users. This had given rise to a new land structure, that co-existed with the old land structure, so each user's grazing land was arranged in a pattern that more or less adjoined the plots in the mountains in northwest to plots in the boreal forest. This followed how the reindeer herds moved to find available grazing over

76 Holmbäck (1922, p. 22).

the year. These new lands, in-between the summer and winter locations, were fairly small compared to the old *skatteland* in the boreal forest, and they were often shared between several users. In numerous court cases from the 1730s to 1740s, where user rights were discussed, it becomes apparent that a user could have numerous lands. For example, one court case shows how Olof Olsson Ainil in Tuorpon, had at least four plots of land.[77] However, since he was not the only user, the questions of how they should be used and by whom had been taken to court. Another court ruling described how Anders Paggesson in Sirkas had been using at least six different lands between 1733 and 1735. Five of them seem to have been used for grazing and at the sixth, he had the right to fish. On each of the five lands used for grazing, there were at least three other users involved which had given rise to conflicts.[78] In a third example, from a court ruling in 1750, it is clear that Pål Eriksson Tulpa, his brother, and another user, all three from Tuorpon, shared the use of at least three plots.[79]

Moving routes between grazing areas seem to have been quite fixed, and it often became an undertaking for the court to decide if users could stay temporarily on another user's land during migration. In the rulings, the court could for example stipulate how many days certain visitors were allowed to stay in a location before they had to move on with their reindeer. In one court ruling from 1733, a user in Tuorpon got the right to stay for seven days in a location that belonged to two users in Sirkas.[80] In another court ruling from 1731, a man in Tuorpon was allowed to use a certain land and some years later, in 1746, he in turn contested another user who had moved over that same land. The court found that the intruder's ancestors had used it earlier, and so it was stipulated that he could stay there for two days during migration.[81] In yet another court case, it was decided that Anders Larsson Lanni in Tuorpon and his son were permitted to stay for one day, or if it was on a weekend for two

[77] Hultblad (1968, pp. 356–357, evidence 25a, b, c, d).

[78] Hultblad (1968, p. 385, evidence 476a, b, c, d).

[79] Hultblad (1968, p. 366, evidence 191a).

[80] Hultblad (1968, p. 385, evidence 476b).

[81] Hultbland (1968, p. 358, evidence 37c).

days, on a certain land when they migrated.[82] The court could not only decide who had the right to what land, it could moreover stipulate that users could not bring *skötesrenar* (reindeer that belonged to other households) on to lands that were shared among several users.[83] The court could also stipulate that users with a great proportion of male reindeer in their herds could not keep them on lands that were shared with users that had a great proportion of *vajor* (female reindeer) since it might be harmful for the latter.[84]

Other matters that the court dealt with were, for example, whether or not land should be divided between users, or if someone should lose rights to use certain lands. An illustration of this comes from a court ruling in 1735 wherein the court said no to a request from Pål Persson in Sirkas to become the sole user of a plot of land. Instead, the court decided that he had to *beta klöv om klöv* (graze hoof by hoof) with another user. However, to be able to share the grazing equally, both users had to arrive at the location around the same time in fall since this was a fall grazing location.[85] In a similar court ruling from 1754, the court stipulated that two users sharing a land in Tuorpon had to arrive around the same time to get a just distribution of grazing.[86] The court could also decide that users with relatively few reindeer had to give up land they did not need for others to graze their animals, and that users with many reindeer could obtain more grazing land when needed. The results of these negotiations were warranted by a phenomenon called *renmakt*, a term that literally could be translated into "reindeer might" or "reindeer power," which meant that users' rights were linked to possession of reindeer. A couple of court cases from the 1770s show how these proceedings could end. One case from 1772 concerns a user, Anders Nilsson Skubb, in Tuorpon who stated that he lacked summer grazing. He was permitted by the court to use a certain land individually, and also to share two lands

[82] Hultbland (1968, p. 356, evidence 18b).

[83] Hultblad (1968, p. 366, evidence 191a). The users should abstain from taking care of Norwegian or Swedish reindeer on the land.

[84] Hultblad (1968, p. 356, evidence 25a).

[85] Hultblad (1968, p. 385, evidence 478a).

[86] Hultblad (1968, p. 357, evidence 25 g).

with three users.[87] It is noteworthy that Nilsson Skubb owned as many reindeer as the other three users together. In another court ruling, two users in Tuorpon, Amma Larsson Tjagge and Per Anundsson, stated that they lacked grazing land and asked if the court could point them to a place that was available.[88] They were referred to a land with summer and fall grazing that no one was using. In a third ruling on the same theme from 1775, a user, Pål Turesson Pirkit, in Tuorpon obtained the right to use a grazing land in spite of protests from two users in Sirkas who claimed that their ancestors formerly had used the land.[89] The court's formal argument for handing over the land to Turesson Pirkit was that he owned many reindeer. All of these cases illustrate ongoing negotiations and renegotiations between users over how grazing resources should be distributed.

For households, it became more and more important to follow approximately the same route every year, to stay in approximately the same locations, and to cooperate with other users as their reindeer herds grew in size. These components, characterized by predictability and reciprocity, contributed to the long-term endurance of an otherwise relatively vulnerable tenure system, which in turn granted a more robust living situation for household members. The inhabitants developed a deep knowhow about the land, such as conditions for grazing, water supplies, and prevalence of other natural resources, as well as familiarity with the best locations for establishing living grounds where they could erect the *goahte* (Lule Sami for the tent that inhabitants lived in). This knowhow was transferred to the next generation, because the same lands were often used for many generations. Households also made investments along their routes, for example, by setting up storage buildings for food and gear at locations they passed during migrations. Many court rulings from the seventeenth century dealt with theft or burglary, and it was not uncommon that the perpetrator had broken into such storage buildings to steal reindeer cheese, cauldrons, fishing gear, clothes,

---

87 Hultblad (1968, p. 369, evidence 259c).

88 Hultblad (1968, p. 370, evidence 261a).

89 Hultblad (1968, p. 375, evidence 354a).

shoes, fabrics, or other items.[90] Food items, such as meat and cheese, could also be stored in mountain crevasses that were situated on the household's land.[91] Firewood was a much-used resource in the household, and shortages could arise, particularly in the mountains where fire materials were relatively sparse. Consequently, it was sometimes important to regulate the use of firewood.[92] Households could also invest in *renvallar* (gathering pens) that were used for milking.[93] All in all, in the largely unpredictable setting that dictated much of the tenure system for reindeer, it was a rational strategy to return to the same locations, and to travel approximately along the same routes every year. Retracing their steps allowed inhabitants to control as many factors as possible in a largely uncontrollable world, and thus make food production more predictable.

Users needed access to many lands with different grazing qualities to be able to keep large herds of reindeer alive and prospering. Grazing was, however, not the only ecological factor that was important to be successful in this tenure system. Another feature was that reindeer prefer to stay in locations where they can avoid insects in summer. Access to these kinds of locations could be negotiated in the local courts, which the following example from 1774 shows. In the ruling, Anders Nilsson Guväla in Sirkas had complained in court that another Sirkas user, Anti Ivarsson Abril, had trespassed onto his land.[94] Ivarsson Abril replied that he lacked "ice and snow land" that could protect his reindeer from

---

[90] A few examples are HRA (1699, pp. 70–75; 1704, pp. 814–818) (in this case, 202 reindeer cheese rounds that belonged to five people had been stolen); HRA (1706, p. 57).

[91] HRA (1701, p. 403). Tomas Amundsson Nabri in Sjokksjokk explained to the court in 1774 that he had lost at least 80 cheese rounds that had been stored under a large stone at his summer grazing land (Hultblad 1968, p. 411, evidence 937b).

[92] Firewood was sometimes in short supply, and the court could therefore apply restrictions on its use. In a conflict where a man from Sirkas and his son had used a land belonging to users in Pite lappmark, the court found that they could use the land in the fall because the users from Pite lappmark only used it in spring and summer. However, they were not allowed to use juniper (*Juniperus communis*) growing there for firewood, but had to bring their own firewood (Hultblad 1968, p. 307, evidence 344c).

[93] Aronsson (1991).

[94] Hultbland (1968, p. 389, evidence 526c). The court ruling mentions mosquitoes, but the word probably was used as a collective term for all insects that were a nuisance to reindeer. It was more likely different types of oestrid flies that caused the worst problem for the reindeer and made them seek out snow and ice patches.

mosquitoes. The court suggested that the two parties exchange lands so both could have lands with access to ice and snow in summer. In a similar case from 1777, user Lars Pålsson Rimpi, in Sjokksjokk, who migrated to the mountains in summer with users from Sirkas, complained that he lacked lands where his reindeer could avoid mosquitoes "in the strongest heat of summer."[95] Pålsson Rimpi got permission by the court to use a land belonging to two other users that they did not need in the middle of summer. The authorization was, however, restricted to seven to ten days.

The last case takes us to the third stage in the establishment of a common-property regime for inhabitants with large reindeer herds in Lule lappmark. In this stage, some users in Jokkmokk and Sjokksjokk had begun to amass larger reindeer herds, and some of them had also started to move to the mountains to find better summer grazing. As mentioned before, the earliest court rulings with descriptions of users in the western parts of Sjokksjokk's boreal forest taking reindeer to the mountains came from the early eighteenth century.[96] During the eighteenth century, it gradually became more and more common for users in villages in the boreal forest to access summer grazing in the mountains. In 1721, two brothers from Sjokksjokk could not guard their reindeer from insects and instead they ended up on a land that belonged to some users in Tuorpon which resulted in the latter filing a trespassing complaint in court.[97] The court resolved the matter by permitting the brothers to use the land, and to move together with the users in Tuorpon, under the condition that the latter were permitted to use lands in Sjokksjokk. It shows that reciprocity had developed regarding the organization of grazing between villagers in the mountains and villagers in the boreal forest. Some users had become dependent on resources that another village controlled, and a functional solution was to share the resources equally between them. It resembled an earlier mentioned situation where the court argued that the users in Sirkas had to tolerate the intrusion of

[95] Hultblad (1968, p. 379, evidence 391b).

[96] HRA (1707, pp. 145–146). Three users in Sjokksjokk told the court that their reindeer had been stolen when their animals were grazing in the mountains in September of 1706.

[97] Hultblad (1968, p. 399, evidence 767a).

users in Sjokksjokk during spring and summer since the former spent winters on lands that belonged to users in Sjokksjokk.[98]

The custom of paying rent for winter grazing in the boreal forest was probably downplayed due to the more reciprocal exchange of user rights between villagers. One court ruling shows, for example, how a land that was situated on the border between two villages was divided to permit users in Tuorpon to also use land situated in Jokkmokk without payment, but only in the fall.[99] Not all attempts made by users from the villages in the boreal forest were successful in establishing grazing rights in the mountains. Nonetheless, these efforts also show how badly users from Jokkmokk and Sjokksjokk wanted summer grazing in the mountains. For example, in a court ruling from 1763, a user in Tuorpon complained that four users in Jokkmokk had repeatedly trespassed onto his land.[100] It resulted in a verdict wherein the court prohibited the latter from this trespassing. In another ruling from 1774, a user in Jokkmokk was prohibited from using a particular land since it belonged to a user in Tuorpon, but he was instead pointed to another land in Tuorpon where he could stay with his reindeer.[101] According to the rulings, one explanation behind why users in the boreal forest had access to grazing in the mountains was that they had obtained permission to graze there directly from the rights holder.[102] Such assurances would discard any potential claims from other users belonging to the same village to let them share the grazing. For the rights holder, it was probably a strategic choice to formally share the grazing land with a user from a forest village, since he or she could get access to winter grazing in the boreal forest in exchange.[103]

---

[98] Hultblad (1968, p. 397, evidence 715a).

[99] RA SH (1769, pp. 504–505). In this case, the users in Tuorpon were only allowed to graze their reindeer on the land, not hunt or fish.

[100] Hultblad (1968, p. 357, evidence 25i).

[101] Hultblad (1968, pp. 357–358, evidence 33b). Other court rulings wherein users in Jokkmokk and Sjokksjokk were allowed to use land in Sirkas and Tuorpon are Hultblad (1968: p. 354, evidence 1a [1753]; p. 358, evidence 45b [1754]; p. 411, evidence 937a [1773 and 1774]; p. 412, evidence 940a [1772]; p 422, evidence 1056a [1774]; p. 425, evidence 1082c [1754]). Some lands were situated in the high mountains (*högfjäll*).

[102] Hultblad (1968, p. 358, evidence 46a).

[103] Hultblad (1968, p. 143).

Another strategy to get access to grazing resources across village boundaries was through strategic marriages. Hultblad showed that the number of intervillage marriages increased after mid-eighteenth century.[104] It had several benefits, including in the short term that it enhanced cooperation between villages that gained both parties, and in the long term that children resulting from these marriages would inherit both winter and summer grazing. Instead of paying rent for grazing, households could form coalitions based on mutual interests. An important factor in reindeer pastoralism was intricate patterns of reciprocity between practitioners, and through strategic marriages some of the necessary bonds could be facilitated, which in turn contributed to a more robust tenure system. As was mentioned in Chapter 3, part of the discussion about the origin of CPRs in mediaeval Europe has focused on the transition from an economy based on family and kinship to an economy in which neighbor relations grew in importance. In this transition, people started to make alliances, mainly with persons with the same occupation.[105] For reindeer pastoralists, it was important to have good relations with one's family and extended family, but it is also clear that relations to users in neighboring villages grew in importance over time.[106] We showed earlier how the use of grazing in the mountains often overlapped in Sirkas and Tuorpon. Eventually, a parallel development took place between users in the mountains and users in the boreal forest. It was a development where the adjacent border between villages in the mountains and the boreal forest started to dissolve, and where the emerging villages took on a more elongated northwestern-southeastern geographic orientation compared to the previously much smaller and more circularly shaped villages. These changes can be interpreted as highly functional responses to the needs created by a new land-use pattern, categorized as reindeer pastoralism, which focused on use of grazing resources.

---

[104] Hultblad (1968, p. 143).

[105] de Moor (2015, p. 3).

[106] Some rights holders continued to collect rent for winter grazing; e.g., Hultblad (1968, p. 365, evidence 178) where one user had paid with a two-year-old reindeer and the other with 16 *skilling*.

Creating a Common-Property Regime

During the eighteenth century, a common-property regime with detailed rules of use had been established with regard to the most important resource for reindeer, i.e., grazing lands, encompassing all villages under the jurisdiction of the local court in Jokkmokk.[107] The regime had many of the characteristics that grant the management of CPRs success, including a vivid and ongoing negotiation among users to try to define a just distribution of resources and who should have the right to use them.[108] These negotiations were based on extensive knowhow about local settings, and were executed by local people who lived in the area under similar circumstances as the plaintiffs and the defendants. The court rulings themselves show that the court worked as a collective-choice arena and that local users were involved in the process of defining the rules of use. Simply put, it was a local arena where inhabitants solved conflicts and disputes regarding natural resource use. The court not only solved conflicts as they occurred, it also facilitated the expansion of reindeer pastoralism. The commonly elaborated rules generated favorable conditions for pastoralists with room for more flexibility and increased mobility. At the same time, the local court warranted continuity, which contributed to reliability and stability for the tenure system. Still, it was not a completely egalitarian system as most of the court's decisions favored users with many reindeer.

Flexibility was created in many ways; one was through a continuing discussion about how land should be used and who had the right to use it. The court's role as a place where user rights could be negotiated and the court's members functioned as mediators and surveyors is important to emphasize. As a collective-choice arena that could decide the conditions for how land could be used, the court also worked as a guide for how other users could solve problems regarding land use, such as access to grazing land. What we, today, can read in the court rulings is most likely only a fraction of all the discussions that took place about land use and grazing rights that happened between users. Reindeer pastoralism,

---

[107] Up to 1751 it also included Kaitum and the northern part of Sjokksjokk.

[108] Ostrom (1990, p. 90; 2005, pp. 258–270).

to function well, required better reciprocal arrangements with other households than fishing and hunting did during the same period. These reciprocal arrangements included marriages between households to obtain access to grazing lands throughout the year, and negotiations and oral agreements between households that involved permission to use other users' lands in case of emergency.

Grazing land in the mountains must be viewed as a CPR with strong user rights. How the land had been used earlier and if a household had used a certain location during a long period of time was important to determine future use, and it was something that the court deliberated. The rulings show that lands could be inherited. However, the court could also decide that a user could lose the right to a land if it had not been used. Or, if a land was underutilized for grazing, the court could decide to redistribute the rights to other users. If someone had many reindeer and contributed to the village by paying tax, the court could consider it more important to afford him or her access to grazing rather than the original rights holder who might have had fewer reindeer and paid little or no tax. Yet, no one was allowed to routinely share lands that already had rightful users if the grazing resources were limited. If a tax-paying household with many reindeer lacked grazing resources for one reason or another, it triggered a search for available grazing where the household could be designated grazing rights by the court. Hence, although the reindeer was private property, the collective natural resource, i.e., grazing lands, that made it possible to manage reindeer was a collective resource.

The conditions for winter grazing in the boreal forest varied a lot over the season, which called for a high degree of flexibility among reindeer herders[109] and implies that winter grazing in the early modern era had to be organized in smaller user groups rather than large settlements as Tanner claimed.[110] Our conclusion is corroborated by Kuoljok, who states that for practical reasons reindeer herds must be divided into smaller groups during winter.[111] Demant-Hatt wrote a book about her year living in a reindeer herder household in Torne lappmark in the

[109] Roturier and Roué (2009).

[110] Tanner (1929) See also Chapter 3).

[111] Kuoljok (2011).

early twentieth century and described winter grazing as a highly flexible system where the family mostly lived on its own and moved with the herds as frequently as every two weeks in winter, in constant search for better grazing.[112] Although she described the reindeer rancher phase of history, it is possible to draw some parallels to our study period, when the pastoralist economy shifted from reindeer milk to meat production. The common denominator is the importance of mobility and flexibility in the grazing regime. Regardless whether the outcome was milk or meat, the main goal for reindeer herders was to find good enough grazing for the reindeer to survive and prosper, as is the central goal for modern-day reindeer herders.[113]

In summary, the tenure system for reindeer that evolved in the seventeenth and eighteenth centuries was based on a collective organization of extensive grazing resources instead of the restricted household territories that had characterized the previous system. In this development, households in Sirkas and Tuorpon had an advantage compared to households in Jokkmokk and Sjokksjokk, mainly due to the former group's access to favorable summer grazing in the mountains.

References

Arell, Nils. 1977. Rennomadismen i Torne lappmark: markanvändning under kolonisationsepoken i fr.a. Enontekis socken. PhD dissertation, Skytteanska samfundet, Umeå, Sweden. http://www.diva-portal.org/smash/record.jsf?pid=diva2%3A616377&dswid=6098.

Aronsson, Kjell-Åke. 1991. Forest reindeer herding A.D. 1–1800: An archaeological and palaeoecological study in northern Sweden. PhD dissertation, Umeå University.

Awebro, Kenneth. 2000. Renmjölkningens betydelse förr. In *Samisk etnobiologi Människor, djur och växter i norr*, ed. Ingvar Svanberg and Håkan Tunón, 179–191. Nora, Sweden: Bokförlaget nya Doxa.

112 Demant-Hatt (1913).

113 Roturier and Roué (2009).

Axelsson Linkowski, Weronika. 2015. Myrar i renbetesland – en kunskapssammanställning om biologisk mångfald. In *Myrens betydelse för renskötseln*, ed. Ann-Catrin Blind, Kajsa Kuoljok, Weronika Axelsson Linkowski, and Håkan Tunón, 51–67. Uppsala: Naptek.

Bergman, Ingela, Olle Zachrisson, and Lars Liedgren. 2013. From hunting to herding: Land use, ecosystem processes, and social transformation among Sami ad 800–1500. *Arctic Antrophology* 50 (2): 25–39. http://doi.org/10.3368/aa.50.2.25

Bjørklund, Ivar. 2013. Domestication, reindeer husbandry and the development of Sámi pastoralism. *Acta Borealia* 30 (2): 174–189. https://doi.org/10.1080/08003831.2013.847676.

Bjørklund. Ivar. 2019. Gollevarre revisited: Reindeer, domestication and pastoral transformation. In *In search of hearths: A book in memory of Sven-Donald Hedman; proceedings of the seminar dedicated to the memory of Sven-Donald Hedman; University of Tromsø—The Arctic University of Norway, March 4, 2016*, ed. Petri Halinen and Bjørnar Olsen, 88–95, Helsinki: The Finnish Antiquarian Society.

Bjørnstad, Gro, Øystein Flagstad, Anne Karin Hufthammer, and Knut H. Røed. 2012. Ancient DNA reveals a major genetic change during the transition from hunting economy to reindeer husbandry in northern Scandinavia. *Journal of Archaeological Science* 39: 102–108. https://doi.org/10.1016/j.jas.2011.09.006.

Danell, Öje, and Mauri Nieminen. 1997. Renen och betet. In *Flora i renbetesland*, ed. Kristina Warenberg, Bengt Ekendahl, and Karstein Bye, 19–30. Nordiskt organ för renforskning (NOR). Oslo: Landbruksforlaget.

de Moor, Tine. 2015. *The dilemma of the commoners*. New York: Cambridge University Press.

Demant Hatt, Emilie, 1913. *Med lapperne i højfjeldet*. Stockholm: Nordiska bokhandeln.

Douglas. 1695. *See* Kungliga bibliotektet in Archival Sources.

Egelkraut, Dagmarmz, Kjell-Åke Aronsson, Anna Allard, Marianne Åkerholm, Sari Stark, and Johan Olofsson. 2018. Multiple feedbacks contribute to a centennial legacy of reindeer on tundra vegetation. *Ecosystems* 21: 1545–1563. https://doi.org/10.1007/s10021-018-0239-z.

Ehrenmalm, Arwid. 1743. *Resa igenom Wäster-Norrland til Åsehle lappmark, anstäld uti julii månad 1741*. Stockholm. Available page by page at http://runeberg.org/resawenoas/index.html.

Eidlitz Kuoljok, Kerstin. 2011. *Den samiska sitan och vinterbyarna. En utmaning*, Dissertations and Documents in Cultural Anthropology, No. 10. Uppsala University.

Ekman, Sven. 1910. *Norrlands jakt och fiske*. Uppsala, Sweden: Almqvist & Wiksell.

Fernández-Giménez, María E. 2002. Spatial and social boundaries and the paradox of pastoral land tenure. *Human Ecology* 30: 49–78. https://doi.org/10.1023/A:1014562913014.

Fjellström, Phebe. 1986. *Samernas samhälle i tradition och nutid*, 2nd ed. Stockholm: Norstedt.

Galaty, John G., and Douglas L. Johnson, eds. 1990. *The world of pastoralism: Herding systems in comparative perspective*. New York: Guilford Press.

Graan, Olaus. 1899. *Relation, eller en fulkomblig beskrifning om lapparnas ursprung, så wähl som om heela dheras Lefwernes Förehållande*. Uppsala, Sweden: Harald Wretmans tryckeri.

Hagemoen, Rolf Iver M., and Eigil Reimers. 2002. Reindeer summer activity pattern in relation to weather and insect harassment. *Journal of Animal Ecology* 71: 883–892. https://doi.org/10.1046/j.1365-2656.2002.00654.x.

Hansen, Thorkild. 2000 [1962]. *Det lyckliga Arabien: en forskningsfärd 1761–1767*, trans. Olof Hoffsten. Stockholm: En bok för alla.

Hansen, Lars Ivar, and Bjørnar Olsen, 2014. *Hunters in transition: An outline of early Sámi history*. Leiden, the Netherlands: Brill.

Hardin, Garrett. 1968. The tragedy of the commons. *Science* 162: 1243–1248. https://doi.org/10.1126/science.162.3859.1243.

Högström, Pehr. 1747. *Beskrifning öfwer de til Sweriges krona lydande lapmarker*. Stockholm: Salvius. http://urn.kb.se/resolve?urn=urn:nbn:se:umu:eod-114.

Holmbäck, Åke. 1922. *Om lappskattelandsinstitutet och dess historiska utveckling*. Stockholm: Statens offentliga utredningar.

Hultblad, Filip. 1968. *Övergång från nomadism till agrar bosättning i Jokkmokks socken*. PhD dissertation, Uppsala University.

Ingold, Tim. 1980. *Hunters, pastoralists and ranchers*. Cambridge, UK: Cambridge University Press.

Khazanov, Anatoly M. 1994. *Nomads and the outside world*, 2 Rev ed. Madison: University of Wisconsin Press.

Kvist, Roger. 1989. Sociala processer i det rennomadiska samhället. *Scandia* 1: 97–111.

Linnaeus, Carl. 1811a. *Lachesis Lapponica or a tour in Lapland, now first published from the original manuscript journal of the celebrated Linnaeus*, vol. 1, ed. J. E. Smith. London: White and Cochrane.
Linnaeus, Carl. 1811b. *Lachesis Lapponica or a tour in Lapland, now first published from the original manuscript journal of the celebrated Linnaeus*, vol. 2, ed. J. E. Smith. London: White and Cochrane.
Linnaeus, Carl. 2003. *Iter Lapponicum: Lappländska resan 1732. I.* Dagboken. Umeå, Sweden: Kungl. Skytteanska Samfundet.
Lundius, Nicolai. 1905. *Descriptio Lapponiæ*. Uppsala, Sweden: Harald Wretmans tryckeri.
Lundmark, Lennart. 1982. Uppbörd, utarmning, utveckling. Det samiska fångstsamhällets övergång till rennomadism i Lule lappmark. PhD dissertation, Umeå University.
Moritz, Mark. 2016. Open property regimes. *International Journal of the Commons* 10: 688–708. https://doi.org/10.18352/ijc.719.
Nordin, Gabriella. 2009. Äktenskap i Sápmi: giftermålsmönster och etnisk komplexitet i kolonisationens tidevarv, 1722–1895. PhD dissertation, Umeå University.
Norstedt, Gudrun, Anna-Lena Axelsson, and Lars Östlund. 2014. Exploring pre-colonial resource control of individual Sami household. *Arctic* 67 (2): 223–237. https://doi.org/10.14430/arctic4389.
Öhrling, Samuel. 1970 [1773]. *Historisk-ekonomisk avhandling om Arjeplogs församling i Lappland*. Arjeplog, Sweden: Silvermuseet.
Ostrom, Elinor. 1990. *Governing the commons, the evolution of institutions for collective action*. Cambridge, UK: Cambridge University Press.
Ostrom, Elinor. 2005. *Understanding institutional diversity*. Princeton, NJ: Princeton University Press.
Rheen, Samuele. 1897. *En kortt relation om Lapparnes lefwarne och sedher, wijd-skiepellsser, sampt i många stycken grofwe wildfarellsser*. Uppsala, Sweden: Harald Wretmans tryckeri.
Roturier, Samuel, and Marie Roué. 2009. Of forest, snow and lichen: Sámi reindeer herders' knowledge of winter pastures in northern Sweden. *Forest Ecology and Management* 258 (9): 1960–1976. https://doi.org/10.1016/j.foreco.2009.07.045.
Ruong, Israel. 1969. *Samerna*. Stockholm: Aldus/Bonnier.
Storli, Inger. 1993. Sami Viking Age pastoralism—or the "fur trade paradigm" reconsidered. *Norwegian Archeological Review* 26 (1): 1–20. https://doi.org/10.1080/00293652.1993.9965550.

Tanner, Väinö. 1929. *Antropogeografiska studier inom Petsamo-området*. 1, Skolt-lapparna. Helsinki: Tilgmanns Tryck.
Wiklund, Karl Bernhard, and Just Knud Qvigstad. 1909. *Dokument angående flyttlapparna, del II*. Kristiania, Norway: Grøndahl & Søns boktryckeri.
Zeder, Melinda A. 2012. The domestication of animals. *Journal of Anthropological Research* 68 (2): 161–190. https://doi.org/10.3998/jar.0521004.0068.201.

Archival Sources

Härnösand Regional Archive (HRA):
Rulings in Jokkmokks District Court, Sweden, 1689–1780.
Kungliga biblioteket (National Library of Sweden), Stockholm:
Douglas. 1695. Skrivelse till Kungl. Maj:t ang. lapparna dat 25 mars 1695, X [1695] 281a:1.
Riksarkivet [National Archives of Sweden]:
Svea Court of Appeal (RA SH). 1712–1780. Rulings in Jokkmokks District Court, Sweden.

8

Other Income Sources

In this chapter, we stress the fact that households' incomes were complex and came together by a mix of activities. To fully understand how households managed their livelihoods, activities other than fishing, hunting, and reindeer herding also need to be considered. Bjørklund has suggested that the inhabitants' livelihood in interior Scandinavia until the nineteenth century was a continual "multifaceted household adaption" made up of a wide range of activities.[1] This view has parallels to analytical concepts to understand early modern agrarian livelihoods, and the latest concept launched is an "integrated peasant economy."[2] The concept stresses that peasants engaging in a wide number of subsistence activities was a prominent characteristic of pre-industrial farms in many regions of Europe and particularly in upland areas. Used in a Sami context, it has shown that diversification was an active and systematic choice for these households, not something they did occasionally.[3] Some of these activities were for subsistence, some for exchange. However, the more engaged

[1] Bjørklund (2013).

[2] Panjek et al. (2017).

[3] Päiviö (2017).

J. Larsson and E.-L. Päiviö Sjaunja, *Self-Governance and Sami Communities*,
https://doi.org/10.1007/978-3-030-87498-8_8

users were in reindeer pastoralism, the less time they had to spend on other activities, and the more they traded.

Several means of livelihood besides herding, fishing, and hunting were part of everyday life for early modern inhabitants in interior northwest Fennoscandia. By and large, people's economy depended on self-sufficiency, so all or most of the food, clothes, and utensils they needed were produced within the household. Any excess products were sold, bartered, or used for paying tax. What households could produce was to a large extent determined by their main mode of production, which in turn was linked to rights or access to resources. Reindeer pastoralist households could thus produce a variety of reindeer products, for example, dried meat, cheese, leather and fur from hides, and wire from sinews. They also transported people, post, and goods. Much of the produced goods were used in the household, but with gradually enlarging reindeer herds, it became more and more feasible to produce a surplus to sell. Fisher households, on the other hand, produced dried fish mostly for household consumption but occasionally, when harvests were especially rich, also for sale. Many households, foremost those that dwelled in the boreal forest, hunted wild mammals and birds that contributed extra food and raw materials, such as furs, meat, feathers, and eggs. They also engaged in gathering of raw materials such as plants, bark, roots, and berries.[4] Market production was probably desirable for all households regardless of economic orientation, since trade generated incomes to purchase products that were difficult or impossible to produce within the household. In the following sections, we describe each of these activities with more detail.

Plants, Berries, and Handcrafts

In the interior of northwest Fennoscandia, the growing season lasts approximately from May to September and gets shorter with increased altitude, which occurs with a clear gradient between the eastern boreal forest and the western mountainous region. During the summer, the

[4] Zackrisson et al. (2000).

short growing season is somewhat compensated by the length of the polar day, as plenty of daylight favors both growth and nutritional content in plants. Sub-zero temperatures, or even snowfalls, are not exceptional during the growing season, but native plants have adapted rather well to the capricious weather. However, frosts in early summer can affect flowering and thus fructification negatively, especially for berry plants, which in turn might reduce the amount of fruit later in the season. For early modern inhabitants, the short growing season meant they only had a few summer months to collect wild plants and berries, and the weather made the returns unpredictable from year to year.

Sources frequently described how early modern inhabitants gathered berries, bark, firewood, wild herbs, roots, and sedges, mostly for their own use but sometimes to sell. Inhabitants collected bilberries (*Vaccinium myrtillus*), cloudberries (*Rubus chamaemorus*), crowberries (*Empetrum nigrum*), and lingonberries (*Vaccinium vitis-idaea*).[5] These were either eaten straightaway, served in milk or fish stews, or stored in cool places for later use. With regard to trade, it is stated that fisher households in Ume lappmark could obtain cheese, reindeer calves, or meat from reindeer pastoralist households in return for berries.[6]

Plants were gathered for different purposes.[7] Some plants were presumably collected because they tasted good and contributed to an otherwise one-sided diet of meat or fish. Among the collected edible plants mentioned in the source material were alpine blue-sow-thistle (*Cicerbita alpina*), common sorrel (*Rumex acetosa*), garden angelica (*Angelica archangelica*), and wild angelica (*Angelica sylvestris*). As with berries, herbs could be eaten as they were or with milk, or be saved for later use. Some plants were considered medicinal, and could be used to treat a variety of conditions and illnesses.[8] Within this group, garden angelica fought off colds, mugwort (*Artemisia vulgaris*) remedied toothaches, tormentil (*Potentilla erecta*) cured stomach pains, and yarrow (*Achillea millefolium*) treated small cuts or wounds (Fig. 8.1).

---

5 Graan (1899, p. 42) and Rheen (1897, p. 21).

6 Lundius (1905, p. 19).

7 Aronsson (2000), Phebe Fjellström (2000), Linnaeus (2003, pp. 91–102), Lundius (1905, p. 11), Rautio (2014, pp. 20ff), Rheen (1897, p. 21), and Svanberg (2000).

8 Phebe Fjellström (2003, p. 255), Linnaeus (2003, p. 95), and Tunón (2000).

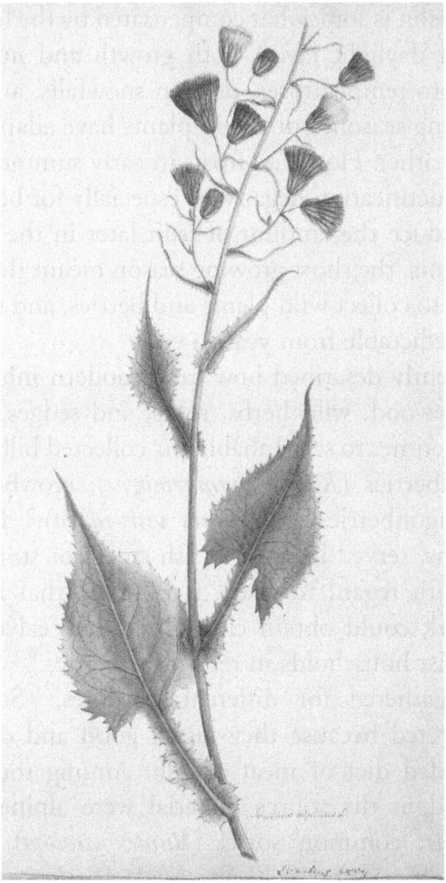

Fig. 8.1 Alpine blue-sow-thistle (*Cicerbita alpine*), depicted in 1695 (*Source* Iter lapponicum, Luefsta MS 92, Uppsala University Library, Sweden. Public domain. https://www.alvin-portal.org/alvin/imageViewer.jsf?dsId=ATTACHMENT-0028&pid=alvin-record:162152)

Although berry picking surely was an activity in almost every household, it is elusive in court rulings. Like most ordinary chores, berry picking was rarely a subject of conflict and in the court cases it is only mentioned a few times to contextualize other events. For example, in 1704 a man from Sirkas stated in court that his sister had gone missing.[9] The sister's husband, who was asked about her disappearance, described that she had gone out one morning late in September, just before Michaelmas, to pick *bär eller lingon* (berries or lingonberries). He had accompanied her to a location roughly one-quarter of a Swedish mile (2 to 3 km) from their living grounds, where *som mästa bären finnes* (most berries were to be found). According to him, she had remained at the berry site and he had gone to search for some lost reindeer. She had not returned home in the evening. The particulars linked to this tragic event contribute useful information about berry picking: it was part of everyday life, it could take place rather late in the season, and inhabitants had comprehensive knowledge about the locations of good berry sites.

When it came to the distribution of rights to resources, berries were hardly ever mentioned in the court material. One exception was in a court ruling from 1770 when a pair of brothers transmitted two lands they had inherited from their father to another user. According to the court records, the lands included two lakes and one *bärbacke* (berry hill).[10] It implies that berries belonged to the user of a land, in contrast to present-day Sweden where wild berries are open access.

Other plants were collected for more practical reasons. In late summer, a couple of particular sedge species (*Carex sp.*) were harvested when the straw had become tall and rich in lignin and therefore durable. After initial clearing from twigs, the sedge was sorted into bundles that were struck against rocks to become soft, and then left to dry. The dried straws were later used as shoe hay in leather boots to keep feet warm and comfortable.[11] Preparation of shoe hay was probably a time-demanding task since household members had to gather enough to last until the following summer. The ready-made shoe hay could be bartered and, at least in Ume lappmark, fisher households exchanged shoe hay with reindeer pastoralist households in return for reindeer products.[12]

Plant parts that were rich in colorfast natural pigments could also be used to produce dye. The root of tormentil was, for example, used

[9] HRA (1704, pp. 819–821).

[10] Hultblad (1968, p. 369, evidence 259b).

[11] Phebe Fjellström (1986, pp. 339–341) and Linnaeus (2003, pp. 90–94).

[12] Lundius (1905, p. 30).

to extract pigments to dye wool red.[13] Fine roots of birch (*Betula sp.*), Norway spruce, or Scots pine were used to twine threads and ropes, and to make baskets.[14] The roots were dug up in summer when the ground was soft. Before use they would be soaked in water to get rid of dirt, and to become soft and more manageable. Beside roots, bark from some tree species was collected for tanning leather, foremost bark from birch, rowan (*Sorbus aucuparia*), grey alder (*Alnus incana*), and sallow (*Salix caprea*).[15] The bark was gathered in early summer when the trees' sap rises, since it makes the bark detach easily from the tree trunk. Aside from tanning, Scots pine bark was also used for consumption and for making storage cases.[16]

Raw materials that were amassed by the household were used in production of clothes, tools, or other utensils that the household members needed. It was mainly the women who turned hides from reindeer and other animals into useful garments, such as hats, cloaks, boots, and gloves sewn with threads of twined sinews. In fact, the manufacturing of threads was a handcraft in itself, and the priest Pehr Högström,[17] who spent time among households in Kaitum in the eighteenth century, described it as an art that was masterly performed mostly by women. Besides garments, a great variety of utensils were handcrafted, such as boats, sleds, chests, boxes, spoons, and baskets.[18]Rheen described that handcrafts such as cloaks, boots, and gloves also were sold at market.[19]

Based on evidence in the sources, poor households with few reindeer were more involved in handcrafts and collection of plants and berries than rich households. According to Högström, reindeer pastoralist households were less engaged in handcrafting, but poor Sami, forced by necessity, could be quite skilled at handcrafts.[20] The explanation is

[13] Linnaeus (2003, p. 59).
[14] Phebe Fjellström (2003, p. 272) and Linnaeus (2003, p. 141).
[15] Phebe Fjellström (2003, p. 272) and Linnaeus (2003, pp. 28–30).
[16] Graan (1899, p. 43), Rautio (2014, pp. 25ff), and Zackrisson et al. (2000).
[17] Högström (1747, p. 88).
[18] Graan (1899, p. 52), Högström (1747, p. 87), and Rheen (1897, p. 57).
[19] Rheen (1897, p. 58).
[20] Högström (1747, p. 87).

probably that poor households had more time and could prioritize gathering and refinement of plant materials since they had few reindeer. For pastoralists, the work-intensive tasks of tending and milking reindeer left little or no time for them.

Cultivation, Livestock, and Caring for Reindeer

Most early modern households in interior northwest Fennoscandia were non-sedentary, which is linked to their extensive use of natural resources. For these households, mobility was a means to optimize use of relatively low-productivity fishing waters, hunting grounds, and reindeer pastures spread out over large areas. Cultivation on the other hand, rests on a different kind of logic, namely intensive land use that maximizes the use of a constrained area. Prerequisites for successful cultivation are soil preparation, fertilization, watering, and weeding, which meant that gardeners/farmers had to invest quite a lot of energy into a plot of land to get a significant output. Besides access to arable land, cultivation demands access to manure, seeds, tools, etc. Moreover, the cultivator has to tend regularly to the growing plants, from sowing to harvest which demands a sedentary lifestyle, at least during the growing season. Toward the nineteenth century, more and more households began to settle in interior northwest Fennoscandia, and it was not until then that cultivation became more dispersed.[21] Due to the climatic constraints at these northern latitudes, it is especially challenging to cultivate on open land, and crop production has never prevailed. Sedentary households, instead, continued to rely on a wide range of subsistence activities, such as keeping of livestock, forestry, fishing, hunting, and small-scale reindeer herding.

All the same, it is evident from the sources that cultivation occurred in the inland from time to time. Lundius described, for example, how

[21] Josefsson et al. (2014) suggest that records of fossil cereal pollen from northernmost Sweden, Norway, and Finland show that cereal was cultivated among inhabitants there in prehistoric time.

inhabitants in Ume lappmark sometimes dug up small plots in the enclosures where reindeer had been milked in order to sow turnip (*Brassica rapa ssp. rapa*) seeds.[22] It was a resourceful cultivation strategy that took advantage of already fertilized and fenced plots. Even a small yield was probably a welcome contribution to the household diet. Turnip cultivation seems especially worthwhile when linked to a statement by Linnaeus, who said that the inhabitants desired turnips so much that they easily would trade a whole reindeer cheese for a single turnip, which he by the way found foolish.[23] From Torne lappmark, Tornaeus stated that "the settlers in the Lappmark sow a great deal of turnip seed, which frequently succeeds very well and produces a plentiful crop."[24] Given the many contacts between Sami and neighboring groups, it is not unlikely that Sami would acquire inspiration, cultivation tips, and turnip seeds from non-Sami settlers.

Besides cultivation, some sources also describe how mostly wealthy reindeer pastoralist households kept livestock during summers.[25] In early summer, these reindeer herders bought cows, sheep, and goats in Norway and took them to the mountains to graze with the reindeer. Like reindeer, livestock was milked daily. Around the time of the first snowfalls in autumn, when accessible grazing for livestock diminished, the animals were slaughtered and the meat stored or consumed. This type of animal husbandry had many similarities to reindeer herding, and could easily be integrated into the households' supply strategy.

The interaction between Sami and other groups also centered around a particular system for management of tame reindeer, so-called *skötesrenar*. It was a common practice, for example, for Norwegian and Swedish peasants, tradesmen from the coast of the Gulf of Bothnia, and non-Sami settlers in the inland to own reindeer that were cared for by Sami pastoralists. In return, reindeer pastoralists got paid with money and products such as salt and flour. According to Hultblad, the custom had

[22] Lundius (1905, p. 27).

[23] Linnaeus (2003, pp. 58 and 60).

[24] Tornaeus (1900, pp. 63–64).

[25] Graan (1899, p. 37), Lundius (1905, p. 32), Högström (1747, p. 118), and Rheen (1897, p. 59).

long historical roots.[26] It was probably an important income source for many Sami households. In 1699, three court rulings in the local court in Jokkmokk concerned relationships between people from Luleå town and Sami in Lule lappmark who took care of, or rented out reindeer.[27] In two of the cases, the death of a reindeer had sparked a discussion about responsibility and compensation.

Trade and Transports

Although it was mostly a subsistence economy, trade has long historical roots in the interior of northwest Fennoscandia, as interactions both between local households and with external tradesmen.[28] Trade implied that households did not have to be entirely self-sufficient, but that they, if they had the means, could barter or buy goods from other producers. In many ways, the seventeenth century was a transitional period with an expansion of trade, and an increased focus on reindeer herding. Around this time, the state had introduced official market places in each lappmark where recurring markets took place in January or February each year. One such marketplace was located in Jokkmokk in Lule lappmark. At these markets, inhabitants sold surplus produce to each other and to non-Sami tradesmen from the nearest Swedish coastal towns. According to the sources, inhabitants primarily sold live reindeer and reindeer meat, reindeer hides and furs, reindeer cheese, and handcrafted products, such as fur parkas, boots, gloves, and cloaks.[29] They also sold dried fish, furs of wild game, and down and feathers.

The tradesmen traveled to these markets for the sole purpose of doing business with Sami. It was surely the increased wealth among reindeer pastoralist households that made them grasp the opportunity to buy reindeer products and to proliferate from sales to a new and growing

[26] Hultblad (1968, pp. 148–150).

[27] HRA (1699, pp. 89–90, 100–101).

[28] Hansen and Olsen (2014, pp. 232–243). As discussed in Chapter 4, trade was a prerequisite for the livelihood of early modern Sami households and for the development of reindeer pastoralism.

[29] Ehrenmalm (1743, p. 91) and Rheen (1897, p. 58).

consumer group. The lists of products that merchants took to these markets included alcohol, axes, brass rings, clay tobacco pipes, coins, copper, fabric, fishing tackle, flour, gunpowder, ox and cow hides, iron, knives, lead, needles, rifles, rope, salt, silver, tar, and tobacco.[30] Aside from written trade lists, pieces of clay tobacco pipes, pottery, and porcelain, as well as needles, metals, and coins which originated from the early modern era, have been found at the ancient market site in Lycksele in Ume lappmark.[31]

The state had awarded Swedish merchants in coastal towns by the Gulf of Bothnia the exclusive privilege to trade with inhabitants in the Swedish lappmark. All trade was, however, not legal, and court cases that deal with illegal trade enable us to study firsthand what inhabitants bought and how they paid for goods. In November and December of 1705, a peasant from Pajala in the parish of Övertorneå traveled to the Sami village of Kaitum in Lule lappmark to do business with the inhabitants there. He was not a tradesman from the designated coastal area and, therefore, was not allowed to trade in the lappmark. In total, eight men from Kaitum were mentioned in court rulings to do with illegal trade with the peasant. For example, one man bought an ax and *brännvin* (hard liquor) that he paid for with *härnskor* (shoes) and *vajrenskinn* (reindeer fur). Another man bought an ax that he paid for with three pairs of gloves, and three *lispund* (around 25 kg) of flour that he paid for with a *vaja* (female reindeer). A third man bought tobacco that he paid for with reindeer fur. A fourth man bought salt that he paid for with gloves.[32] Although these transactions were illegal, they probably give a valid picture of what kinds of goods inhabitants would buy, and how they would pay for them in legal trade.

Some reindeer pastoralists acted as middlemen or forwarding agents in trade between Swedish and Norwegian merchants. When the reindeer grazed in Norway, or in the mountains on the border, some pastoralists took the opportunity to visit Norwegian markets to do business. These markets took place twice each year: around midsummer and in

30 Ehrenmalm (1743, p. 91) and Rheen (1897, p. 59).

31 Huggert (2009, 2010), and Rydström (2006). The marketplace in Lycksele was in use only until 1785.

32 HRA (1706, pp. 50–51).

November. Reindeer pastoralists could sell both self-produced goods, such as reindeer hides and meat, and goods they had bought or bartered from Swedish merchants or Sami households in the boreal forest, such as feathers and down.[33] These middlemen took advantage of the fact that some merchandise, for example, silver, tobacco, and woven wool blankets, were cheaper in Norway. They also brought dried sea fish with them back to Sweden, that they eventually could sell to Swedish merchants.

Most of the barter between households probably took place outside the market on a day-to-day basis whenever people crossed paths. Bartering between local households included, for example, reindeer meat, cheese, shoe hay, berries, dried fish, down, feathers, and turnips.[34] Some court rulings also give insights into how goods changed hands between households. More specifically, barter is sometimes mentioned in cases that dealt with theft, or when someone had to account for how he or she had obtained a certain food item. As always in court, we cannot decide whether the defendants were telling the truth or not, but the point to make here is that they had to tell a story that aligned with the proper way to go about it in similar situations in order to convince the lay-judges. All lay-judges were well-acquainted with barter and could, probably rather effortlessly, determine if the defendant's story seemed reasonable or not. A court ruling from 1704 about a stolen *rana* (a woven wool fabric that was used as a cover on the *goahte* or a blanket) revealed several barter deals. The plaintiff, Anders Nilsson who was the original owner of the stolen *rana*, had found it at Anders Pålsson's home. Pålsson claimed that he had bartered it from a third person, Tore Andersson, in return for two reindeer. Andersson in turn, claimed that he had gotten the *rana* from Anders Nilsson (unclear if it intended the plaintiff or someone else by that name) in return for 1½ *riksdaler*, 1 reindeer fur, and ten reindeer cheese rounds.[35]

---

33 Ehrenmalm (1743, p. 91), Lundius (1905, p. 40), and Rheen (1897). In a court ruling from 1701, a man had sold "fresh meat" in Norway in 1699. The meat came from 10 reindeer and had been stored under a stone slab in the mountain in Sweden when it was stolen (HRA 1701, pp. 403–404).

34 Ehrenmalm (1743, p. 91), Lundius (1905, p. 40), Rheen (1897), and Tornaeus (1900, pp. 63–64).

35 HRA (1704, pp. 810–811). Tore Andersson was convicted.

The routes through interior northwest Fennoscandia were difficult to travel, which made visitors dependent on local guides if they wanted to go there. Many transports were in fact ensured by local households with access to pack and draft reindeer, and Högström in Kaitum even described transports during market season as a good income source for some Sami households.[36] In addition to draft reindeer, local pathfinders had attained an invaluable sense of direction that guided them along passable routes in rugged terrain in both summer and winter. Most transports of goods were carried out on snow sleds in winter, this circumstance surely contributed to the timing of the annual market in January or February. An important contributing factor was that reindeer pastoralist households grazed their reindeer in the boreal forest that time of year, and thus had temporary settlements near marketplaces. The inland markets would probably have been considerably more difficult for external tradesmen to access without the local reindeer pastoralists with draft reindeer and sleds. In summer, post and people mostly came inland on foot, although boat transports along lakes and rivers surely mitigated transport and travel.

Parallel with the market, when almost all inhabitants in the lappmark were gathered in the same place at the same time, the state took the opportunity to collect the yearly tax, and to have proceedings in the local court. Local inhabitants, therefore, also transported official representatives from the state, such as the bailiff, judge, and court clerk.[37] These transports were considered duties and stood in relation to the household's status or economic position. The duties also included transports of priests and other church staff year-round. The duty to transport officials could be unpopular, as a court record from 1706 shows. The case concerned Lars Nilsson in Tuorpon, who for many years had been defiant of the order to let his reindeer transport state representatives. The *länsman* (sheriff) related to the court that Nilsson had told him that he would rather accept a fine than perform these transports, and when he at times had sent reindeer to do transports, they turned out to be incapable and useless as draft animals. His verdict was to pay a fine in both

36 Högström (1747, p. 86).

37 Fellman (1910, p. 347).

reindeer and cash and he was told that if he continued to disregard his transport duties, he would be penalized even harder.[38] This was not the first time the court fined a person for refusing to do transport duties. In 1704, Olof Joensson in Jokkmokk was fined,[39] and the same year Lars Nilsson in Tuopon was convicted. Henrik Eriksson in the same village was fined for twice neglecting to do his duties.[40] In some places, such as Nasafjell in Pite lappmark, inhabitants could also have duties related to mining transports. Although these transports provided incomes, they were mostly seen as unwelcome and dreaded burdens by the inhabitants.

Relative Importance of Various Subsistence Activities

Both reindeer pastoralist households and fisher households took part in various gathering activities, and sold products that were manufactured from gathered resources. Even so, gathering seems to have been more important for fisher households. Among reindeer pastoralist households, social stratification likely gave rise to varying economic strategies within the group. For example, poor households appear to have been more active in handcrafting, fishing, and hunting. The rational explanation here is probably that the poor needed several income sources to make ends meet.

The illustration in Fig. 8.2. shows that households in interior northwest Fennoscandia were engaged in a wide range of economic activities, such as reindeer herding, fishing, hunting, handcrafting, cultivation, livestock keeping, gathering, trade, and transport. Diversification of activities was part of an economic system and not just occasional tasks performed randomly. However, this was not equally distributed between pastoralist and fisher households.

38 HRA (1706, pp. 53–54).

39 HRA (1704, p. 812).

40 HRA (1706, p. 59).

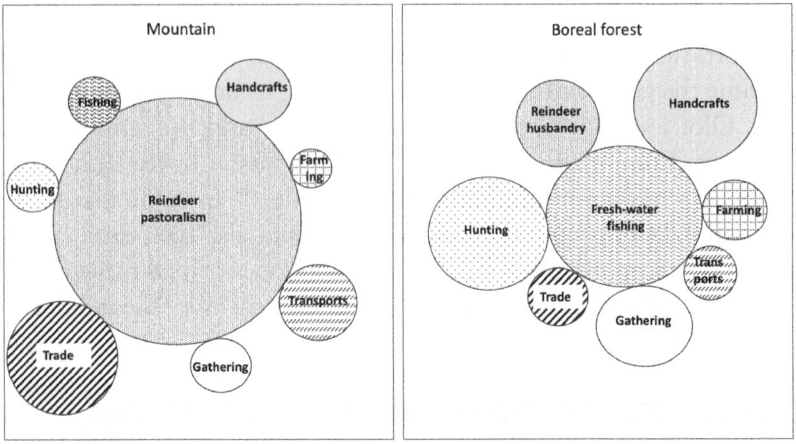

Fig. 8.2 Model showing the relative importance of various subsistence activities in pastoralist and fisher households in interior northwest Fennoscandia in the seventeenth and eighteenth centuries (*Source* Adapted from E.-L. Päiviö [2017, p. 155, with permission])

References

Aronsson, Kjell-Åke. Å. 2000. Användning av ängssyra (Rumex acetosa) bland samerna. In *Samisk etnobiologi Människor, djur och växter i norr*, ed. Ingvar Svanberg and Håkan Tunón, 253–258. Nora, Sweden: Bokförlaget nya Doxa.

Bjørklund, Ivar. 2013. Domestication, reindeer husbandry and the development of Sámi pastoralism. *Acta Borealia* 30(2): 174–189. https://doi.org/10.1080/08003831.2013.847676.

Ehrenmalm, Arwid. 1743. *Resa igenom Wäster-Norrland til Åsehle lappmark, anstäld uti julii månad 1741*. Stockholm. Available page by page at http://runeberg.org/resawenoas/index.html.

Fellman, Isak. 1910. *Handlingar och uppsatser angående Finska Lappmarken och lapparne*. Helsinki: Finska Litteratursällskapets Tryckeri.

Fjellström, Phebe. 1986. *Samernas samhälle i tradition och nutid*, 2nd ed. Stockholm: Norstedt

Fjellström, Phebe. 2000. Fjällkvannen (Angelica archangelica) i samisk tradition. In *Samisk etnobiologi*, ed., Ingvar Svanberg och Håkan Tunón, 241–252. Nora, Sweden: Nya Doxa.

Fjellström, Phebe. 2003. Etnologisk kommentar. In *Iter Lapponicum.* Lappländska resan 1732, II Kommentardel, ed. Carl Linnaeus, 250–287. Umeå, Sweden: Kungl. Skytteanska Samfundet.

Graan, Olaus. 1899. *Relation, eller en fulkomblig beskrifning om lapparnas ursprung, så wähl som om heela dheras Lefwernes Förehållande.* Uppsala, Sweden: Harald Wretmans tryckeri.

Hansen, Lars Ivar, and Bjørnar Olsen. 2014. *Hunters in transition: An outline of early Sámi history.* Leiden, the Netherlands: Brill.

Högström, Pehr. 1747. *Beskrifning öfwer de til Sweriges krona lydande lapmarker.* Stockholm: Salvius. http://urn.kb.se/resolve?urn=urn:nbn:se:umu:eod-114.

Huggert, Anders. 2009. Danska mynt funna på kåtaplats i Tärna socken, Lappland. *Svensk Numismatisk Tidskrift* 7: 159–161.

Huggert. Anders. 2010. Kyrk- och marknadsplatsen Lyksälie under 1600–1700-talen. *Svensk Numismatisk Tidskrift* 1: 6–10.

Hultblad, Filip. 1968. *Övergång från nomadism till agrar bosättning i Jokkmokks socken.* PhD dissertation, Uppsala University.

Josefsson, Torbjörn, Per H. Ramqvist, and Greger Hörnberg. 2014. The history of early cereal cultivation in northernmost Fennoscandia as indicated by palynological research. *Vegetation History and Archaeobotany* 23: 821–840. https://doi.org/10.1007/s00334-014-0446-2.

Linnaeus, Carl. 2003. *Iter Lapponicum: Lappländska resan 1732. I.* Dagboken. Umeå, Sweden: Kungl. Skytteanska Samfundet.

Lundius, Nicolai. 1905. *Descriptio Lapponiæ.* Uppsala, Sweden: Harald Wretmans tryckeri.

Päiviö, Eva-Lotta. 2017. Livelihood diversification in early modern Sami households in northern Sweden. In *Integrated peasant economy in a comparative perspective: Alps, Scandinavia and beyond*, ed. Aleksander Panjek, Jesper Larsson, and Luca Mocarelli, 137–159. Koper, Slovenia: University of Primorska Press.

Panjek, Aleksander, Jesper Larsson, Luca Mocarelli, eds. 2017. *Integrated peasant economy in a comparative perspective: Alps, Scandinavia and beyond.* Koper, Slovenia: University of Primorska Press. https://www.hippocampus.si/ISBN/978-961-7023-02-2.pdf.

Rautio, Anna-Maria. 2014. People-plant interrelationships: Historical plant use in native Sami societies. PhD dissertation, Sveriges lantbruksuniversitet, Umeå, Sweden. http://urn.kb.se/resolve?urn=urn:nbn:se:slu:epsilon-e-2168.

Rheen, Samuele. 1897. *En kortt relation om Lapparnes lefwarne och sedher, wijd-skiepellsser, sampt i många stycken grofwe wildfarellsser*. Uppsala, Sweden: Harald Wretmans tryckeri.

Rydström, Gunhild. 2006. *Det äldsta Lycksele - Öhn: rapport över genomgång och bearbetning av fyndmaterial från undersökningar åren 1949–2001, raä nr 343, Gammplatsen, Lycksele socken, Lappland*. Lycksele, Sweden: Skogsmuseet.

Svanberg, Ingvar. 2000. (Lacta Alpina) i Samiskt kosthåll. In *Samisk etnobiologi Människor, djur och växter i norr*, ed. Ingvar Svanberg and Håkan Tunón, 259–265. Nora, Sweden: Bokförlaget nya Doxa.

Tornaeus, Johannes. 1900. *Berättelse om Lapmarckerna och Deras Tillstånd*. Uppsala, Sweden: Harald Wretmans tryckeri.

Tunón, Håkan. 2000. Botemedel inom samisk medicin. In *Samisk etnobiologi Människor, djur och växter i norr*, ed. Ingvar Svanberg and Håkan Tunón, 126–163. Nora, Sweden: Bokförlaget nya Doxa.

Zackrisson, Olle, Lars Östlund, Olavi Korhonen, and Ingela Bergman. 2000. The ancient use of *Pinus sylvestris* L. (Scots pine) inner bark by Sami people in northern Sweden, related to cultural and ecological factors. *Vegetation History and Archaeobotany* 9 (2): 99–109. https://doi.org/10.1007/BF01300060.

Archival Sources

Härnösand Regional Archive (HRA):

Rulings in Jokkmokks District Court, Sweden, 1689–1780.

Part III

Synthesis

9

From Private to Common: Coevolution of Land-Use Practices and Property Rights

In this concluding chapter, we synthesize the results from the previous chapters and discuss how changing land-use regimes among Sami in interior northwest Fennoscandia interrelated with the development of property rights between 1550 and 1780. The focus is mostly on fishing, hunting, and reindeer grazing, but some other economic activities are also described. During this period, a new tenure system, categorized as reindeer pastoralism, emerged where some users could have hundreds or thousands of reindeer. For households that had amassed large reindeer herds, it became crucial to access both large pastures in the mountains and in the boreal forest to have enough grazing. Eventually, this led to the establishment of common-property regimes in both the mountains and the boreal forest, where grazing became a CPR. For users, the strategy enabled possession of large herds of reindeer on relatively low-yield grazing lands that would otherwise have been impossible. Moreover, the new tenure system required mobility, flexibility, and reciprocity to further optimize the grazing, and to make risks and uncertainties, for example, of weather and grazing conditions, more manageable. At the same time, to assure that everyone's access to resources within the new system was relatively predictable and corresponded to household needs,

J. Larsson and E.-L. Päiviö Sjaunja, *Self-Governance and Sami Communities*,
https://doi.org/10.1007/978-3-030-87498-8_9

both during the year and from year to year, users had to develop joint strategies to designate enough grazing to individual users, and to mitigate potential conflicts between users. The emergence of this kind of common-property regime is therefore best described as a bottom-up process as it assumes that local users design and implement institutions for common use that all or most users adhere to.

The new governance structure was tightly linked to changes in the users' economy, as many households during that time went from a livelihood based on resources that were considered private, mostly fish and wild game, to a livelihood that was based on CPRs, mostly extensive grazing. Converting from one regime to another was not a quick and uncomplicated leap that all inhabitants made simultaneously. At the same time as more and more households enlarged reindeer herds and needed access to more grazing, many households, especially in the boreal forest, continued to live as before, on fishing and hunting. The governing institutions that emerged had to design tailored property rights for Sami users with different subsistence modes so they could co-exist and access natural resources needed to survive and prosper. Changes in the Sami economy and governance structures were moreover linked to events on a higher institutional level in the surrounding society, such as the introduction of new state tax codes, the government's inauguration of yearly markets in the lappmark, and an increase in Sami population in the first half of the eighteenth century.

Hunting and Fishing to Reindeer Pastoralism

For most users in Lule lappmark the economy changed profoundly between 1550 and 1780. These changes took place first among users in the mountains and later encompassed many users in the boreal forest. The introduction of a tenure system for keeping reindeer in large herds evoked a focus on grazing resources which came to change the distribution of the Sami villages. To better suit new needs, the villages were eventually reshaped from previously roundish areas, roughly situated either in mountains or boreal forest, to elongated areas that stretched from the northwest mountains to the southeast boreal forest. These new villages made it possible for users with reindeer to access both summer and winter grazing within their villages' borders.[1]

In the sixteenth century, hunting still made up the backbone of Sami economy and any surpluses that households accumulated could foremost be attributed to hunting. Before the seventeenth century, as discussed in Chapter 6, hunting had largely been considered a collective enterprise. In fact, it has been suggested that Sami villages came about as a response to the joint organization of hunting. In northern Fennoscandia, the economic importance of hunting peaked around 1570 and thereafter rapidly lost significance as a major income source for most households. Nonetheless, especially small-game hunting continued to be part of the economy in some households, especially among those that stayed in the boreal forest year-round. The boreal forest generally offered more habitats for different wild game species which must have facilitated the perpetuation of hunting. Moreover, wild reindeer seem to have disappeared first from the mountains, which further downplayed the role of hunting there.

As for hunting, the prerequisites for fishing were also more favorable in the boreal forest than in the mountains. Compared to extremely nutrient-poor fishing waters in the mountains, lakes, rivers, and streams in the boreal forest offered both a greater diversity of fish species and larger catches overall. In the seventeenth century, fresh-water fishing was the major food and income source for numerous households in interior northern Fennoscandia.[2] Albeit, it is more difficult to estimate the role of fishing in preceding centuries. Although fishing probably had been essential for a long time, some evidence indicates that its importance increased and maybe also culminated in the seventeenth century. Tax records from mid-sixteenth century show how particular fishing waters situated west of the lappmark border periodically were used lawfully by coastal peasants from the Gulf of Bothnia.[3] Later in the sixteenth century, this practice ceased, at least officially, and in the beginning of the seventeenth century, the government began to counteract coastal peasants' fishing

---

[1] Vorren (1980).

[2] Norstedt et al. (2014).

[3] Göthe (1929, pp. 3–8), Hultblad (1968, p. 38), and Bergman and Ramqvist (2017, p. 11).

in Sami waters. Although we know little about these events and what preceded them, it seems likely that Sami users gained, or regained, access to these waters in the late sixteenth century, and that this speaks to an increased importance of fishing among Sami inhabitants. One hypothesis could be that the waters had not been in demand by Sami users in the early sixteenth century as profitable hunting had taken up more of their time. In sum, fishing and hunting continued to be important for users in the boreal forest throughout the seventeenth century. In 1671, the government tasked a cadastral surveyor and a clerk to map and describe all resources connected to lands belonging to tax-paying Sami in Ume lappmark.[4] The resulting map and its associated description show that the valued resources on Sami lands predominantly were linked to fishing and hunting.

In the sixteenth century, the majority of households in interior north Fennoscandia had small numbers of tame reindeer to use as decoys in hunts for wild reindeer, and for transportation and milking. The animals also provided furs and meat, but the bulk of these commodities nevertheless came from hunting of wild reindeer. In the early seventeenth century, some households had started to amass more tame reindeer but the number per household was still quite modest, on average. Yet, by then, the number showed a noticeable difference between tax-paying Sami in mountain villages and tax-paying Sami in forest villages. In Lule lappmark, users in Sirkas and Tuorpon had almost twice as many reindeer as users in Sjokksjokk and Jokkmokk—twenty-seven or so to about fourteen, respectively. Later in the seventeenth century, the gap had increased, and herds of hundreds or thousands of reindeer had developed foremost in the mountains. Certain ecological advantages surely augmented the expansion of animal numbers among users with access to grazing in the mountains compared to users whose grazing was restricted to the boreal forest. First, the mountains offered access to relatively nutritious and energy-rich localities for summer grazing, such as open alpine heaths, grasslands, willow thickets, and mountain birch forests that stretched out over enormous areas.[5] Second, the combination of a normally cold

---

[4] Norstedt (2011) and Norstedt et al. (2014).

[5] Skarin et al. (2010).

summer climate with a lot of wind, and a multitude of icy and snowy patches in the mountains, offered the reindeer relief from flying insects, especially oestrid flies. If reindeer cannot escape the flies, they significantly reduce their peaceful grazing and hence their growth. Third, the typically open mountain landscape made gathering the herd less work intensive, compared to the boreal forest, which was an especially advantageous feature when reindeer were being milked every day. Fourth, in the initial phase of reindeer pastoralism, it was probably relatively easy for households with many reindeer to access winter grazing in the boreal forest since most users who lived in the forest year-round had few reindeer and there was thus no or little competition for winter grazing. They might even have welcomed leases for renting out a resource they did not need. Leasing winter grazing could have been a continuation of an older custom that we unfortunately know little about. There were at least two possible options for winter grazing in the preceding tenure system: one was that users moved seasonally with their small reindeer herds to find grazing in the boreal forest, and the other was that they spent winters in the low mountains. Small herds of tame reindeer could probably survive the winter on old vegetation in the mountain birch forests or on ground lichens in windswept higher terrain.

The question of what caused the transition to reindeer pastoralism has been much debated in Sami historical and archaeological research. We adhere to those who argue that trade was a catalyst behind this transformation. Pastoralism implies some sort of economic specialization among users, and pastoralists typically depend on connections with surrounding societies. Pastoralists require contacts with the outside world to sell surplus products and to get food and other commodities they cannot produce themselves.[6] As users with access to mountain grazing grew their herds, fishing and hunting lost most of their economic importance. Partially, the shift from hunting was a consequence of the extinction of wild reindeer in the mountains, which had been one of the economically most important prey animals for users there. Overall, conditions for fishing and hunting of other game were also considerably less favorable

[6] Khazanov (1994, p. xxxi).

in the mountains compared to the boreal forest. But even more important was the fact that pastoralists, to become successful, had to engage almost all of their time and energy into the management of livestock, so they had relatively little time for other activities. Fishing and hunting simply became less prioritized.

Pastoralist groups need dependable trading partners. It is therefore not surprising that the expansion of reindeer pastoralism coincided with a growing interest in northern Fennoscandia from adjacent peoples. Gradually, the inhabitants became more tightly linked to different markets in Sweden, Norway, and Russia, not least through the establishment of official trade networks. In Lule lappmark, the Swedish government had taken a more active role in Sami trade starting in the mid-sixteenth century. Nevertheless, reforms, including the establishment of yearly markets in each district of the lappmark in the first decades of the seventeenth century, played a significant role in trade. In 1605, Jokkmokk became the hub for trade in Lule lappmark, and in 1621 the town of Luleå was established on the shore of the Gulf of Bothnia. The government granted some merchants in Luleå unique privileges to trade with the Sami inhabitants in Lule lappmark. The establishment of trade networks with tradespeople in Luleå was probably beneficial for the inhabitants in the lappmark as well, as it secured a steady inflow of sought-after goods, and assured them buyers for the surplus produce they marketed. This trade was based on long-standing traditions through the *birkarl* system. The inhabitants could also buy and sell products in Norwegian markets in summer and fall, just across the border from Lule lappmark. However, none of these trade networks was a one-way relationship that routinely subordinated Sami producers. Sami inhabitants, especially those with many reindeer, were important trade partners because they produced appraised market goods and they had strong purchasing power. So, reindeer pastoralism became a dominant factor and a prerequisite for trade in this region. A more practical aspect to do with trade is that it requires transportation of goods. Also, in this regard, Sami were the main actors, since they had unique capabilities, including draft reindeer, sleds, and local knowledge, needed to transport goods.

The seventeenth century saw progress in reindeer pastoralism for many users in the mountains at the same time as fishing and hunting became more firmly established among many users in the boreal forest. Thus, there were several parallel, ongoing production modes. In several written accounts from the late seventeenth century aimed at describing Sami livelihoods, religion, and customs, the inhabitants were often characterized as either *Mountain Sami* or *Forest Sami*,[7] a dichotomy that has often been repeated and reused in research about Sami cultural history (see Chapter 3).[8] Here we point to an additional problem related to these concepts. In the late seventeenth century, the economic gap between so-called Mountain Sami and Forest Sami were probably at its largest. As reindeer pastoralism became more widespread in the upcoming century, it also spread to many users in the boreal forest, and by then the two groups began to converge economically. As it turned out, some users in the boreal forest continued to live on fishing and hunting while others amassed large reindeer herds. The differences were, however, strictly economic and not cultural. Inhabitants' cultural affiliation was instead foremost linked to which part of the lappmark they belonged to. So geographical factors, not subsistence mode, seem to have been the deciding factor for language, attires, and customs.

If users were efficient and somewhat fortunate, owning many reindeer could give rise to a substantial surplus that was much more profitable than the gains retrieved from fishing and hunting. The attraction and expansion of reindeer pastoralism in the eighteenth century can perhaps best be understood by the fact that it gave extraordinary incomes that households could spend on utensils and luxury goods, such as silver jewelry, tobacco, and alcohol. Relatively soon, it must have become apparent to everyone that it was possible to become really wealthy as a reindeer pastoralist, and if possible, other inhabitants would not hesitate to follow in the same developmental track. Besides the good profit margin, a tax reform in 1695 also contributed to favorable economic conditions for reindeer pastoralists. The reform stated that the tax level henceforth would be fixed and no longer linked to the taxpayers' assets. In the cadastral book, most tax-paying Sami were connected to a specific

[7] Several of the authors were commissioned by Johannes Schefferus as groundwork for his book *Lapponia*.

[8] See, for example, Marklund (2015) and Norstedt (2018).

piece of land, but in reality, it was difficult or even impossible for the government to discern exactly how these lands were used, which assets they contained, or even their size. This made individual tax levies arbitrary. So, in 1695, after several attempts to elucidate a more transparent tax levy for individual taxpayers, the government finally abandoned its old strategy and decided on a tax on the Sami village. Thereafter, it became the village's responsibility to deduce each member's tax capacity, collect the tax, and then hand the total levy over to the government's bailiff. Since the tax had been fixed, it did not increase when users amassed more reindeer. The individual levies basically remained unaffected by changes in users' assets, which had not been the case in the old tax system. Nevertheless, in the new tax arrangement, trusted men in the village who were responsible for deducing, collecting, and forwarding the tax had to stay well-informed about each tax-paying member's economic condition.[9] At the same time, this mandate gave them leverage as a governance institution. With more tax-paying members, the individual user's tax burden would decrease. On the village level, the joint tax became an incentive to use resources as efficiently as possible, and if necessary, redistribute resources to new users, or to returning users. On the other hand, if the number of tax-payers decreased, levies would increase for those remaining. It was rational for the village to strive toward a reasonable resource distribution, so members could have bearable incomes to support their households, and contribute to the village's joint tax. All in all, the mid-eighteenth century was a very successful period for Sami reindeer pastoralists in interior northern Sweden,[10] which largely became possible through changes in the property regime.

Property Rights

The expansion of reindeer pastoralism set off complex negotiations among users over common grazing rights. This was a fundamental reorganization of rights in a society that previously had been focused on

[9] Arell (1977, p. 64).

[10] Kvist (1989, p. 9).

hunting and fishing on mostly private lands. Users who had amassed large reindeer herds needed access to summer grazing in the mountains, winter grazing in the boreal forest, and pathways for migration in spring and fall, each with its own more or less unique ecological requirements.

In the boreal forest, the property-rights regime for hunting and fishing was based on the individual user's right to fish and hunt within a *skatteland*. In this property regime, fish and game were considered private goods, and it was relatively easy to exclude others from using the resources. Within that *skatteland*, grazing resources also belonged to the landholder. Originally, these lands had been organized so each provided enough resources for fishing and hunting for households to survive and have a surplus. It had been strategic for users to have control over resources within these large but well-defined territories. However, larger herds required larger, contiguous pastures with larger migration paths to optimize grazing resources seasonally. The new needs did not square with an old land division based on fishing and hunting.

When users expanded their reindeer herds in the seventeenth century, members in the villages in the mountains often had to lease winter grazing from members in villages in the boreal forest. It meant that the former paid a fee for the right to graze their animals on the latter's lands. This kind of leasing arrangement continued into the eighteenth century, but as more and more members in villages in the boreal forest also expanded their reindeer herds, more fundamental changes in user rights became inevitable. In the mountains, the division into individual lands had not been as strict as in the boreal forest, or was completely missing. Therefore, reindeer pastoralism did not impose the same challenges on user rights there as it did in the boreal forest. Regardless, as users in their respective villages needed access to more of each other's grazing land, they started to develop reciprocal arrangements to solve the problem, which eventually led to changes in property rights. This is exemplified by an answer from the local court in Jokkmokk in 1765, when users from Sirkas complained that users from Sjokksjokk were intruding on their grazing. The court argued that the villagers from Sirkas had to tolerate trespassing by villagers from Sjokksjokk in spring and summer since Sirkas villagers, in great number, spent winters on lands in Sjokksjokk.[11]

The *skatteland* was a resource area for households, or kinship groups, mainly for fishing and hunting that could be inherited.[12] Conflicts around use of these lands that were taken to the local court often involved a few people who lived quite close to each other. For the court, it meant that they often had to determine the boundaries of the *skatteland* and the user group.[13] In comparison, conflicts that concerned use of grazing lands often involved extensive areas and many users, sometimes from different villages. To become successful, they needed to build alliances with other users in similar situations, including neighbors. It could also involve strategic marriages, which enabled access to strategic grazing, as well as other benefits from an extended kinship network. Robust social relationships beyond the household became a prerequisite when grazing included both mountain pastures and boreal forests. Hence, the common-property regime that was created required participation from all Sami villages within the court district to work properly.

It is important to acknowledge that throughout the process of creating a new property regime for grazing, users could keep their old individual rights to fishing and hunting. Even though the property regime was contradictory in some regards, it favored users to have private rights to fishing and hunting within well-defined territories and at the same time access to grazing areas far apart; it was possible to combine them within the same property-rights system. Sometimes it required that the rights to different resources were divided among users. If a user had many reindeer, it was possible for him or her to have access only to grazing on a land while another user could have access to fishing waters or hunting grounds. It is striking how rights to resources were renegotiated by local users, and how people's needs often were a guiding principle for the local court. Also, inheritance was a strong right and a land could often belong to the same family or kinship group for several generations, as long as

---

[11] Hultblad (1968, p. 397, evidence 715a) See also Chapter 7.

[12] Holmbäck (1922), Kvist (1990, p. 280), and Korpijakko-Labba (1994, p. 53).

[13] The boundaries of the resource area and the user group are aligned with Ostrom's design principle 1 (Ostrom 1990, p. 90; Cox et al. 2010).

they had continued to use it. If it was used too little, the court could assign it to another user, or tell the original user to share it with someone who needed it more.

In the boreal forest, fishing and hunting continued to be organized on private lands until the late nineteenth century.[14] By then, government interventions turned private fishing and hunting rights into collective rights through the Reindeer Grazing Act of 1886. The new common user rights that included grazing, fishing, and hunting were intended for inhabitants who were engaged in reindeer pastoralism, or already had converted to reindeer ranching, and belonged to a newly contrived Sami village. This institution should not, however, be confused with the historical concept of Sami village as we have used it in this book. The Reindeer Grazing Act did not recognize the intrinsic property-rights system that indigenous inhabitants had developed over time. In the early modern era, Sami users had "split property rights," which could include all resources on a piece of land, or rights to resources on a spatial or temporal basis. Eventually, the Swedish government came to favor a decisively more comprehensive property-rights system for Swedish Sami that only included reindeer herders.

Already in the early modern era, the Swedish government had attempted to create uniform legal rules. Conversely, to a large extent, customary and local rules survived and local users retained a strong influence over legal practices. This epoch is best characterized by its great blend of different legal influences.[15] Regional features of rules persisted, and could be effectively enforced. In Lule lappmark, we have seen how rules regarding hunting, fishing, and reindeer pastoralism were developed by local users who tailored them according to their changing needs.

As discussed in Chapter 2, property systems are usually divided into four basic regimes: state, private, common, and non-property.[16] In theoretical models, pastoral systems are usually defined as *common-property regimes*, but many pastoralists have practically no restrictions on access to grazing land, making it similar to a non-property regime. This implies

[14] In some areas the use of these lands continued into the twentieth century, foremost in Ume lappmark district.

[15] Ågren (1997).

[16] Bromley (1991).

that pastoralists have open access to land, which would automatically equate pastoralism with the "tragedy of the commons."[17] However, studies of pastoralists in Africa and Asia suggest that open access in that context does not mean absence of rules, nor leads to depletion of grazing resources.[18] In the debate about pastoral tenure systems and how well common-property theory can explain those systems, it has been argued that one set of characteristics distinguishes common property from what has been called *sovereign pastoral commons*: the resource size is small with well-defined boundaries and the ownership group is small with clearly defined membership.[19] In a pastoral tenure system, areas are extensive with contested boundaries, users are in networks of relationships, and membership is often contested. Hence, an indigenous pastoral tenure system does not fit the "design principles" and is unlikely to be effective common property. Many scholars acknowledge that pastoralist governance systems do not conform to the assumption of mainstream scholarship on common property.[20] To better categorize the property regimes used, new concepts have been launched to describe pastoralism as an *open-property regime*[21] and a *complex-mosaic regime*.[22] In the latter, different types of property rights do not need to be allocated on an all-or-nothing basis and tenure and property rights form only one type of governance institution. To explain how land-tenure regimes work, one needs to add the social processes and governance mechanisms.

The dichotomy of pastoralism is that livestock holders need secure user rights and spatial and social flexibility due to the often relatively large natural variations in resource access in the landscapes where their animals graze.[23] Tenure to land was often informal, other rights more secure. Tuareg people who are nomadic pastoralists in Mali, as an example, returned to the same grazing land with their livestock each year.[24] Even

[17] Hardin (1968).

[18] Moritz (2016) and Robinson (2019).

[19] Behnke (2018).

[20] Moritz (2016), Behnke (2018), and Robinson (2019).

[21] Moritz (2016).

[22] Robinson (2019).

[23] Fernández-Giménez (2002, p. 52).

[24] Berge (2001).

though they had established a customary right to the land, they had no exclusive right. However, they did have exclusive rights to use man-made wells during the dry season.

How do the property regimes created in Lule lappmark compare to what has been said above? We argue that the property regime to regulate reindeer pastoralism in Lule lappmark during the eighteenth century is best described as a common-property regime. Unlike some other pastoralist systems, it was relatively easy in Lule lappmark to determine the members who shared the resource. Almost all Sami were members of the Sami villages, and each village had representatives in the local court where many conflicts over land use were solved. Even if, in other settings,[25] huge areas were seen as a problem in the development of common-property regimes, the vast area that Lule lappmark encompassed did not seem to have been a problem in determining rules for the common use of grazing. Like other pastoralists, reindeer pastoralists needed both spatial and social flexibility and secure rights to be able to optimize their resource use. Access to suitable seasonal grazing, both long term and short term, was a strategy that led to more predictability, and thus increased food security for households. Another part of the predictability was the establishment of a governance system wherein users trusted one another, the customary rules, and the local institutions.

Governing

For a common-property regime to function well, users have to trust the governing institutions at different levels. It is difficult for us today to grasp all the details of the early modern governing infrastructures for natural resources. We assume that most decisions regarding land use were based on deliberations and interactions between users or user groups. Fortunately, preserved court rulings from the early modern local court in the lappmark make it possible to uncover some of the negotiations and arguments that were put forward by users who wanted to defend or claim rights to land or water. These rulings reveal a lot of interesting

[25] See, for example, Moritz (2016) and Behnke (2018).

details about the reality that users operated in, not least around how inhabitants practiced hunting, fishing, or reindeer herding. Nonetheless, some land-use conflicts ended up in court because users wanted the court to settle user rights since the ruling in itself became an official affirmation of the right. It was, for example, common for defendants or plaintiffs to refer to old court rulings during trials as a means to strengthen their own cases. Hence, the local court was an arena where collective-choice rules were made.[26]

For the local court, it was important to uphold and maintain a just and robust local economy. Since most users' livelihoods depended on common-pool resources—fishing waters, hunting grounds, and reindeer grazing land—it was the court's duty to rule in a manner that supported a smooth operation of these activities. To accomplish this, rulings to do with resource use had to be based on a substantial knowledge about both prior and ongoing land use. For the court's head judge, who was appointed by the government and only stayed in the lappmark for a short period of time each year, much of this knowledge must have been inaccessible. Instead, the court relied on trusted indigenous lay-judges from different Sami villages within the court's jurisdiction who possessed vital knowledge for the court to function as intended. Many of the court rulings reveal just how seriously lay-judges or other trusted men took their court assignments, and how meticulously evidence was weighed before they reached a verdict. In especially complicated cases, the procedures often paused for a year between court sessions so the concerned parties and a couple of lay-judges could have time to visit the location of the disputed land or water to gather information and try to resolve the matter on site. Moreover, during the trial, it was common to engage witnesses who could contribute valuable information to help reach as fair a verdict as possible.

The local court in Lule lappmark can be described as a low-cost arena for solving conflicts, which implied that it encouraged users to take conflicts to court.[27] Since there was only one court session per year, in

[26] Ostrom (2005, pp. 58–59).

[27] Having a low-cost arena to solve conflicts is part of Ostrom's design principle 6 (Ostrom 1990, p. 90; Cox et al. 2010).

January or February, it did not inflict a particularly large loss of working time for the inhabitants. Furthermore, the yearly court proceedings coincided with market and church services, which enticed a large proportion of the population in Lule lappmark to visit Jokkmokk around that time of year. It was also the time for state tax collection in the seventeenth century, which might not have enticed people to come but was obligatory to participate in.

Sometimes it took several years for the court to resolve a land-use conflict. However, from the court's perspective, it was more important to act credibly or to align deliberations with peoples' perceptions than to come to a quick ruling.[28] Simply put, in this kind of legal culture, where conflict resolution around land use was based wholly on customary practices, it was indispensable that the inhabitants within a court district be included in and accept the results of the court proceedings. The basic principle behind this legal approach can be expressed in the maxim *Quad omnes tangit ab omnibus approbari debet* (what touches all must be approved by all), a norm that had been established within medieval law in Sweden.[29] Obviously, the principle was still applicable in the early modern court in Lule lappmark, at least when it handled collective-action problems concerning land use. Like other early modern courts in Europe, another role of the court was to foster good neighborhoods.[30]

The open and transparent handling of court cases during the yearly court sessions conveyed guidelines for individuals and communities with similar problems. In the long run, this learning process surely decreased the number of conflicts that were taken to court. During the open, transparent process, the court clarified the underlying reasonings behind their rulings for all users in the district, lowering the efforts and costs associated with upholding the land-use regime. Due to their concurrence with the yearly market and church services, court sessions were well attended, which increased their impact and made it likely for audiences to give

[28] J. Larsson (2016, p. 1114).

[29] Korpiola (2014).

[30] Rodgers et al. (2011, p. 37) and J. Larsson (2016, p. 1114).

honest reports of what had occurred when they discussed court cases with non-participants.

The jurisdiction of the court coincided, to a large extent, with the inhabitants' resource areas and encompassed both the boreal forest and the mountains. The court district's boundaries followed how its inhabitants migrated or otherwise utilized the landscape. This was particularly true for reindeer pastoralists who needed access to different types of grazing lands depending on the season. Eventually, the entirety of the court district turned into a common-pool regime for grazing, where land-use decisions in one region might impact land use in other regions. By then, the representation of lay-judges from all Sami villages became an even more valued asset since they brought experience of using resources on different landscapes. User groups continued to be rather small, but decisions about how lands and waters should be used, required consideration by more users, and over larger geographical areas than before.

Nonetheless, court districts embraced large areas with relatively few and dispersed users. Even if governance of extensive and coherent grazing pastures was advantageous for reindeer pastoralists, it seems to have been a rather smooth process to divide the court district in Lule lappmark into Jokkmokk in the south and Gällivare in the north in 1751. The relative lack of friction was perhaps due to the fact that the newly established districts were adapted to where inhabitants in the respective districts already utilized land and water. Both districts were elongated and stretched from northwest to southeast, and thus encompassed lands for winter and summer grazing for reindeer pastoralists. One can only imagine what turmoil would have occurred if one court district had covered the boreal forest and the other the mountains. For users, the division into two districts was beneficial for two main reasons: (1) the northern court's sessions were closer to inhabitants around Gällivare, simultaneously with an additional location for winter market, tax collection, and church services in the newly established parish[31]; and (2) the split of the original court district meant that the number of inhabitants

[31] Bergling (1964, p. 272).

in each district remained manageable despite an overall increasing Sami population, thus more court cases, in Lule lappmark. Preservation of small user groups also made it possible to continue the customary judicial principle of transparency and local influence over rulings.

Social Justice

The transition from an economy based on hunting and fishing to an economy based on reindeer pastoralism created larger social differences between inhabitants in Lule lappmark. The shift increased the gap between rich and poor households. It is likely that fishing and hunting gave more predictable and thus reliable income sources over time, because they were not as exposed to risk as reindeer pastoralism. At the same time, the latter was often much more rewarding given that users were good at managing the herd, and had a certain degree of luck. It explains why many users turned to reindeer pastoralism in the seventeenth and eighteenth centuries, which made it possible for them to influence the development of new property regimes in the region. Reindeer pastoralism yielded many products that gave good incomes, but it also required a lot of work. The herders had to take the reindeer to places where there was rich grazing, protect them against predators, gather and milk the reindeer cows every day, and not least process the milk into cheese. It thus required work efforts by all members of the household and, if possible, by employees. Reindeer pastoralist households often included young men and women from other families who herded and milked reindeer and performed other household chores in return for food, clothes, and reindeer of their own. Even within the pastoralist group, the economic gap between households eventually grew, and some became wealthier than others.

One feature that distinguishes reindeer pastoralists from other pastoralists is its focus on managing only one particular type of livestock.[32] Most other pastoralists combine herding of several different

[32] The only exception in Lule lappmark was that a few cows, goats, or sheep were sometimes kept with the herd during summer. See Chapter 8.

livestock, although one species may outnumber the rest and be considered more economically important.[33] There are several strategic reasons for pastoralists to have different types of livestock; it can, for example, be a way to spread risks since pests or shortages of grazing do not affect all species equally. Also, the capability to regenerate the livestock herd after a crash in numbers can be quicker for some species than others. For example, goats and sheep regain in numbers faster than camels or cows.[34] Different species can also provide different goods for its owner, and have different grazing strategies that optimize the use of grazing resources. Albeit, reindeer pastoralists had little choice but to rely on only reindeer since no other livestock can survive on grazing during winters in the circumpolar north. But this reliance on just reindeer also put pastoralists in interior northern Sweden at great risk, and contributed to a certain degree of unpredictability in their household economy. As discussed in Chapter 4, this was one argument not to tax Sami in relation to the number of reindeer they owned. The unpredictability was part of the nature of reindeer pastoralism. A deep understanding of a wide range of factors, such as weather, grazing conditions, and reindeer's behavior, were crucial to become successful as a reindeer herder, but even skilled users could have bad luck and loose much of the herd in just a short time.

The property-rights regimes that developed in Lule lappmark also addressed questions about social justice and equity. How much and what kinds of resources should poor users have access to? How should young people, who had not yet established their own household, get access to resources? There were also extremely poor inhabitants in the lappmark who owned practically nothing. They had the option to leave and, for example, go live along the Norwegian coast or at the Gulf of Bothnia in Sweden and live on whatever incomes were available there.[35] Some of the early modern sources also tell us that "very poor" Sami, unlike the rest of the Sami population at the time, became sedentary by lakes where they survived on fishing and hunting year-round.[36] In the boreal forest,

33 Galaty and Johnson (1990, p. 7).
34 McCabe (2004, p. 80).
35 Hultblad (1968, p. 39).
36 Öhrling (1970 [1773], p. 11).

the local court could grant underprivileged users the rights to use traps for hunting birds or small game on lands even though the rights holder opposed it. Poor Sami could also spend winters in the mountains where hunting was open access and snare ptarmigans. For young Sami with few resources, an option, if available, was to work in a pastoralist household where they could receive reindeer as payment and eventually amass their own herds.

Final Remarks

As we have seen, despite the early modern Swedish state's colonial ambitions, local users in interior northwest Fennoscandia developed sophisticated rules for use of natural resources. This was a locally driven process that led to adjusted rules as the economy changed. Users in Lule lappmark managed a complex economy in common, and tailored rights to different resources based on users' demands and needs. When reindeer pastoralism increased in economic importance, lands from the boreal forest into the mountains became managed as one large CPR in regard to which users had both rights and duties. To survive and prosper, reindeer pastoralist households had to migrate with their herds to access different types of grazing depending on the season. By using the local court in Lule lappmark as a collective-choice arena, they could be granted rights to grazing in the mountains, in the boreal forest, and along the migration route. At the same time, the court could consider rights to fish and hunt for other users. In the late eighteenth century, most of this self-governance was lost when the government moved these kinds of decisions to state servants at *Länsstyrelsen* (the County Administrative Board).

In the nineteenth century, indigenous users who had been proficient at building self-governance institutions through a bottom-up process encountered the Swedish government's top-down view of property rights. The fact that the inhabitants previously had distributed rights to resources dynamically, based on users' customary practices and present needs, was completely overshadowed by the government's legal discourse and view of ownership over land. What undermined the indigenous population's positions when it came to determining uses of land and water was the government's interpretative prerogative in the view of what ownership of land meant. Thus, early modern Sami self-governance systems based on customary use for hunting, fishing, and grazing were disregarded and eventually abolished, making it much harder for indigenous users to steer their economies and to co-exist. This was part of an overall development in Sweden in the nineteenth century, when private and state properties were favored and there was little to no understanding of the rationality behind common-property regimes. In these circumstances, it is not surprising that the Swedish government did not recognize a complex property-rights system like the one Sami in Lule lappmark had developed. Sami experienced what many other indigenous people and pastoralists around the world have experienced: that modern nation-states could not and were not willing to see their property-rights systems as functional and rational, or even understand them all.

References

Ågren, Maria. 1997. *Att hävda sin rätt. Synen på jordägande i 1600-talts Sverige, speglad i institutet urminnes hävd*. Stockholm: Institutet för rättshistorisk forskning.

Arell, Nils. 1977. Rennomadismen i Torne lappmark: markanvändning under kolonisationsepoken i fr.a. Enontekis socken. PhD dissertation, Umeå, Sweden: Skytteanska samfundet. http://www.diva-portal.org/smash/record.jsf?pid=diva2%3A616377&dswid=6098.

Behnke, Roy. 2018. Open access and the sovereign commons. *Land Use Policy* 78: 708–718. https://doi.org/10.1016/j.landusepol.2018.02.054.

Berge, Gunnvor. 2001. Tuareg notions of space and place in northern Mali. In *Politics, property, and production in the West African Sahel*, ed. T.A. Benjaminsen and C. Lund, 182–207. Uppsala, Sweden: Nordafrikanska Institutet.

Bergling, Ragnar. 1964. Kyrkstaden i övre Norrland: kyrkliga, merkantila och judiciella funktioner under 1600- och 1700-talen. PhD dissertation, Uppsala University.

Bergman, Ingela, and Per H. Ramqvist. 2017. Farmer fishermen: Interior lake fishing and inter-cultural and intra-cultural relations among coastal and interior Sámi communities in northern Sweden AD 1200–1600. *Acta Borealia* 34 (2): 134–158.

Bromley, Daniel W. 1991. *Environment and economy, property rights and public policy*. Oxford, UK: Blackwell.

Cox, Michael., Gwen Arnold, and Sergio Villamayor Tomás. 2010. A review of design principles for community-based natural resource management. *Ecology and Society* 15 (4): 38. http://www.ecologyandsociety.org/vol15/iss4/art38/

Fernández-Giménez, María E. 2002. Spatial and social boundaries and the paradox of pastoral land tenure. *Human Ecology* 30: 49–78. https://doi.org/10.1023/A:1014562913014.

Galaty, John G., and Douglas L. Johnson, eds. 1990. *The world of pastoralism: Herding systems in comparative perspective*. New York: Guilford Press.

Göthe Gustaf. 1929. Om Umeå lappmarks svenska kolonisation: från mitten av 1500-talet till omkr. 1750. PhD dissertation, Stockholm University.

Hardin, Garrett. 1968. The tragedy of the commons. *Science* 162: 1243–1248. https://doi.org/10.1126/science.162.3859.1243.

Holmbäck, Åke. 1922. *Om lappskattelandsinstitutet och dess historiska utveckling*. Stockholm: Statens offentliga utredningar.

Hultblad, Filip. 1968. *Övergång från nomadism till agrar bosättning i Jokkmokks socken*. PhD dissertation, Uppsala University.

Khazanov, Anatoly M. 1994. *Nomads and the outside world*, 2 rev. ed. Madison: University of Wisconsin Press.

Korpijaakko-Labba, Kaisa. 1994. *Om samernas rättsliga ställning i Sverige-Finland. En rättshistorisk utredning av markanvändningsförhållanden och -rättigheter i Västerbottens lappmark före mitten av 1700-talet*. Helsinki: Juristförbundets förlag.

Korpiola, Mia. 2014. Not without the consent and goodwill of the common people. *The Journal of Legal History* 35 (2): 95–119. https://doi.org/10.1080/01440365.2014.925173.

Kvist, Roger. 1989. Rennomadismens dilemma, det rennomadiska samhällets förändring i Tuorpon och Sirkas, 1760–1860. PhD dissertation, Umeå University.

Kvist, Roger. 1990. Beskattningen av samerna i Sverige 1695–1860. In *Älvdal i norr: människor och resurser i Luledalen 1300–1800*, ed. Sune Åkerman, Kjell Lundholm, 264–305. Umeå, Sweden: Umeå Studies in the Humanities, Umeå University.

Larsson, Jesper. 2016. Conflict-resolution mechanisms maintaining an agricultural system: Early modern local courts as an arena for solving collective-action problems within Scandinavian Civil Law. *International Journal of the Commons* 10 (2): 1100–1118. https://doi.org/10.18352/ijc.666.

Marklund, Bertil. 2015. Det milsvida folket. Skogssamernas samhälle i omvandling, 1650–1800. PhD dissertation, Umeå University.

McCabe, J. Terrence. 2004. *Cattle Bring us to Our Enemies, Turkana Ecology, Politics, and Raiding in a Disequilibrium System.* Ann Arbor: University of Michigan Press.

Moritz, Mark. 2016. Open property regimes. *International Journal of the Commons* 10: 688–708. https://doi.org/10.18352/ijc.719.

Norstedt, Gudrun. 2011. *Lappskattelanden på Geddas karta. Umeå lappmark från 1671 till 1900-talets början.* Umeå, Sweden: Thalassa förlag.

Norstedt, Gudrun. 2018. *A land of one's own.* PhD dissertation, Swedish University of Agricultural Sciences, Umeå. https://pub.epsilon.slu.se/15451/1/norstedt_g_180502.pdf.

Norstedt, Gudrun, Anna-Lena Axelsson, and Lars Östlund. 2014. Exploring pre-colonial resource control of individual Sami household. *Arctic* 67 (2): 223–237. https://doi.org/10.14430/arctic4389.

Öhrling, Samuel. 1970 [1773]. *Historisk-ekonomisk avhandling om Arjeplogs församling i Lappland*. Arjeplog, Sweden: Silvermuseet.

Ostrom, Elinor. 1990. *Governing the commons, the evolution of institutions for collective action.* Cambridge, UK: Cambridge University Press.

Ostrom, Elinor. 2005. *Understanding institutional diversity*. Princeton, NJ: Princeton University Press.

Robinson, Lance W. 2019. Open property and complex mosaics. *International Journal of the Commons* 13 (1): 804–826. https://doi.org/10.18352/ijc.903.

Rodgers, Christopher P., Eleanor A. Straughton, Angus J. L. Winchester, and Margherita Pieraccini. 2011. *Contested common land: Environmental governance past and present*. London: Earthscan.

Skarin, Anna, Öje Danell, Roger Bergström, and Jon Moen. 2010. Reindeer movement patterns in alpine summer ranges. *Polar Biology* 33: 1263–1275. https://doi.org/10.1007/s00300-010-0815-y.

Vorren, Ørnulf. 1980. Samisk bosetning på Nordkalotten, arealdisponering og resursutnytting i historisk-økologisk belysning. In: *Nord-skandinaviens historia i tvärvetenskaplig belysning. förhandlingar vid symposium anordnat av Humanistiska fakulteten vid Umeå universitet den 7–9 juni 1978*, ed. Evert Baudou and Karl-Hampus Dahlstedt, 235–261. Umeå, Sweden: Almqvist & Wiksell.

Archival Sources

Härnösand Regional Archive (HRA):
  Rulings in Jokkmokk District Court, Sweden, 1689–1780.
Kungliga bibliotektet (National Library of Sweden), Stockholm:
  Douglas. 1695. Skrivelse till Kungl. Maj:t ang. lapparna dat 25 mars 1695, X [1695] 281a:1.
Riksarkivet [National Archives of Sweden]:
  Svea Court of Appeal (RA SH). 1712–1780. Rulings in Jokkmokk District Court, Sweden.
  Kammararkivet: Jordeböcker 1750.
  Kammararkivet, Mantalslängder 1643, 1667.
Uppsala University Library:
  Iter lapponicum, Luefsta MS 92.

J. Larsson and E.-L. Päiviö Sjaunja, *Self-Governance and Sami Communities*,
https://doi.org/10.1007/978-3-030-87498-8

Index

J. Larsson and E.-L. Päiviö Sjaunja, *Self-Governance and Sami Communities*,
https://doi.org/10.1007/978-3-030-87498-8

The manufacturer's authorised representative in the EU is Springer Nature Customer Service Centre GmbH, Europaplatz 3, 69115 Heidelberg, Germany. If you have any concerns regarding our products, please contact ProductSafety@springernature.com

Printed and bound by CPI Group (UK) Ltd, Croydon, CR0 4YY
30/09/2026
02225499-0009